INTERNATIONAL LIBRARY

GIULIO BEDESCHI

SCIENCE OF MEDICINE

COLLINS · PUBLISHERS FRANKLIN WATTS, INC.
London · Glasgow   New York

© 1975 International Library
© 1975 Rizzoli Editore, Milan

First Edition 1975

ISBN 0 00 100173–6 (*Collins*)
SBN 0–531–02122–X (*Franklin Watts*)

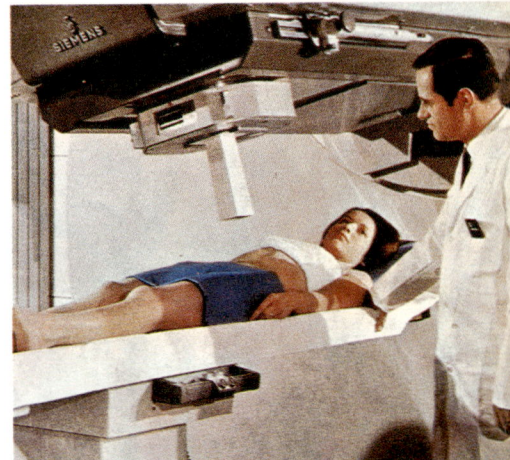

No part of this work may be reproduced without the permission of the publisher. All rights reserved.
Printed and bound in Great Britain by Jarrold and Sons Ltd., Norwich
Library of Congress Catalog Card Number: 74–12752

CONTENTS

Chapter 1
BENEATH OUR SKIN . . . *page* 7

Chapter 2
MEDICAL SCIENCE
THROUGH THE AGES 11

Chapter 3
IN THE TWENTIETH CENTURY . 25

Chapter 4
THE CONQUEST OF MEDICINE
IN OUR CENTURY 37

Chapter 5
TODAY'S DEATH-DEALING
DISEASES 59

Chapter 6
SURGERY AS A MEDICAL TOOL   87

Chapter 7
HEALTH SERVICES 107

Chapter 8
SPACE MEDICINE 119

INDEX 125

CHAPTER 1

BENEATH OUR SKIN

Our skin is a living, protective sheath that encloses our bodies. This outermost surface forms the most obvious point of contact between the human body and its natural environment. Recently, some extraordinary and unexpected defence mechanisms of the skin have been revealed. It has been shown experimentally that if 30 million microbes are distributed over a man's epidermis, as the outer surface of the skin is called, only about 720,000 of them still survive after one hour, and no more than 7,000 are left after two hours.

This finding concerns a part of the human body immediately in view yet only accessible to us with the help of a microscope. It took thousands of years during which man has had to record his observations and theories, discover natural laws and invent numerous tools before he was able to see and understand what was taking place before his very eyes. The difficulties encountered by man in the course of his history, in his attempts to elucidate at least some of the natural laws governing the organization of his body and its relationship with the surrounding world, have been enormous and are by no means at an end.

In the unceasing quest for knowledge, the limits of what can be discovered seem to recede into the distance as scientific knowledge increases. Our investigations take us even farther into the worlds of the infinitely small and the infinitely large.

In an area of study like the biological sciences, which constitute a seemingly fathomless pit of exploration and surprises, all conclusions must be provisional, based on whatever stage of knowledge has been reached at any particular time. We should always be aware that what, at the moment, seems to be an almost incredible achievement could soon be reduced to a very much taken-for-granted kind of concept.

None the less, the scientific knowledge acquired to date, especially during the last hundred years, can be considered as little short of astonishing. Modern biological findings have substantially altered our lives by changing the previous relationships between health and sickness, and indeed, life and death.

Before we can even begin to understand what is currently known of human biology, we must briefly glance at the road man has travelled since the dawn of civilization.

From primitive medicine man to modern specialist the medical practices of every period of civilization have brought progress in knowledge of anatomy, use of drugs and standards of hygiene. Humanity's earliest medicine was a form of nature cure. As man's herbal lore expanded it

A 17th-century miniature showing the Rolandi teachers of surgery at the Salerno School in Italy.

became tinged with magic. Beginning with these natural and supernatural methods of healing, man resorted to hypnosis, dream interpretation, and the treatment of illness through rest and diet. The history of Western medicine demonstrates how abstract principles, superstitions and fads governed the theories of healing; these theories were at the root of all medical practices right up until the middle of the 19th century. It was only the persistence and dedication of men like, Morton, Semmelweiss, Koch, and Pasteur and the development of anaesthetics, asepsis and the germ theory of disease that finally brought man out of the dark ages of medicine into the science we know today as medicine.

The history of biology embraces and defines man's own history, since it is the study of the way in which he is made, the way in which his organs function, the rules which govern the physical and mental existence of a healthy or sick individual, and the interactions between man and his environment.

The skin clothes and protects an entire universe which we carry within us: a complex of systems in a continual state of renewal. These systems are kept in equilibrium through physical and chemical reactions which maintain the living process. To comprehend the essential nature of these phenomena, we need only think of breathing—a function which, if it is stopped for just a few minutes, leads to death.

With the space age already under way, everything that is now happening confirms that man's increasing pursuit of cosmic goals must entail a deeper understanding of his own body. He must become even more familiar with its basic constitution, since the human body is the starting point for every undertaking.

We are accustomed to thinking of our bodies in terms of outward appearances; our image of ourselves is the one most obvious—our reflection in a mirror or our picture in a photograph. However, beneath this exterior, there is a living organization of unimaginable complexity. Whenever we see photographs or anatomical drawings of our internal organs, we may well find it difficult or unpleasant to accept the idea that we are actually composed of such things as stomach, kidneys, lungs and so forth. Yet this, too, is a crude and inaccurate picture of reality. In the light of our present knowledge the human body is not only an edifice containing highly differentiated structures but also a vast laboratory in which millions of physical and chemical interactions are taking place at every moment of our lives. If we had to reproduce by artificial means even the processes that we fully understand and keep them operating simultaneously, we should need the equipment and facilities of a vast factory.

Inside the human body, substances and organs are in a state of perpetual motion. The blood, a thick fluid containing millions of cells, is pumped around the body by the heart in order to reach all the tissues, covering some hundreds of miles in the course of twenty-four hours. In one year carrying out this activity, the heart produces sufficient energy to raise an object weighing many tons. The blood can be thought of as a continually flowing stream within us, so distributed that it bathes and nourishes even the smallest living area of our bodies.

While we are alive, there is little visible on the surface to suggest the intense activity going on inside us. Only through hundreds of years of observation and research has man gradually succeeded in throwing

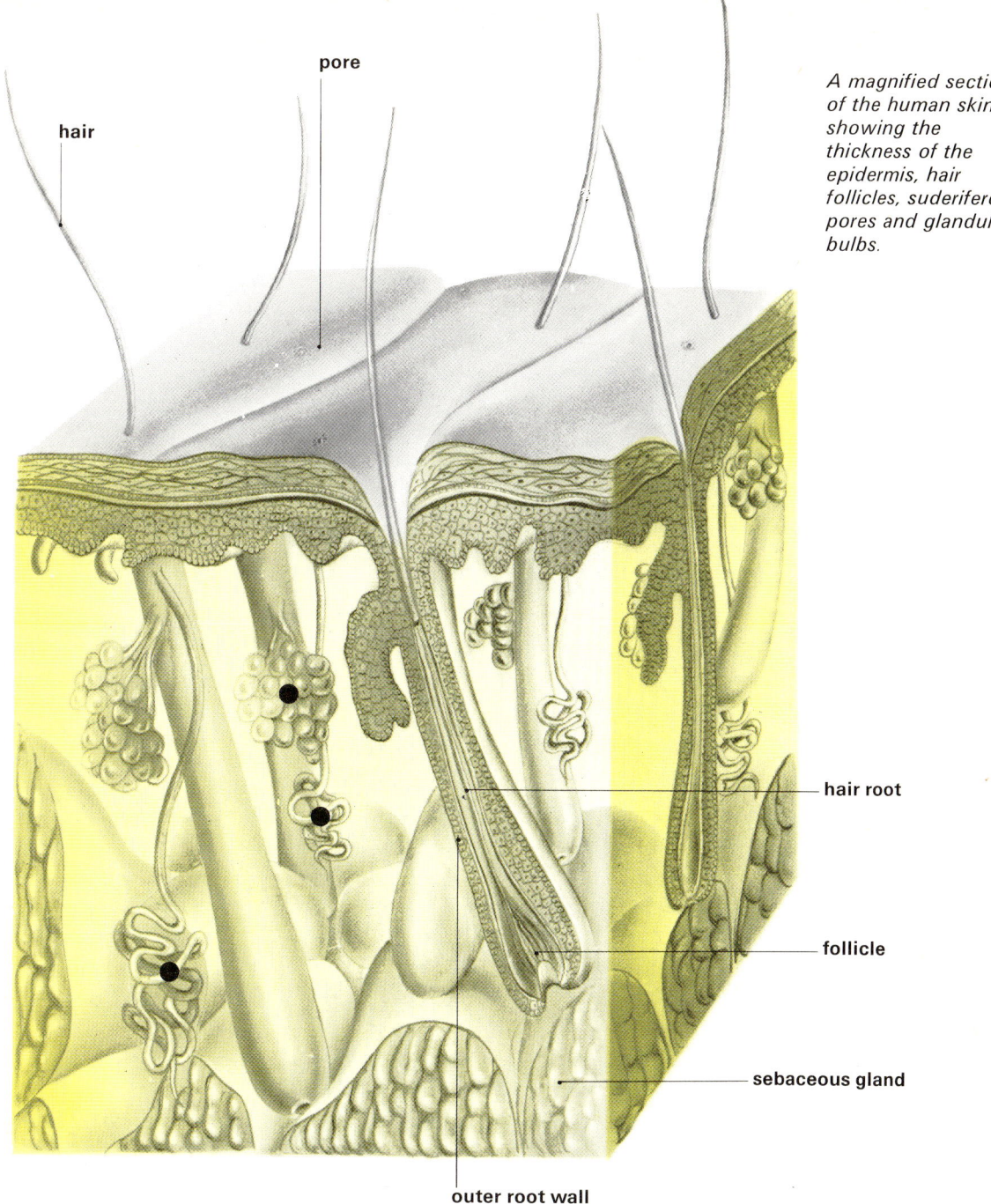

A magnified section of the human skin showing the thickness of the epidermis, hair follicles, suderiferous pores and glandular bulbs.

light on the physical mysteries within him, enabling him to recognize the characteristics of what constitutes the human body in health and disease. When we look at the drawings and descriptions of the human body that have come down to us from the scholars of anatomy in ancient times, we may be amused by their naïve combination of insight and ignorance. But we must emphasize that the increased knowledge over the last few decades has opened up such vast perspectives for the future that our present scientific advantages should be regarded with humility in relation to what appears to lie ahead.

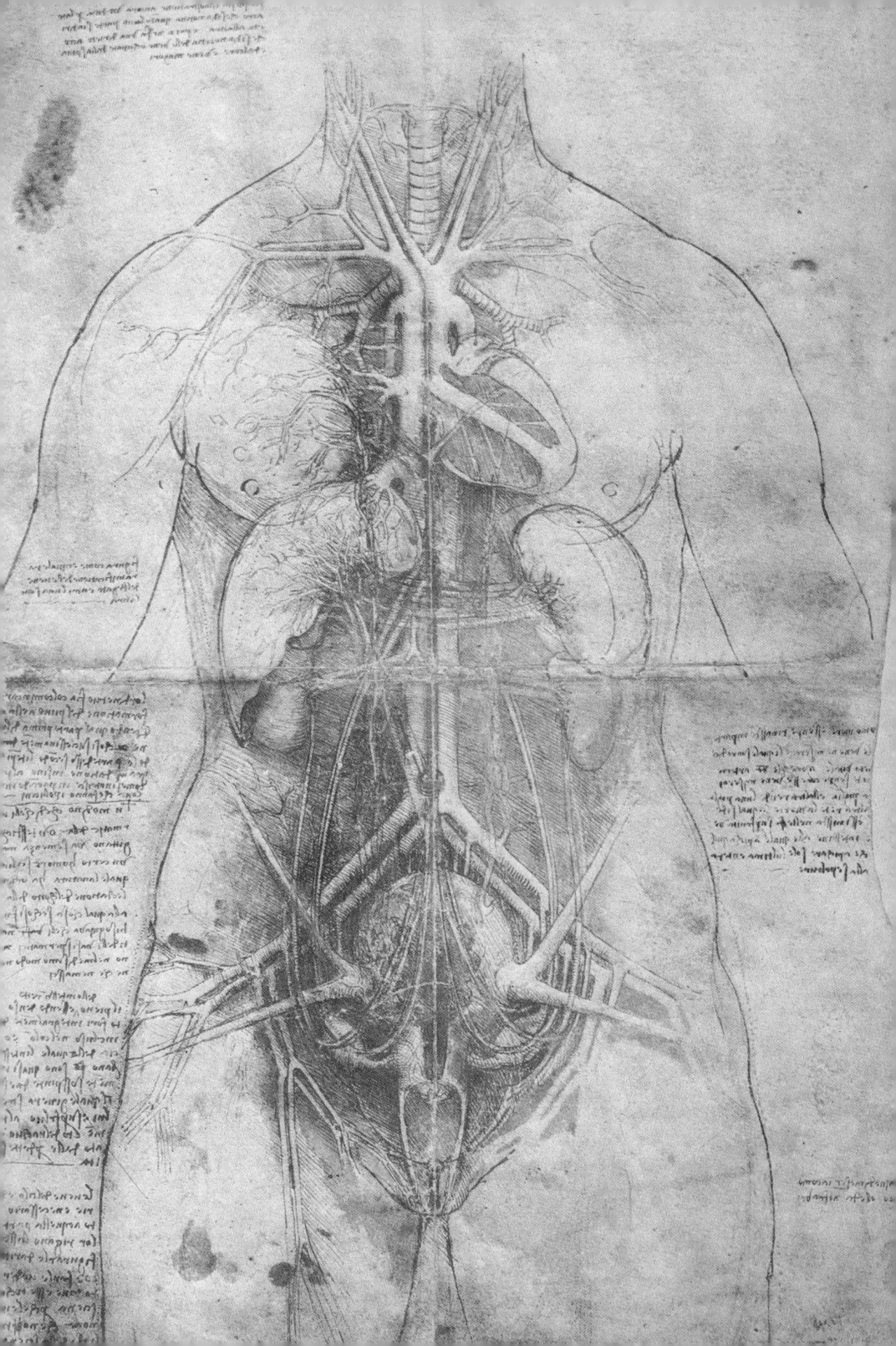

CHAPTER 2

MEDICAL SCIENCE THROUGH THE AGES

Even in the Stone Age, our ancestors must have been aware of the presence of a particularly hard and rigid framework that supported the body. We now call this the skeleton, and we know that it is made up of bone tissue. A fracture of the lower limbs, especially one accompanied by protrusion of broken bone and an inability to stand on the injured leg must inevitably have demonstrated the supportive function of the bones. Again, the sight of skeletons would have told them a good deal about the overall shape of the human body framework.

Even before the dawn of civilization, primitive man was already sufficiently familiar with the conformation of the skeleton to attempt the practice of cranial trepanning. This entailed opening up the skull roof and was probably carried out as part of witchcraft-like rituals intended to drive out evil spirits from diseased individuals. Presumably these spirits were thought to be hidden inside that mysterious closed box, the cranium or skull.

Despite the fact that these surgical techniques were carried out only with sharpened flint blades, numerous human skulls have survived from these times clearly showing healed-over bone scars around the edges of the trepanned hole, unmistakable evidence that the operated person had survived long after the operation was carried out.

The concept of the skeleton as a supporting structure was followed by the idea that bones also served for locomotion. Here the apparatus consisted of the bone joints and muscles, or more roughly those muscles which could be seen beneath the skin contracting and enlarging at every step taken and with every effort made.

It took thousands of years before man's powers of observation had reached a point where he could identify and attribute a specific and definite function to the various organs and internal systems within the outward form. He began to separate them into respiratory, digestive and urinogenital systems, to distinguish between the central and peripheral nervous system, to locate the heart and the blood vessels, to differentiate arteries from veins, and to identify the mysterious external and internal secretory glands.

Throughout ancient times, witch doctors, priests and physicians vied with one another to provide an explanation for the innumerable mysteries posed by observation of the human body. Only by about 4000 BC did human civilization reach a level where historical records were kept. Experiments carried out over several thousand years by the priest-doctors of Eastern civilization gradually multiplied, and knowledge of

An anatomical drawing of a human female by Leonardo da Vinci. Leonardo's scientific investigations of body structure finally established anatomy as a science.

their results eventually reached the land of Greece. Here they provided the basis for the Greek schools of medicine which together gave rise to so-called *Hippocratic* medicine.

By the 6th century BC, Alcmaeon of Crotona had already compiled the first book on human anatomy, but not until the following century did the genius of Hippocrates of Cos bring medicine out of the realm of superstition and practical remedies. Hippocrates was the first to describe the method of systematic diagnostic investigation, based on observation and reasoning. He showed that the doctor's rightful place was not in the temple but at the bedside of the sick man, and laid down solid foundations for the way in which treatment should be conducted logically. Together with Aristotle, the great philosopher, Hippocrates must be considered as the father of biology, the science which studies the nature of the living organisms by observation and experiment.

A bust of Hippocrates (Capitoline Museum, Rome). He opposed the empirical medical thinking which was prevalent during the 5th century BC in favour of systematic diagnostic investigation.

However, nations rise and fall, and as Greek political power declined and the Roman Empire rose to power, so medical science fell into decay. Pliny wrote that for the first six hundred years of their history, the Romans lived without doctors. The practice of the medical arts was left to educated slaves, and it was not until the year 46 BC, in the reign of Julius Caesar that Roman citizenship was granted to foreign doctors.

Dioscorides, Celsus and Galen co-ordinated and deepened medical knowledge in various fields during the succeeding centuries. The Moslem world contributed greatly to medicine through the work of Avicenna and Averroes, two great Arabic doctors. In Italy, the Salernitana school which existed from about AD 1000 to AD 1300 was the greatest centre for study and teaching in the Christian world, and must be considered as the mother of the universities. Saint Augustine and Saint Ambrose preached the duty of caring for the sick, while Saint Benedict imposed it on his monastic order at Monte Cassino and in all his other abbeys. In this way, the hospices came into being; medicinal herbs were grown, preserved and rationally used.

In the mid-1300s, an epidemic of bubonic plague which spread from the East, swept over Europe and caused at least 25 million deaths in five years—a quarter of the population then inhabiting the European continent. Shaken by this scourge, civilized society felt impelled to bring about new hygienic and sanitary measures (a thousand years of neglect had passed since citizens of imperial Rome had been supplied with heated bath-houses, sewage mains and fourteen aqueducts had provided each inhabitant with more than 500 litres of fresh water a day).

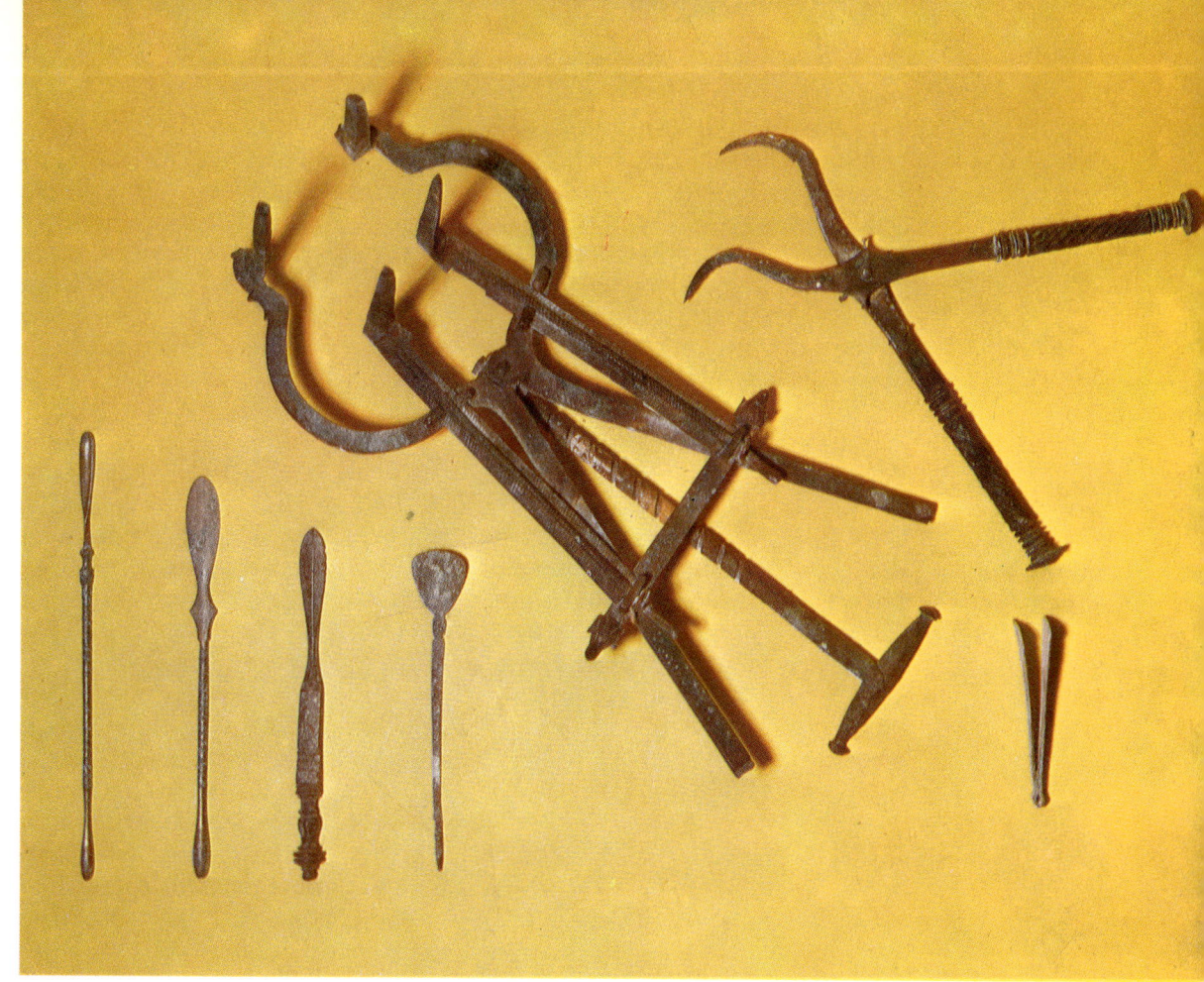

Roman surgical instruments found in Pompeii (now in the National Museum, Naples).

Fever hospitals, leper houses and general hospitals were finally built, while medical ethics and a code of medical conduct were born: the doctor undertook to treat all sick persons against payment allocated for this purpose by the public authorities.

However, even by the time of the great Dante Alighieri—the author of the *Divine Comedy*—methodical research on corpses for the purpose of furthering knowledge was still not permitted. In those days students of anatomy were considered as violators of dead bodies, and were condemned by law as such. It was not until 1315 that the first official dissections were performed at the University of Bologna, followed by a description given in a treatise on anatomy. Only in the Renaissance period, around 1500, was the study of anatomy finally reborn, expanding under the genius of Leonardo da Vinci who applied scientific methods to the investigation of body structure. There was a universal burgeoning of science, and the universities of Padua and Bologna became centres of learning for scholars from nineteen nations. Latin had become an international language and a means of disseminating culture and the invention of printing gave science and scholarship an impetus hitherto unknown. In the field of medicine, Andreas Vesalius, Fallopio, Eustachio, Fabrizio d'Acquapendente, Botallo and Varolio increased our knowledge of anatomy, physiology and surgery. The French surgeon, Ambroise Paré, was beginning to develop a method of stopping the bleeding of wounds and cuts by ligaturing or tying off blood vessels.

Just as the 16th century was the one in which the foundations of anatomy as an exact science were laid down, so the 17th century was the century of physiology. The fanciful and generally erroneous theories of ancient times, based on the writings of a Greek physician named Galen, were beginning to die out as more and more experiments and dissections were made. Finally came a true understanding of how the blood circulated in the body. This was established step by step, beginning with the Spaniard Michele Servetus, and the Italian Andrea Cesalpino, and definitively by the Englishman William Harvey. Looking back from our present standpoint, it is hard to understand how learned men should for so long have failed to interpret correctly the observed phenomena relating to the circulation of blood. Blood-letting or phlebotomy operations had been performed for centuries and they must have noticed the veins in the forearm swell and stand out when they applied a tight tourniquet, and watched the blood spurt from incisions made by their lancets.

The 17th century was a time of fundamental conquests. It was the time outstanding for its brilliant minds. In 1610 Galileo Galilei adapted the optical instrument he used for studying the skies to produce enlarged images of many small, close-up objects, and thus made the transition from telescope to microscope. Marcello Malpighi immediately made use of this new scientific instrument.

Under the microscope, he observed that living organisms consisted of different tissues each with its distinct characteristics, and that each tissue was in turn composed of many units, invisible to the naked eye. He termed these units "saccules". These "saccules" were the *cells*, the fundamental units of living matter which play a leading role in biology, a science that from then on was to expand almost unceasingly. Malpighi founded microscopic anatomy, studying and describing the layers of the skin; he discovered the network of fine blood vessels or capillaries in lung tissue, and provided the scientific basis for studying the detailed organic exchanges that take place in living matter.

In addition to perfecting the microscope, the Dutchman Van Leeuwenhoek—lacking in academic training, but a reliable and dedicated observer—discovered what he termed "little animals of infusions", or *Infusoria*, microscopic life forms that included many single-celled animals and bacteria. He opened the door to another new branch

A Persian miniature depicting Avicenna lecturing to his medical students.

The construction of this jigsaw puzzle demonstrates how man's knowledge of medicine has evolved. Each new piece fitted confirms previous thinking and shows the way to new developments.

of medical science—*microbiology*.

As the 18th century began, Giovanni Battista Morgagni contributed the fruits of his great genius to medicine, a subject that was now emerging from the uncertainties and approximations of the past, as a true science. Morgagni conducted exhaustive studies in the area of anatomy, and it has been said that if all his anatomical discoveries had been named after him, more than a third of human anatomical structures would have to bear his name. He never once allowed his intellect to be diverted from a rigid analysis of facts. His method involved the comparison of constantly recurring clinical symptoms in patients with the organic modifications he found in their bodies after death. He compared healthy with diseased organs and described the differences. He thus formulated not only the science of pathology, but through his method provided the foundation for all modern medicine.

At about the same time, the naturalist Lazzaro Spallanzani, one of the greatest experimenters the world has ever known, made his own great contribution to scientific methods, and together with the Swiss scientist von Haller, founded modern experimental physiology.

The Frenchman Bichat, in the 19th century, increased and carried on the legacy of Morgagni. He promoted advances in the new branch of science termed *histology* which is the study of cells, both normal and diseased. The time was now ripe to confirm the doctrine of "*contagium vivum*" (which translated from the Latin means "live contagion"), or the idea that living organisms passed from one person to another can cause disease. The field of medicine was finally freed from the kind of superstition and ignorance that attributed outbreaks of disease to demoniacal powers, spells, the evil eye, and miasmas or impurities in the air.

In the middle of the 19th century, the Italian Pacini discovered and described the first microbe to be specifically connected with human disease, the cholera organism *Vibrio comma*. But the great story of microbiology and all its scientific repercussions unfolded over a period of time covering all of the second half of the 19th century; the two names most intimately bound up with establishing these developments are the Frenchman Louis Pasteur and the German Robert Koch.

Pasteur was a chemist who devoted his time to studying fermentation in milk and alcoholic beverages in an

A self-portrait of Leonardo da Vinci (Milan Art Gallery).

Marcellus Malpighi, the discoverer of tissues and cells.

Domenico Di Bartolo's painting of a 15th-century hospital ward (Sienna Hospital).

attempt to find better ways of preserving wines and beer. In a flash of intuition, he realized that fermentations, like infections, were due to living micro-organisms, and proceeded to substantiate this theory with rigorous experiments. From this starting point, Pasteur went on to explore the unknown and immense world of microbes, to the study of which he devoted all his energies for the rest of his life. He held out with unceasing tenacity against the opposition and hostile reactions of other scholars whose ideas were still rooted in the old schools of thought. Pasteur remained inflexible, continuing to affirm his beliefs while producing ever more convincing and finally incontrovertible proof that microbes do not arise spontaneously from putrefying and decaying material, but breed from pre-existing microbial individuals. Under the lens of his microscope, he isolated the *pathogenic agents* of various diseases, but his greatness was not limited solely to the discovery of microbes.

It is worth setting out in some detail how Pasteur probed into the life systems of micro-organisms, often progressing intuitively, and related these systems to the natural laws governing our own lives. As a result of his investigations, medical science in the 19th century at last had the possibility of using effective methods to combat successfully those epidemics that had wrought havoc to mankind since ancient times.

Pasteur was making experimental studies on cholera in hens. One day in the laboratory, he came across an evaporating dish, forgotten for several weeks, which in fact contained a culture of cholera bacilli, the bacterial organisms which cause the disease. Rather than discard the culture he decided to try inoculating it into a healthy hen. Contrary to what usually happened, the hen did not die, but merely exhibited a few mild signs of illness. Pasteur waited for some time, then injected the same hen with a further quantity of cholera bacilli, this time taken from a freshly prepared and highly virulent culture. The hen developed no

Lazzaro Spallanzani, the father of experimental physiology.

Anton van Leeuwenhoek, the Dutchman who was the first to see infusoria through the microscope.

Gian Battista Morgagni, the founder of modern pathological anatomy.

signs of illness. Pasteur deduced from this that the virulence of the bacilli he had first injected had become attenuated with age; the effects of the first mild attack of illness had immunized the hen, mustering its body's defences so that it was protected from developing cholera even when large quantities of virulent bacilli were injected. Pasteur conducted further experiments in which he conclusively demonstrated the scientific validity of *preventive immunization*. This was the process first used empirically by the Englishman Jenner, when he deliberately infected his patients with cowpox in order to prevent a later occurrence of the frequently deadly and disfiguring disease of smallpox. Pasteur went on with his experiments in immunization, and opened up a whole range of applications in this field of preventive medicine. He himself developed the anti-rabies treatment involving the use of an appropriate serum.

So began the great battle against pathogenic agents, some of which had now been isolated and identified. At last it was within man's power to defend himself against the enemies that were invisible to the naked eye but present everywhere in his environment, threatening his existence and burdening it with disease. Merely by breathing and eating, man carried (and carries) micro-organisms into his body that are capable of destroying him. The time had finally arrived when really effective weapons were being forged against infection, rather than mere palliatives that only served to relieve the severity of the symptoms. It was becoming increasingly apparent that medical science could not just confine itself to treating diseases once they had become obvious in individuals, but that certain rules of hygiene would have to be introduced into everyday life and social organization. Observance of these rules would help to protect the individual against contagion and prevent various diseases from exploding into epidemics.

For example, Pasteur himself perfected a technical process, later termed pasteurization, whereby milk and other liquids are brought to fairly high temperatures for a specific time at a certain pressure, which renders them safe for consumption. The process kills the disease bacteria responsible for tuberculosis and typhoid, which are sometimes found in milk, and also delays the development of other bacteria that lead to spoilage.

Robert Koch carried on the work of Pasteur and developed many of his findings. He was twenty years younger than Pasteur, and while still a general practitioner in a small German town, he pursued his studies in a wretched, almost makeshift laboratory whose lack of equipment was overcome only by Koch's passion for science. He developed a precise technique by which he was able to isolate various kinds of microscopic organisms from sick animals. He kept these microbes alive in colonies of pure cultures that grew in artificial media which Koch himself developed and prepared. When he inoculated other animals with these isolated organisms, Koch found that the disease was reproduced. He was thus able to demonstrate scientifically that diseases are passed from one animal to another by the transmission of a specific organism. This infective agent is called the *pathogen*.

Wars were common during those years, and there was an appalling loss of life from the infectious complications of wounds sustained on the battlefield. The German health authorities grasped the importance of Koch's studies and invited him to work in Berlin in the Department of Health, where he finally had at his disposal the facilities and equipment necessary to continue his research. In the decades which followed, Koch intensified his studies and became surrounded by students who helped to pursue microbial investigations until they too became well-known researchers and teachers. However, one of the most difficult tasks fell to Koch himself: the discovery of the pathogenic agent responsible for tuberculosis, a disease that had always been widespread, insidious and apparently invincible. Signs of this disease had even been found in Egyptian mummies. In 1882, Koch finally announced the discovery of this bacillus, which became known throughout the world simply as "Koch's bacillus".

Having isolated the causative organism of the disease, Koch went on beyond the confines of bacteriology, devoting himself to attempting to discover a treatment for tuberculosis. After several years, he had developed a remedy based on a substance called *tuberculin*. This was not the final answer to the problem, and the fight against tuberculosis was to go on into the present century. However, the work done under Koch's direction paved the way for today's developments, which will be discussed in the chapter on *serotherapy* and *immunology*.

Koch died in 1910. The discoveries made by him and Pasteur aroused the enthusiasm of scientists all over the world, and the intensification in study and experiment that followed produced great advances in medicine and its practical applications. While surgeons in the 19th century still dressed in black and worked with bare hands in the operating theatre, the new and certain knowledge of the real causes of infection resulted in techniques of disinfection coming into general use. Aseptic and antiseptic practices now became the standard in the operating theatre. Only on this basis, in conjunction with the discovery of anaesthesia, could surgery progress and reach achievements unimaginable only a few decades before.

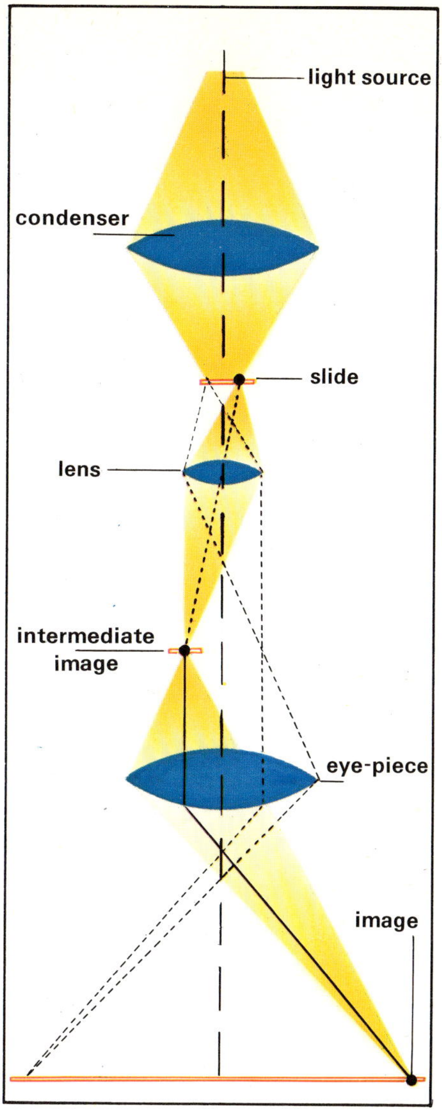

Scientific research having proliferated to such an extent, doctors and research men in all branches of medicine throughout the world could now see the lines to pursue for tackling many of the outstanding problems. Most importantly, the

This diagram shows the direction of light rays through an optic microscope.

Louis Pasteur, the famous French chemist, working in his laboratory.

means of developing an almost unlimited number of new techniques were at hand. Today, in fact, the doctor finds himself facing a new difficulty—that of keeping sufficiently well informed and up to date, despite the mass of information published daily on recent advances in medicine.

Contemporary medicine

At the beginning of our century, the first steps were taken towards a new branch of medicine. In 1901, the German physicist Wilhelm Roentgen was awarded the Nobel Prize for his discovery of certain rays which he termed X-rays, on account of their being previously unknown.

A few years before, Roentgen had observed that a screen coated with barium platinocyanide became luminescent in the dark when a nearby vacuum tube was discharging. He realized that the rays emitted from the cathode of this Crookes' tube would pass through any solid object of a non-metallic nature, and would reveal its internal structure by way of differences in shadow cast on a sensitive photographic plate behind the object. Roentgen presented the photograph of a hand, which became famous and the astonished world heard his now famous description: "If the hand is held between the discharge apparatus and the screen, the darker shadows of the bones can be seen in the lighter image of the hand."

Doctors all over the world began to apply the newly discovered principle, and so *radiology* was born. In the course of a few decades examination techniques became so refined that not only was a complete picture of the skeleton obtainable, but also a detailed and clear image of all the internal organs and systems such as the digestive tract and the kidney apparatus. These soft parts show up in X-rays when they are made to absorb certain kinds of barium and iodine salts.

Almost at the same time, the French husband and wife team, Pierre and Marie Curie, discovered radium which also emitted rays. It was found that X-rays and radium could be used as therapy for some forms of tumours, since both were able to destroy tumour cells. Unfortunately, these radiations also destroyed skin tissue, and the radiologists themselves began to suffer from radiation injuries. They developed areas of skin irritation that worsened, leading to severe skin and eventually to internal tissue de-

generation that sometimes became lethal. It was never imagined, at the start of the century, that these few early victims, who were exposed to radiation through their scientific work, were the predecessors of those many who were to be killed by the fall-out from atomic bombs a few decades later. Nor was it conceivable that radioactive contamination would rapidly become such a serious problem for the safety and survival of successive generations.

At the same time as scientists were achieving a more profound and better understanding of the way in which the human body functioned through X-ray examinations, the Austrian doctor Sigmund Freud was advancing some very revolutionary theories on the workings of the human mind. His ideas soon spread widely and created a new understanding of the factors governing man's mental activity.

Freud re-examined some of his earlier intuitive ideas to give them a

Robert Koch, the discoverer of the bacillus popularly known as Koch's bacillus

Mycobacterium tuberculosis

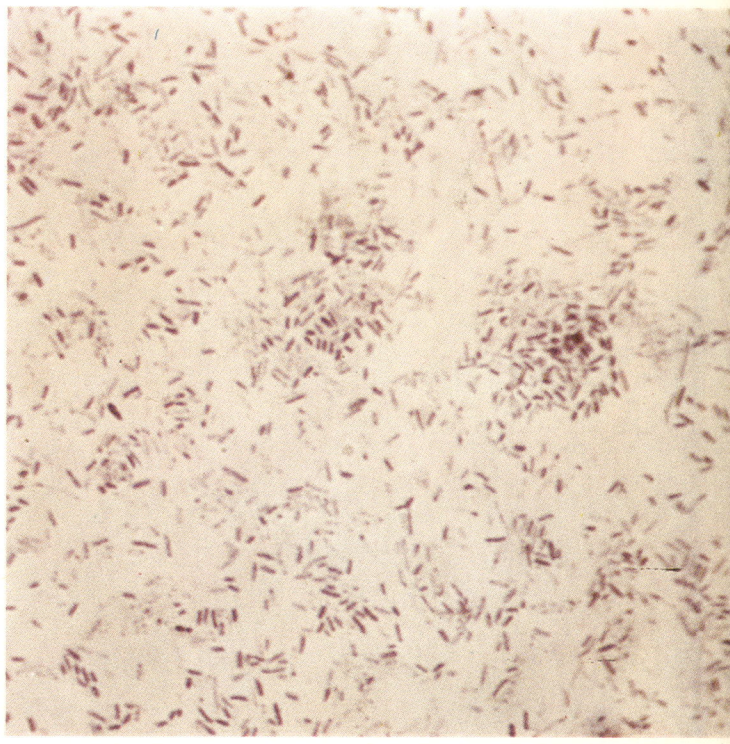

Wilhelm Conrad Roentgen who discovered X-rays.

Marie and Pierre Curie whose discovery of radium had a profound effect on the treatment of some forms of tumours.

more scientific basis and correlated some of them with what he had observed when visiting the hospital for mental disorders run by the celebrated physician Charcot in Paris. Freud then made his own original deductions. One of his major theories was that certain important mental activities and processes take place in man, of which the conscious mind is unaware. After long studies and observation of many patients, Freud concluded that in the normal course of our life, and as a reaction to it, a combination of impulses, feelings and ideas is born and stored in a part of the mind called the "subconscious". These impressions are not openly expressed but remain submerged in the form of repressed emotions, which do not come sufficiently near the surface to be consciously recognized and identified by the individual.

As a consequence of this repression, the stronger repressed emotions seek relief—which they sometimes find, but only by interfering with the whole psyche and disturbing its balance, thus producing neurotic symptoms and illnesses.

Freud applied these hypotheses to the practical field and developed a special investigation technique. This is an interchange between doctor and patient, through which the patient is helped to release his repressed emotions in a balanced sort of way. Eventually the patient learns to see consciously the deep underlying cause or causes of his mental disturbance. In theory, this should then free him of his neuroses and psychosomatic ills.

This technique was given the name *psychoanalysis*. It opened up an unknown world to medical science, extending the treatment of mental

Sigmund Freud, the father of psychoanalysis.

ills far beyond its previously narrow confines, and influencing practically every sector of medical thought. The implications of Freud's theories are that man is a totality, in which mind and body are indivisible. This means that there is a constant interplay of mental and physical factors, each influencing the other, and giving rise to a host of actions and reactions in both spheres.

Freud's ideas were initially met with misunderstanding and hostility, yet today he is considered a great innovator. His theories and clinical techniques, now somewhat altered and refined by the disciples of the school he founded, have enormously extended the scope of psychiatry, the medical field that deals with the mind. Providing a more profound understanding of the human psyche, Freud's ideas gave rise to new interpretations and insights in areas outside the strictly medical field, such as sociology. More generally, Freud illuminated the relationship between the single individual and his fellow, and laid the basis for modern concepts of mass psychology.

To sum up, the methods of scientific study that had begun so slowly, uncertainly, and with such difficulty in the dawn of civilization, were developed and perfected in the first quarter of this century. Countless scholars, famous and unknown contributed over the centuries to the refinement of the art of medicine. Finally, it now rested on a truly scientific basis, instead of the realm of approximation and clever guesses or hypotheses. Now only that which could be incontrovertibly and scientifically demonstrated was considered valid.

A 19th-century caricature of the process of obtaining vaccines.

cathode
condensing reels
object
revolving lens
aperture
polarized enlarger
intermediate image
focuser
image

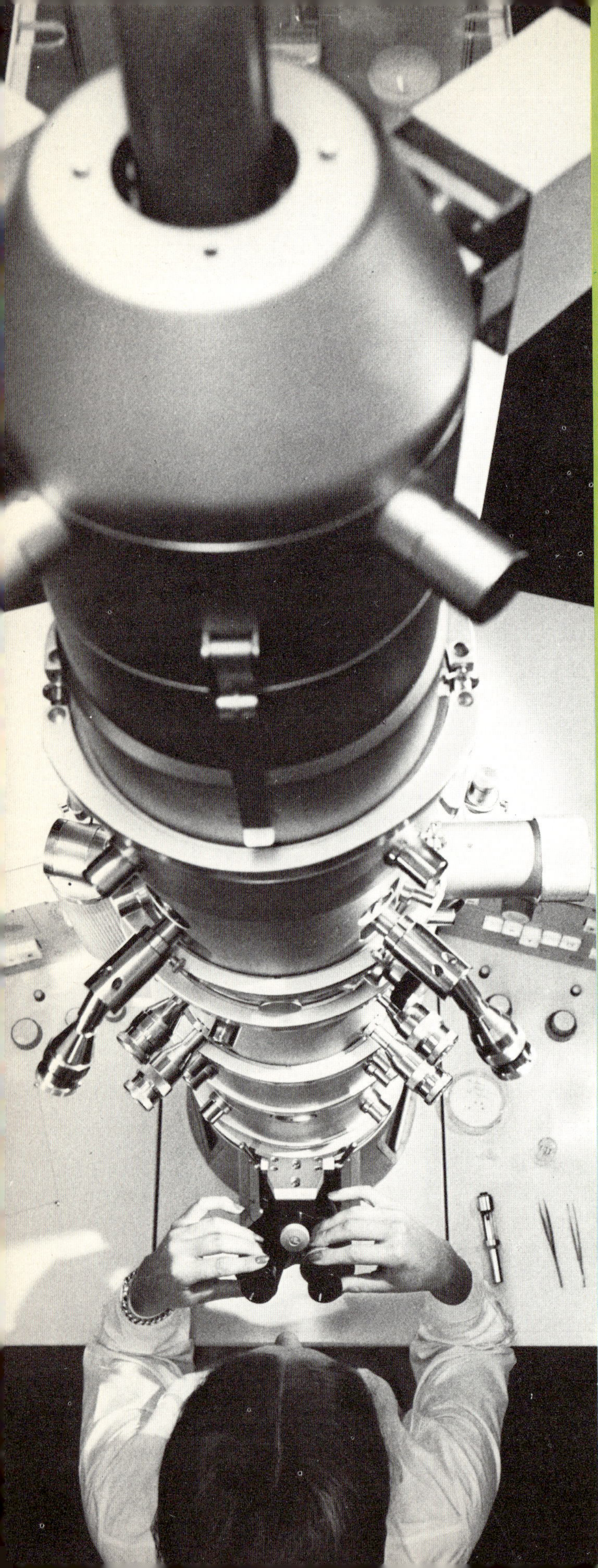

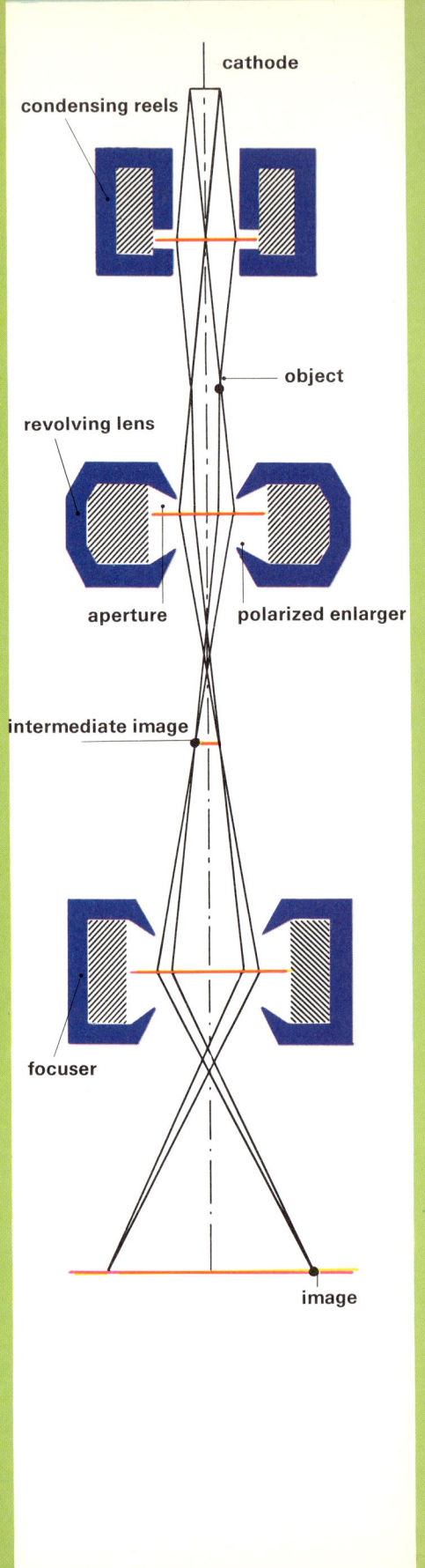

CHAPTER 3

IN THE TWENTIETH CENTURY

With the advantages made available in technology, medicine made tremendous advances in the second quarter of this century. This brings us to the present day when, despite the achievements of recent years, many goals still seem far distant and not even clearly defined. However, our knowledge of biology has advanced so far that without question it will transform medical know-how and modify the tenor of man's life on earth.

Just as a building is made up of vast numbers of bricks placed next to and on top of one another, so all living tissue is made up of millions of fundamental units, each of which is called a *cell*.

Cells were first seen and described three centuries ago by Marcello Malpighi. The years that followed saw the birth of histology and microscopic anatomy, sciences that study the structure of cells and the different kinds of tissues. These studies took an enormous and fundamental step forward with the advent of the electron microscope in the 1930s. The maximum magnification obtainable with the standard optical microscope was 2,500 times, but now this amazing new instrument dramatically increased man's powers of observation, permitting the human eye to see and study the infinitely small. The resolving power, that is the capacity to reveal details, of the electron microscope is actually some two-thousand times greater than that of the optical microscope.

Unlike the optical microscope, which uses visible light and the magnifying power of the lens, the electron microscope generates a minute beam of electrons (particles which possess an electric charge) and focuses it on the material being examined. Bombarded in this way, the examined material reflects the electrons which are then collected and conveyed to a cathode ray tube which transforms them into an image. This image is then magnified, this time by electromagnetic, rather than optical, lenses. Finally projected on to a fluorescent screen, the image has now been made accessible to the human eye.

In an alternative system, the fluorescent screen is replaced by a photographic device, so that a permanent record can be obtained of whatever the microscope reveals. Using special filters and additional technical devices to increase the effects, the degree of magnification gained has enabled single atoms to be distinguished within the cell. An English firm has recently produced and supplied several universities with a gigantic electron microscope which requires 1 million volts to function. This microscope is so powerful that details with dimensions as minute as 500 millionths of a

Far left: the Elmiskop 102 electron microscope which enlarges an object four and a half million times. Near left: a diagram showing how the microscope works.

The cell and its components: 1. cellular membrane; 2. vacuoles; 3. lysosome; 4. DNA; 5. nucleolus; 6. mitocondrium; 7. nuclear membrane; 8. Golgi apparatus; 9. ribosomes; 10. labyrinthine areas of cellular membrane.

Opposite: A few molecular structures.

centimetre (about 830 millionths of an inch) can be distinguished.

By producing such highly perfected instruments, it is possible to gain a much deeper knowledge of living and non-living matter, to extend the boundaries of our knowledge to an almost unimaginable extent, and to verify in detail much of what was already known. It is a constantly observed fact that, once the means of investigation and experimentation has been refined, much knowledge, which until then has been regarded as fully defined, reveals unsuspected depths, and new paths of study are opened up.

The range of size in living beings is immense, and the ratio of the smallest to the largest may be 1:1,000 million. If we consider the order of size of that which is visible under the optical microscope, we find we are dealing with entities to be measured in *microns*, that is in thousandths of a millimetre (1 mm. = .039 in.): we are in the range of average cell size. There are whole organisms that consist of only a single cell, while the human body is composed of countless thousands of millions of cells. In each case, however, every cell is a living individual entity, the smallest single living unit, and is capable of an independent existence under the right conditions. All cells are differentiated to some extent, in accordance with the functions they perform, but all of them share certain essential characteristics. Cells are bounded externally by a membrane that allows exchanges to take place between the cell and its surrounding environment; enclosed within this boundary membrane, like the flesh of a fruit, is the *cytoplasm*. This jelly-like substance in turn contains other discrete structures that constitute distinct functional systems. The best-known of these cytoplasmic structures are the *endoplasmic reticulum* (a system of fine canals), the *mitochondria* and the *ribosomes*, each of which have their own functional role in the life of the cell. Deep within the cell, like the stone within a fruit, is the *nucleus*; this is the most vital part of the cell and without it the cell dies; it too is enclosed in its own membrane.

When the living matter of the cell itself is examined and analysed, today's instruments are able to reveal the composition and structure of the very molecules that make up this

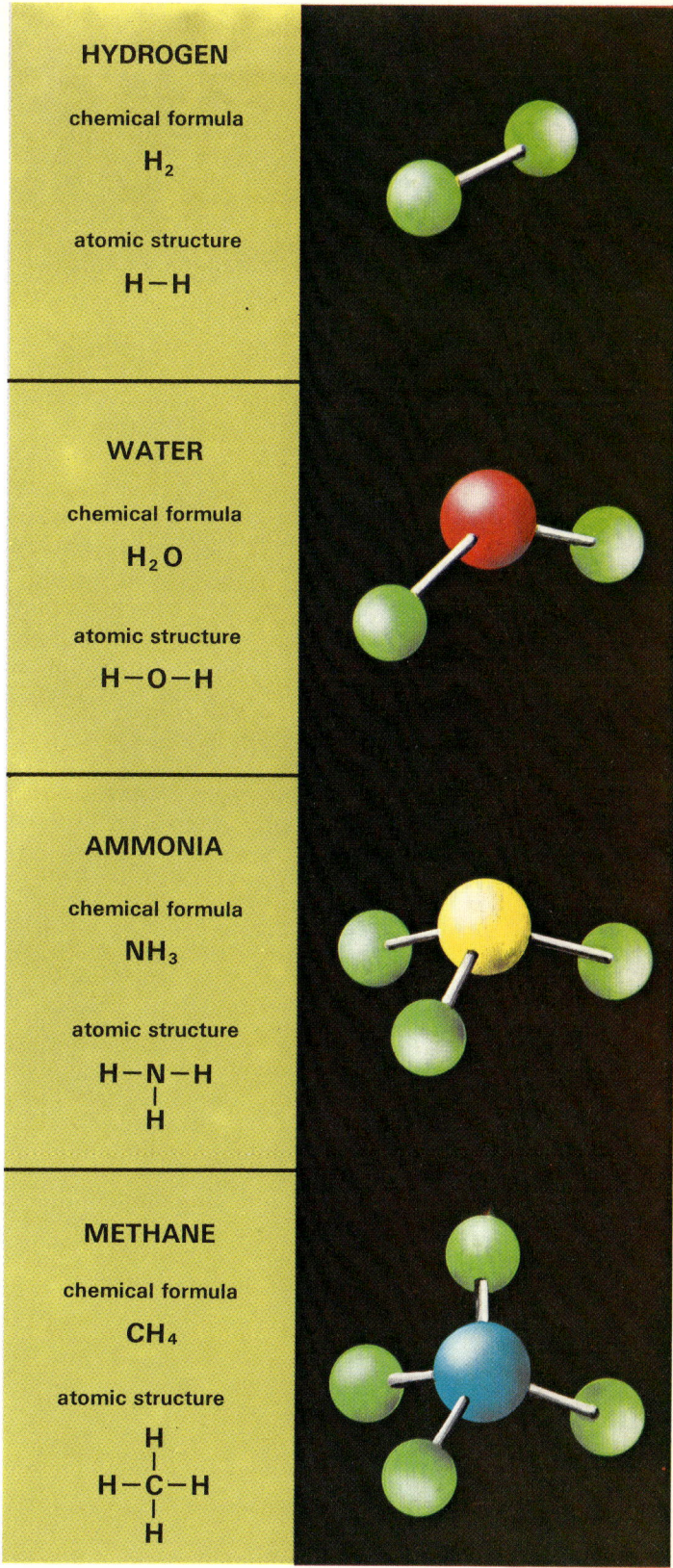

HYDROGEN

chemical formula

H_2

atomic structure

H—H

WATER

chemical formula

H_2O

atomic structure

H—O—H

AMMONIA

chemical formula

NH_3

atomic structure

H—N—H
    |
    H

METHANE

chemical formula

CH_4

atomic structure

    H
    |
H—C—H
    |
    H

living substance. These molecules are called *organic molecules*, in contrast to the inorganic molecules that make up non-living materials. Molecular variety and arrangements within the cell are almost unlimited, but many of these ultimate components of living matter are now understood in terms of their physical atomic structure and also in terms of their interrelated biological functions within the cell. In other words, we now know how some of these molecules are put together chemically, and we also know how they work inside the cell.

We have thus gradually come down to the realm of the smallest measurable units of which life is composed. These molecular and atomic structures exhibit seemingly unlimited complexity and variety. Certain specific molecules are composed of chains of vast numbers of atomic structures exhibit seemingly different from one another, and whose geometric relationships appear infinitely varied. Step by step, we have descended into what seems like an abyss, where the infinitesimally small repeats the pattern of the infinitely large relationships we have become used to considering when examining space. It is indeed an abyss, for we have reached the sphere of *biochemistry*, the science that probes the fundamental processes of life, molecule by molecule, cell by cell, tissue by tissue. Biochemical processes take place without interruption deep within us, and as long as they function regularly, the body maintains a normal state of health. But if they are disturbed, illness results. Such a disturbance may come about through internal organic changes, or by external environmental factors such as infection by viruses or bacteria that cause disease.

We now know so much about the nature of the components, and the arrangement of the various atoms in different molecules, that we can reproduce structural models of certain molecular substances. However, despite the many discoveries already made we are really only beginning, as the field of molecular biology includes an incredible number of these *macro-molecules*, so called because of their relatively large size and complexity. It is calculated for example that in a single cell the number of atoms of oxygen, hydrogen, carbon and nitrogen (the most common elements present in the molecules which make up living cells and tissues including that of the human body) may add up to some hundred of thousands of millions. Remember that all these atoms are contained in a single cell so small that four of them together would only measure a hundredth part of a millimetre.

We seem to be on the fringes of science fiction in trying to imagine the unlimited conglomeration of these tiny yet exceedingly active worlds contained in our body, living parts of ourselves, yet parts which individually we neither control nor feel. Although we are not normally aware of these chemical molecules it is along the path of biochemistry that the future lies.

The symptom that serves to identify an illness (a localized pain or rash, for example) is an outward manifestation, an empirical piece of information that has come down to us from past centuries of experience as the traditional element of recognition. However, the key to future progress in medicine lies in the understanding and control of the chemical phenomena that are continually taking place deep within us, and which are at the root of these outward symptoms. If we are able to observe matter in the appropriate manner, it can tell us much; it

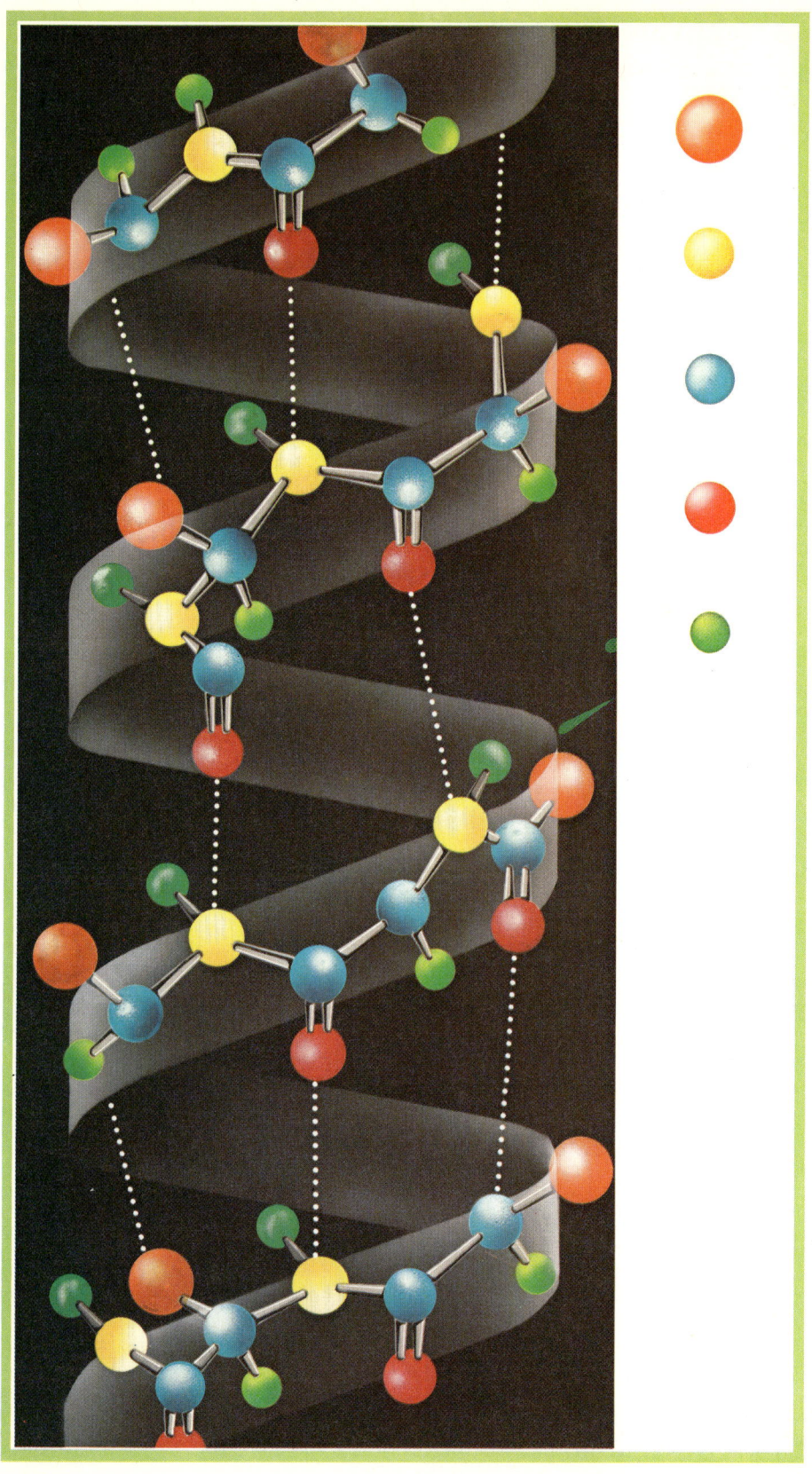

A "spiral" model of a protein molecule.

29

communicates with us, showing itself through its constitution and its observable state of activity. Considering living matter on a molecular level, it can be said to have its own comprehensible and decipherable language, based on the way the atoms of the molecule are distributed, arranged and connected with one another. This atomic and molecular framework can be likened to a page of writing, in which every graphic symbol and the arrangement of words on each line have a precise meaning, which results in an overall pattern that conveys the meaning of the whole page of writing. Conversely, every variation or substitution modifies the sense of these same words, and alters the meaning in some way.

This kind of comparison between molecular make-up and symbolic expression of meaning (as in writing) will be useful later on in helping us to understand the principles of *genetics*.

Macromolecules: the proteins and nucleic acids

Of the many groups into which macromolecules are subdivided, modern biology has paid particular attention to two: the *proteins*, and the *nucleic acids*. The proteins are large molecules, composed of long chains of chemical substances called *amino acids* which are linked to one another. There is not a vast number of different atoms constituting matter on earth and there is an even more limited number common to living matter. The amino acids—of which there are only twenty common ones—are all composed of only a few different atoms: carbon, hydrogen, oxygen, nitrogen, and in two cases sulphur as well. The way in which these atoms are arranged in a three-dimensional lattice-like pattern is characteristic of, and unvarying for, each amino acid. These relatively few amino acids are the basic building units for the proteins, but they can be linked to one another in such a variety of ways that the number of different proteins that can result is practically infinite.

One of the most important characteristics that differentiates one cell from another, e.g. a muscle cell from a nerve cell, and in turn from any other cell, is the type of protein that each cell contains. All these cells are alive and performing their functions, which consist in a complex of specific reactions and chemical transformations of substances that are in continuous flux with the cell's environment. This building up and breaking down of materials is called *cell metabolism*.

None of these chemical reactions would be possible within our bodies if the proteins did not include a special category of organic molecules known as *enzymes*. These enzymes have a very special property: they direct and control the entire activity of the cell, as they have the ability to initiate and accelerate specific chemical reactions and regulate their outcome. Every metabolic process is controlled by a specific enzyme, of which there are over a thousand, all working in harmony with one another.

But, in order to perpetuate itself, living matter has not only to maintain itself through metabolic activity, it must also be able to reproduce itself. This is where the second class of macromolecules comes in, the nucleic acids present in the nucleus of every cell. Although these acids had been known for a long time, it was not until the late 1950s and through the 1960s that their exact structure and role was described and determined. The most important nucleic acid within the nucleus is *deoxyribonucleic acid*

Mendel's Laws. Example of transmission of two characters (colour and surface) in successive generations of peas (above).

Form of transmission of another plant character (flower colour, either red or white).

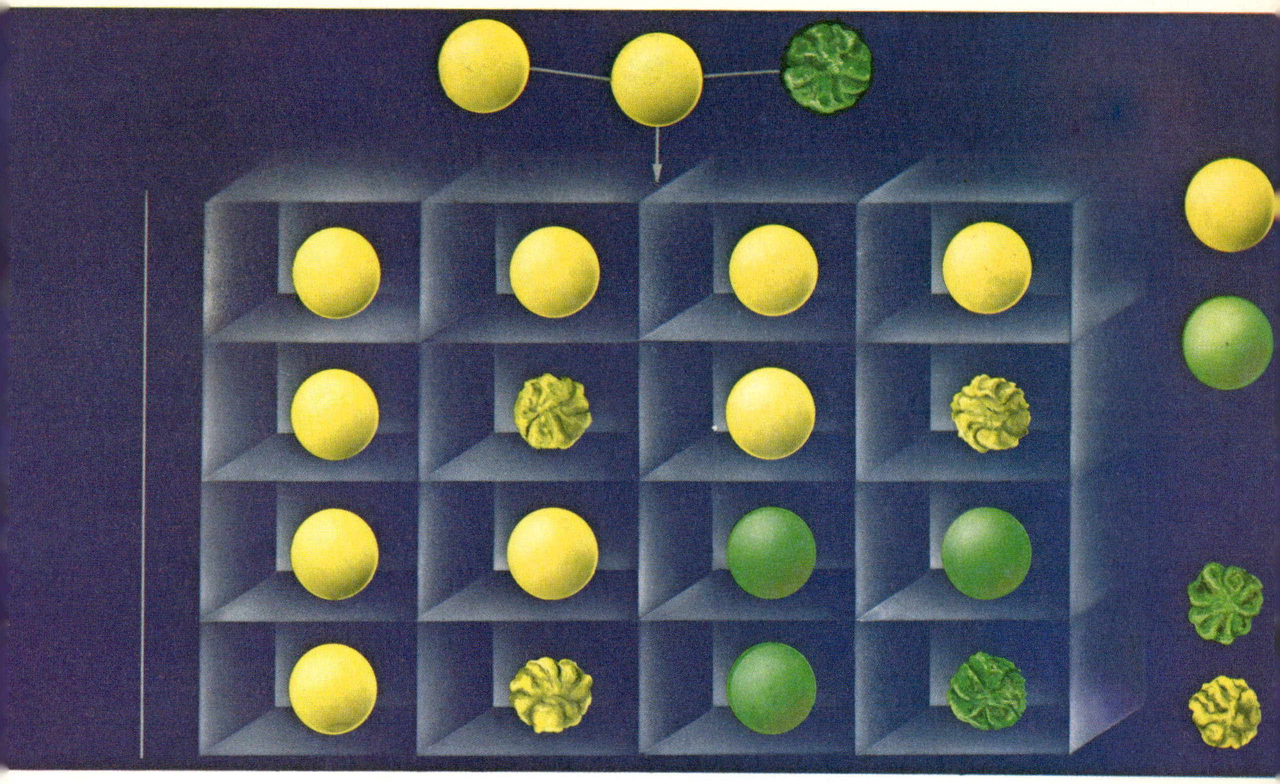

31

(abbreviated to DNA). DNA has been found to possess the extraordinary and exclusive ability to build up and duplicate those chemical molecules upon which the transmission of hereditary characteristics depends. DNA has a very characteristic molecular structure shaped like a double helix or spiral, and it is especially active when cells enter their reproductive phase. DNA is an integral and essential part of the cell nucleus and it is the major constituent of the *chromosomes*. The chromosomes are structures that become visible in the nucleus during certain stages of cell division, and they are responsible for passing on the hereditary information that every cell transmits to all the cells derived from it. The double helix of DNA has the ability to unwind and to make two twin copies of itself, thus giving the necessary instructions to the two new cells that are derived during cell division. DNA is the fundamental and irreplaceable molecule that forms the hereditary pattern of all living things. It not only copies itself during cell division, but it also provides the basic pattern for another nucleic acid, *ribonucleic acid* (abbreviated as RNA) whose structure and composition is similar to DNA. Some of the RNA molecules which are formed by the DNA molecules serve as "messengers" into the cytoplasm outside the nucleus where they determine the chemical formation of the proteins and enzymes necessary to the living process of a cell. The ribosomes, mentioned earlier, play an important role during the manufacture of proteins.

During cell division, there is a doubling of the DNA material in the nucleus, so that two new nuclei, each with the same hereditary characters as the "mother" cell, are formed. This process ensures the preservation of a species' specific characteristics from one generation to the next.

However, such a strict duplication of hereditary materials does not always take place. Mistakes can occur during the duplication of the DNA. When such errors happen during the formation of the germ cell that provide the beginnings of a new generation, they are called *mutations*. Most mutations are harmful and lead to the crippling or death of the developing embryo, but some of these "mistakes" form the basis of viable variations in structure and function. When the environment in which a species lives changes, some of these variations may turn out to be exactly right for the new conditions of existence. And in this fashion, mutations are at the root of all biological progress and evolutionary change.

The role of DNA then is a twofold one: first, to copy itself and to pass on to other generations the directions it contains; second, to control the chemical reaction of the cells of which it is part, thus controlling the functioning of the entire organism.

The DNA molecule is the most important, as well as the largest molecule present in all living organisms, including the human species. Its three-dimensional structure was first described in the 1950s as a double helix, rather like a spiral staircase, by two scientists working together: the English chemist Francis Crick and the American biologist James Dewey Watson. Today DNA is being studied with a view to one day modifying the structure itself. The aim is to substitute healthy chromosomal formations for defective ones so as to do away with the hereditary transmission of certain malformations, defects and diseases.

A diagram representing the translation of the genetic "message" into protein. The top shows the DNA, in which the genetic message is eucoded. The next section shows a molecule of RNA polymerase (the ball) attached to the DNA. RNA polymerase molecules move along the DNA (third section) making molecules of RNA which are copies of one strand of the DNA; these RNA molecules act as intermediary messengers. The bottom shows the messenger RNA attached to ribosomes (the "factories" in the cytoplasm where the proteins are made) where its copy of the genetic message is translated into protein.

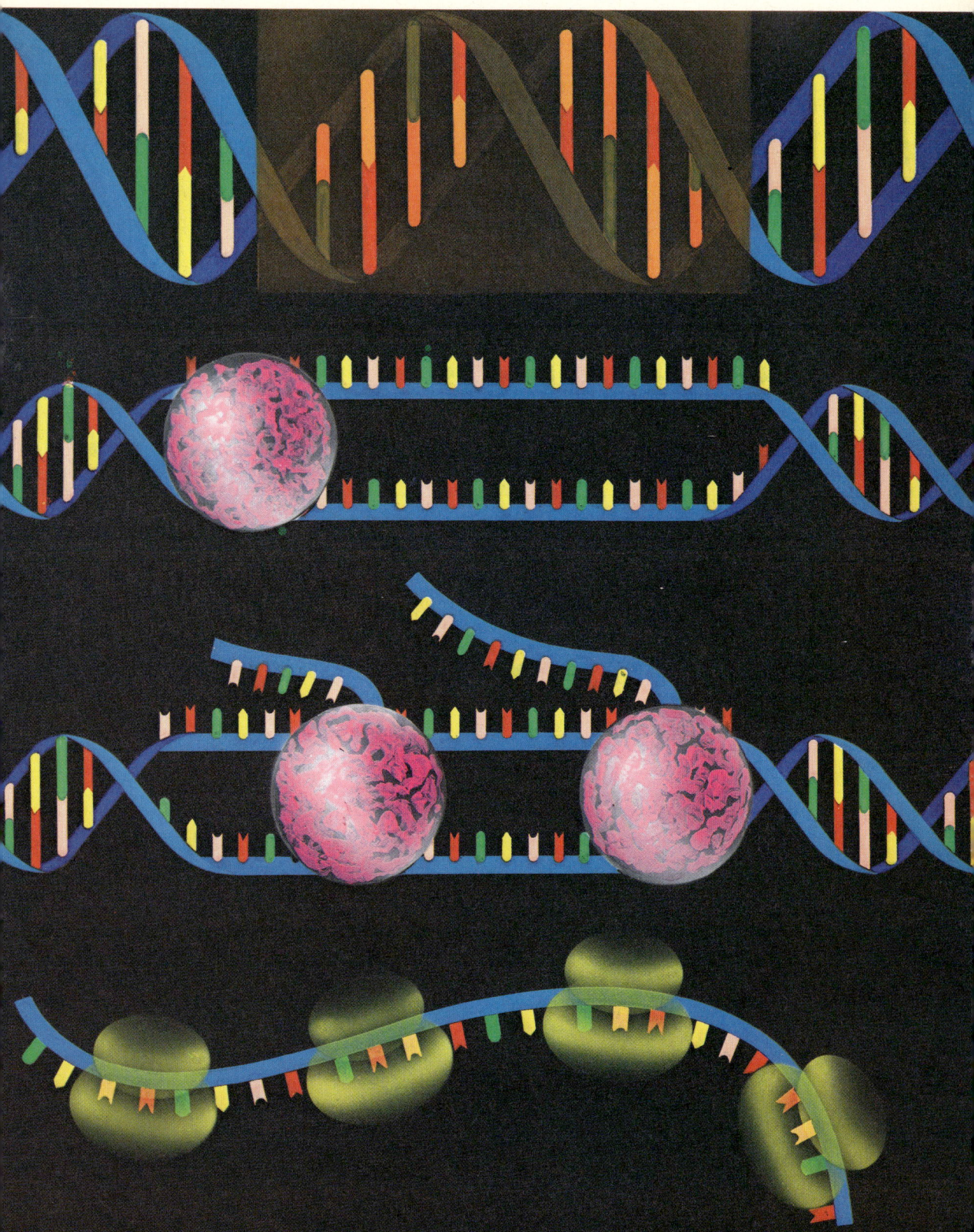

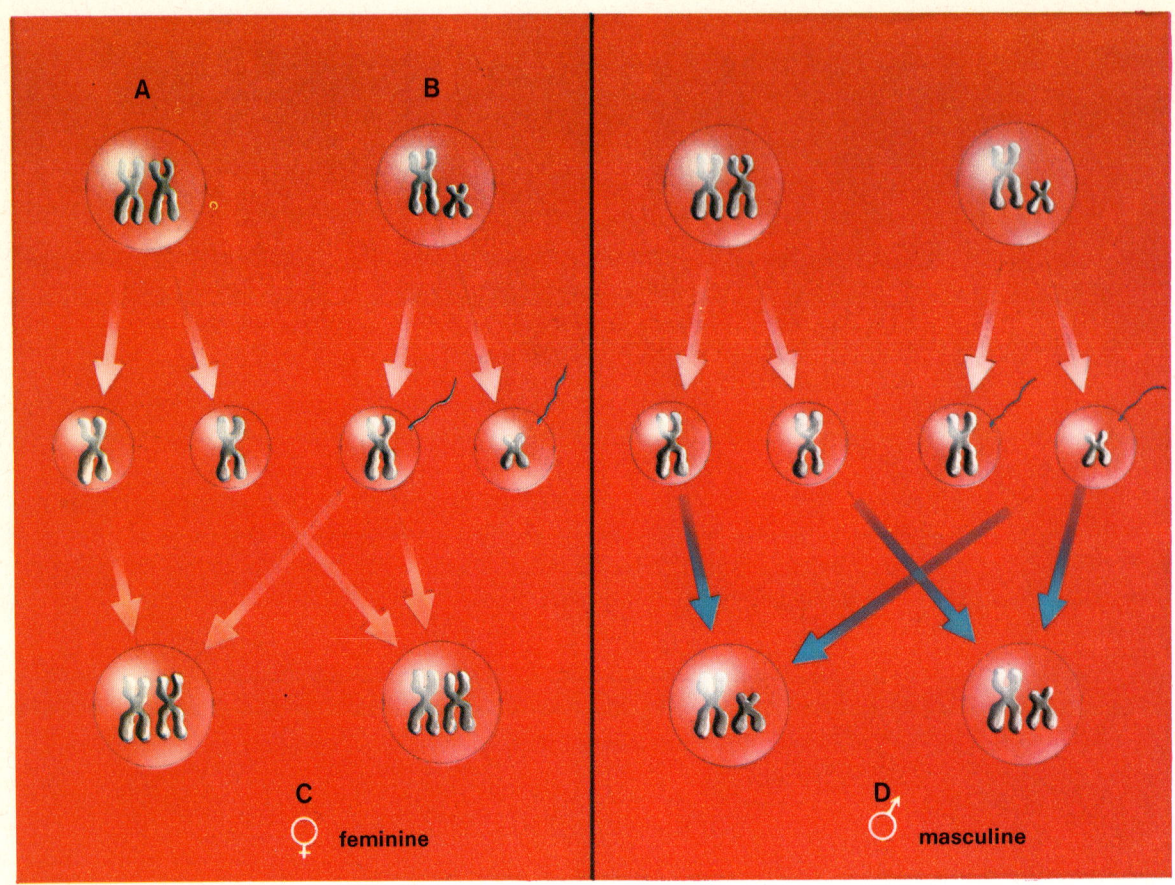

Female ovules containing the male and female chromosomes which together determine sex.

In order to understand this aim more fully, some points should be made clear. The chromosomes, as we have seen, are the storehouses of genetic information responsible for transmitting the hereditary characteristics to successive generations of cells. There is normally a fixed number of chromosomes for each animal species: the nucleus of human cells, for instance, has 46 chromosomes arranged in pairs, derived originally from two sets of 23 chromosomes, each set being provided by the germ cells of the respective parents. These germ cells, one male (the sperm) and one female (the ovum), only have half the normal number of chromosomes, so that when their nuclei fuse at fertilization, the resulting fertilized cell has the full number of chromosomes. Each chromosome is elongated in shape and looks like a small, bent rod. Each rod is itself composed of a great many distinct sections or units strung together that are called *genes*. Each gene in turn has its own information and has the capacity to control single and distinct hereditary features such as the colour of skin and eyes or the conformation of the various internal organs. Genes, which are sections

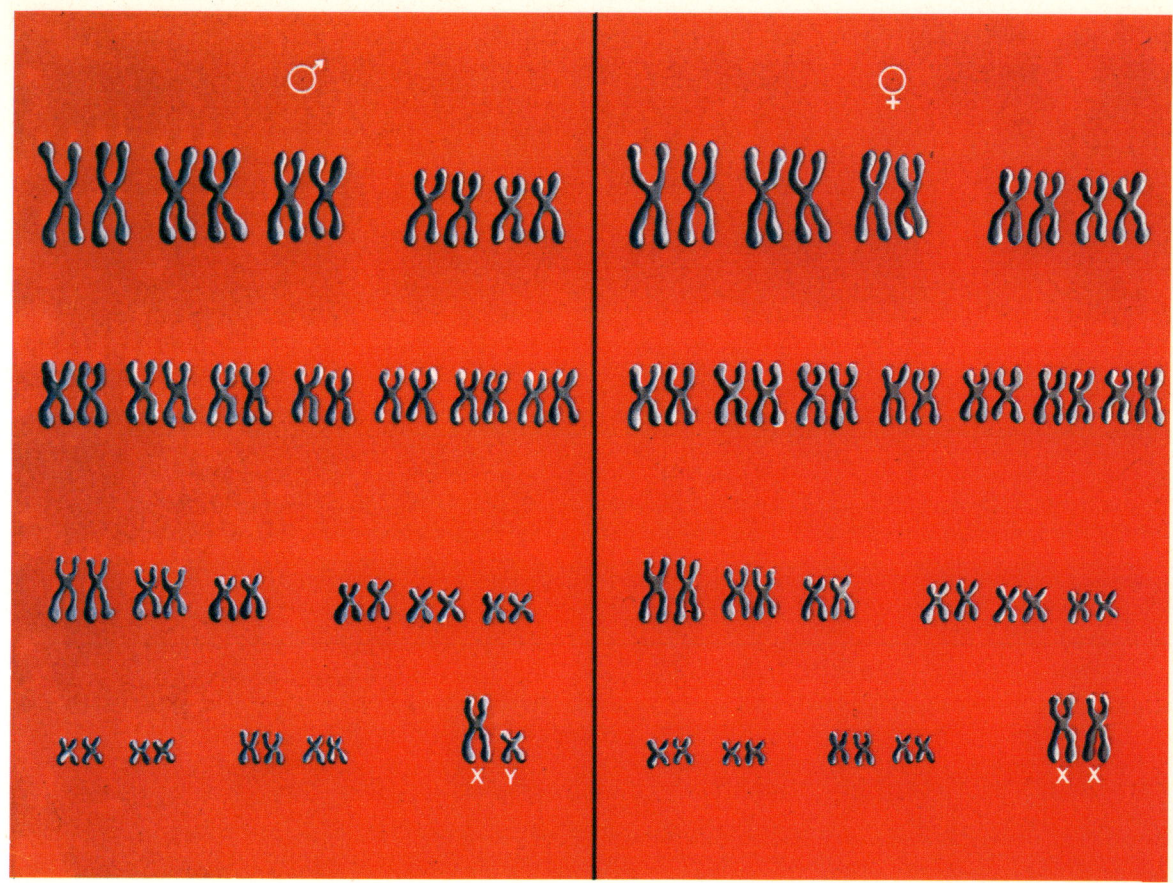

Series of male and female chromosomes.

of DNA, are basically responsible for determining the formation of the various enzymes that in turn control the overall functioning of the vast biochemical laboratory that structures and sustains life in all organisms. We can now return to the subject of modifying DNA structure for correcting genetic abnormalities. With the help of microsurgery we might eventually be able to get at the nucleus of a single cell and substitute a normal gene for that section of DNA that is responsible for a given metabolic error or any other hereditary defect. In theory, all the generations of cells arising from the operated cell would then reproduce the new characteristics and be restored to normality.

Of course, all these possibilities for future medical progress presuppose that we will be able to fully understand the molecular sequence, made up of millions of separate units, of all the DNA in the human species. Although such a goal lies in the distant future, it is not just a vague fantasy. With the knowledge we already have in the field of molecular biology and heredity, direct interference with the nucleic acid molecules may certainly become a reality.

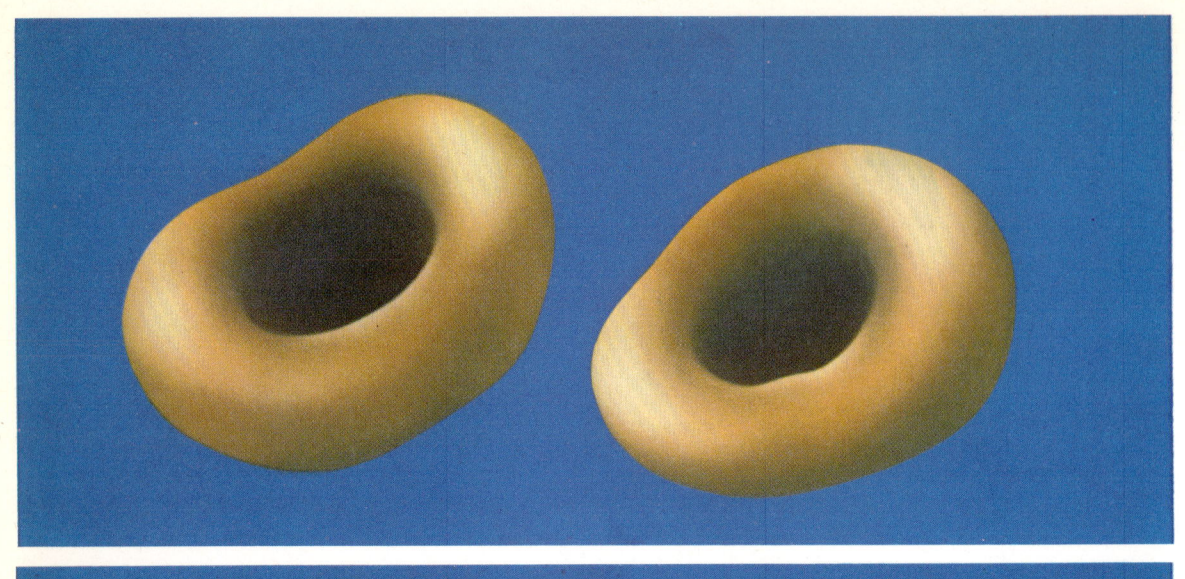

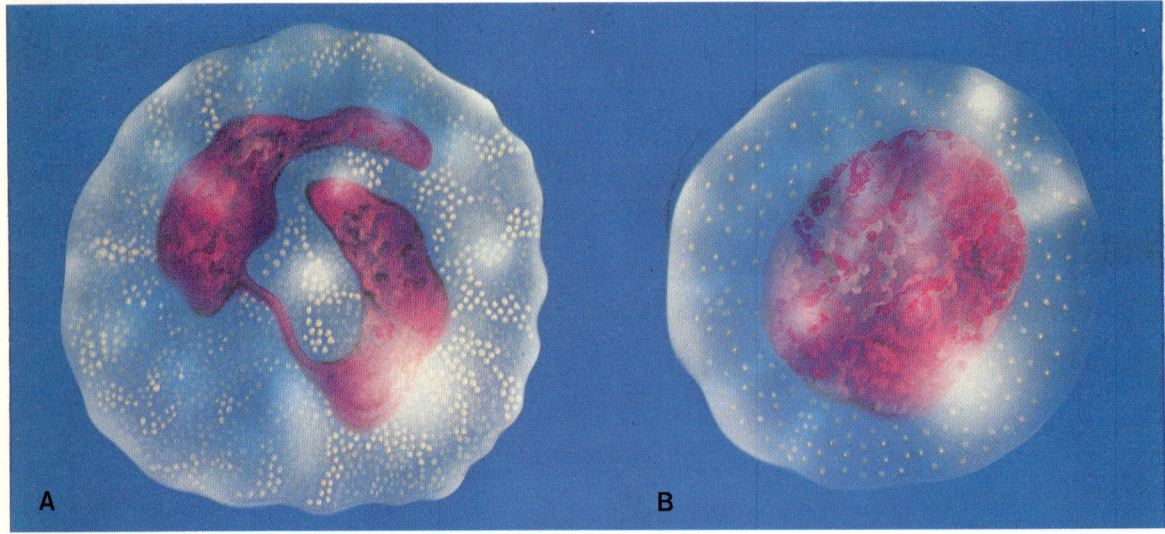

A B

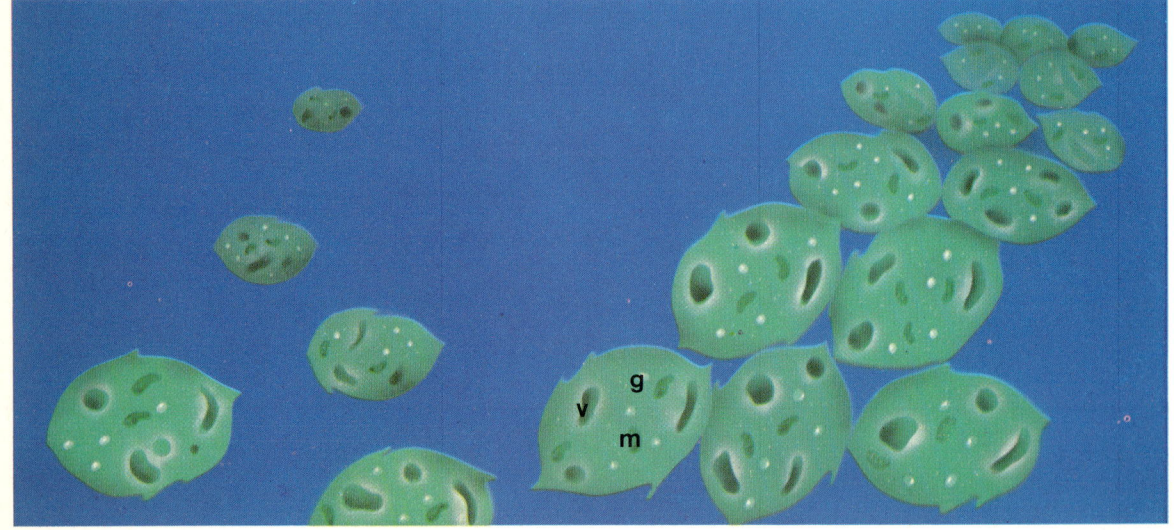

g
v
m

CHAPTER 4

THE CONQUESTS OF MEDICINE IN OUR CENTURY

In the first decades of our century, when the pace was somewhat slower, the most important medical discoveries were made in the area of infectious diseases. After the deaths of Pasteur and Koch, bacteriologists continued the research of these two great men. The French schools, following Pasteur, worked mainly on problems concerned with immunization against various diseases. The German schools systematically continued to search for, isolate, identify and culture in the laboratory those bacilli which they suspected might be the causative factors of infectious diseases. Their aim was to learn the characteristics and essential requirements of these micro-organisms so as to strike at the vulnerable points in their life cycle and prepare substances that could destroy them.

In the area of immunity, successive studies showed that the serum (cell-free) fraction of the blood of an animal that had been immunized by Pasteur's techniques would, if injected into a second animal, make this animal immune in its turn. In this way sera were prepared that would immunize against tetanus and diphtheria. Used in large amounts at a sufficiently early stage, or better still preventatively, these sera proved capable of suppressing the majority of cases of these diseases which had wrought such havoc for so long.

Having confirmed the existence of *toxins*, that is poisonous substances secreted by disease-causing bacteria, and using special filters that retained the bacteria but allowed the toxins to pass through, the latter were finally isolated. It was observed that when toxins were injected into an animal in increasing doses, they eventually immunized it against the disease.

Rather than studying *serotherapy*, other research workers devoted their efforts to *vaccine therapy*, injecting specially treated (usually dead) germs. It was found these too would confer immunity. Using these methods a third group of terrible diseases capable of inflicting great casualties—namely typhoid and paratyphoid A and B—became less of a menace and were no longer inevitably fatal.

However, in contrast to these successes, the majority of infectious diseases resisted all efforts to combat them; their disease-causing agents proved almost unaffected by serotherapy and vaccine therapy. Unfortunately, these could be said to represent the majority of the bacterial army that attacked mankind, the everyday adversaries, some causing septic infection of wounds, others attacking certain organs of the human body, and others again multiplying so rapidly that they killed the patient by general poison-

Corpuscular elements of the blood seen through an electron microscope: red corpuscles (top); leucocytes; granulocytes (A), lymphocytes (B) (centre); plates (below).

ing of his system. Confronted with these many different kinds of disease-causing micro-organisms the doctor was almost powerless and his position was not too different from that of physicians of ancient times. He knew full well that certain disinfectants such as carbolic acid were quite capable of killing bacteria where this was necessary for disinfecting the skin. However, he could not use such agents internally, precisely because they were poisonous or caustic.

Bacteria are classified into a large number of categories: according to the way they appear under the microscope, they are termed *cocci* if rounded, *bacilli* if rod-shaped, *spirilla* when they are shaped like spirals. Bacterial defence against unfavourable environmental conditions consists of producing and enclosing their cell body in a kind of resistant membrane, and in this case they are called *spores*.

Particularly in the spore state, many bacteria remain alive for as long as twelve hours, even when immersed in boiling water. Bacteria of one sort or another are found everywhere and there appear to be almost no environmental restrictions. It is calculated that a cubic centimetre of common soil contains over 20,000 million bacteria. Water, milk and other liquids all contain considerable numbers of bacteria, as does our saliva, our skin and some of our internal organs. This is particularly true for our intestine, where some of the digestive processes could not be completed without the presence and biological activity of an abundant bacterial population.

We can infer from this that man lives surrounded by, and virtually impregnated with an incalculable quantity of bacteria. The latter are by far the most numerous living creatures on earth, and are able to reproduce themselves with unparalleled rapidity. But of course the majority of bacteria are harmless, and many are in fact necessary and beneficial. If this were not the case mankind would long ago have lost the battle and disappeared from the face of the earth. Only certain species of bacteria are responsible for producing diseases: they are called *pathogenic bacteria*.

The sulphonamides

At the beginning of this century, scientists began to fight these pathogenic bacteria with new weapons, developed not only by brilliant research workers isolated in their own laboratories, but also through the use of the technological facilities provided by industry. *Chemotherapy* was thus born. This is the treatment of diseases with drugs based on chemical substances of accurately defined structure. These are designed and obtained in scientific research laboratories, extensively tested on animals first and when proved safe and effective, tested on patients. Finally they are produced and distributed throughout the world by the various pharmaceutical houses. A basic premise for the use of chemotherapeutic products is that they should be able to seriously harm or kill the bacteria in the human body without damaging the body itself.

One of the first chemotherapeutic agents was developed by the German Paul Ehrlich and the Japanese Noguchi. They synthesized a chemical compound derived from arsenic called *Salvarsan*, which proved highly effective in the treatment of syphilis, a venereal disease that until that time had been treated with the most primitive and usually ineffective methods. In the years which followed, chemotherapeutic agents, such as *Plasmochin* and

The two defence mechanisms of the organism. (A) the "immune response"; a cell that produces antibodies (green sphere) comes into contact with an antigen (orange cone) and remembers it; through this memory it will later be able to recognize this antigen and fight it. (B) A white corpuscle recognizes a bacterium, surrounds it (phagocytosis), and destroys it by means of special enzymes.

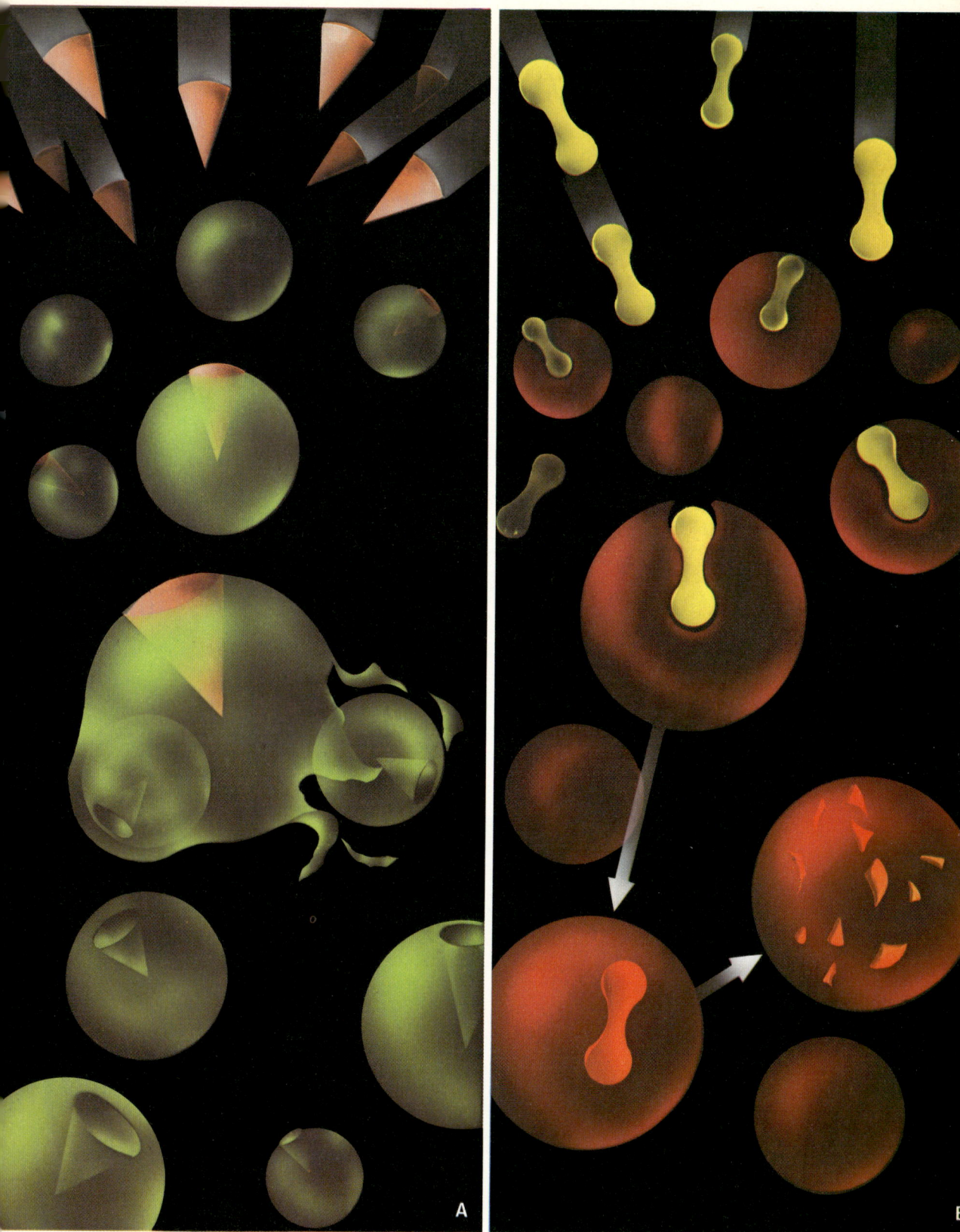

A B

39

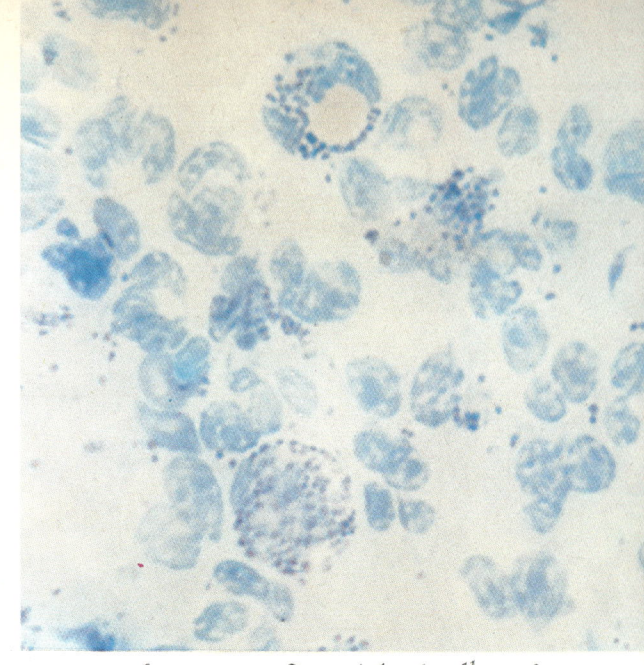

*Top left: cocci (*Diplococcus gonorrhoeae*).
Top centre: bacilli (*Bacillus anthracis*).
Top right: spirilla (spirillaform bacteria of stagnant water).*

Below: detail of the bacteriological laboratory of the Karolinska Hospital in Stockholm.

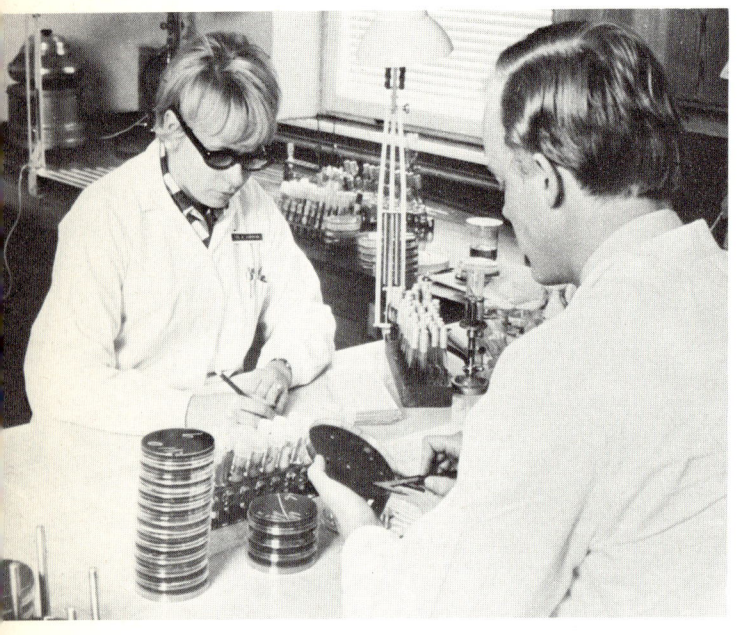

Atebrin were discovered and put on the market to combat malaria. These replaced the Peruvian bark preparation called *quinine* that had been used for centuries. Effective medicines were also discovered to treat various tropical diseases such as sleeping sickness and amoebic dysentery.

But it was during the 1930s that chemotherapy began to achieve its most impressive successes. Research by the German Domagk and other doctors, confirmed the deadly action of chemicals called sulphonamides on the development and multiplication of various pathogenic agents. Among these were the streptococci and staphylococci, bacteria that caused some of the most serious and widespread infections, and which in addition had proved to be especially resistant to vaccine therapy and serotherapy.

In order to appreciate the exchange of ideas which, from the 1930s on was to benefit and accelerate the reciprocal relationship between medical science and industry, let us look briefly at the steps which led up to the production of *Prontosil*. This sulphonamide has rightly become famous and is in use throughout the world. An Austrian industrialist had synthesized—namely obtained in the laboratory—a chemical compound which could fast-dye woollen fabrics red. The complex formula for this compound was worked out and modified by other research workers, until some of them perfected a new preparation that was given the name Prontosil. With the possibility of its medical application in mind, Domagk used Prontosil experimentally, administering it to groups of rats that had previously

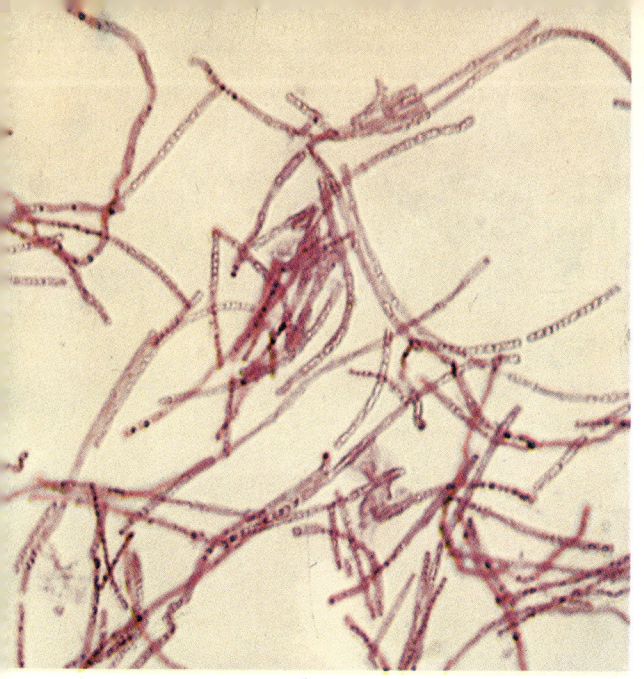
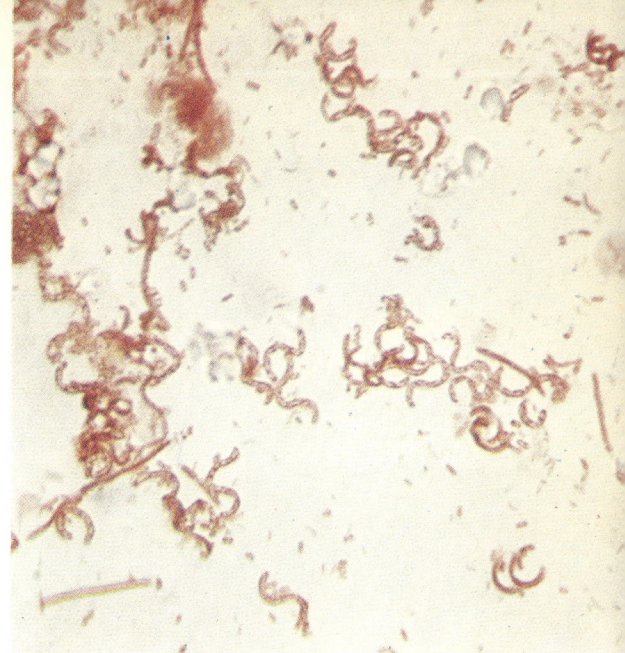

been injected with fatal doses of streptococci.

The consistent result was as follows: the groups of rats treated with Prontosil survived and recovered, and the other groups died. Prontosil was distributed and used throughout the world, while research workers of every nationality vied with one another to elucidate the mechanism of its biochemical and pharmacological activity. Eventually, it was noticed that when Prontosil reached the tissues of the human body, it dissociated into two separate chemical compounds, one of which remained inert, while the other was harmful to streptococci. Oddly enough, the active substance was precisely the same one as had been used by the industrialist years before for dyeing wool.

In the years which followed, research workers became involved in the search for other sulphonamides that could provide potent and effective treatment for particular types of infection caused by specific bacteria. Thus in 1938, for the first time in history, a severely ill patient was treated and cured of an illness against which doctors had been powerless. Until that time doctors had to confine their efforts to relieving the symptoms and leaving the patient's fate to his own body's natural defences. This disease was *pneumonia*, and since then it has ceased to be the invincible enemy that had led to so many fatalities.

The group of sulphonamides has grown consistently, including ever more specialized and active compounds against all kinds of infectious diseases, even *tuberculosis*. Used in association with one another certain sulpha drugs can exert a wider range of activity than they can singly. Such combinations can attack the *anaerobic* bacteria, that is bacteria whose life cycle does not involve the use of oxygen, and which are responsible for the most serious and untreatable infections, such as *gas gangrene*. Some sulphonamides have only *bacteriostatic* action, that is they are unable to destroy bacteria outright; they merely interfere with the life cycle in such a way that bacterial activity is reduced and multiplication inhibited. But even this limited effect is useful in maintaining health and survival in certain cases. During World War II the sulpha drugs proved a tremendous help to the countless wounded; they inhibited the development of gangrene, and reduced the number of

Domagk, discoverer of sulphonamides.

amputations necessary because of septic complications.

However, it is part of the natural process that all living things, from single-cell organisms to man, tend to adapt to their environment. When the surroundings change for the worse certain members of a given species frequently develop a resistance to the hostile factors as part of their defence mechanism. These individuals will be the ones to increase and eventually come to represent the species as a whole. This is just what happened with certain micro-organisms. Over recent decades many groups of bacteria have developed an increasing capacity to defend themselves against the new drugs, a property termed *sulphonamide resistance*.

Man was therefore still very far from having found the complete answer to disease, even in this respect. The wisest course of action in the light of the foregoing was to use the sulphonamides in combination with the older therapeutic measures. The latter included vaccine therapy and seroteraphy, together with a more modern immunization technique called *non-specific protein therapy*. The interesting result was that, in addition to their own immunological action, these modes of treatment often removed the bacteria's ability to build up resistance to sulphonamides.

But the advent of antibiotics was not far distant on the horizon of medical science.

The antibiotics

It is a well-known fact that folk medicine, whose traditions have been handed down to us over the centuries, has always used pastes of earth, mud, bark or plant, concoctions of seaweeds and moulds to be applied to wounds in order to heal them. These customs are found not only among people far removed from civilization but also among ordinary country people who treat wounds by spreading old dust from attics or spiders' webs collected in damp places over them.

It is interesting that in relatively modern times (1895) an obscure doctor in the Italian Navy, Vincenzo Tiberio, published an account of his own studies in which he described the marked antibacterial action exerted by factors present in certain moulds known as *Penicillium* and *Aspergillus*.

Such research remained isolated and virtually unnoticed. However, in 1928, the Scotsman Alexander Fleming directed his attention to an apparently commonplace incident and provided the cornerstone on which a vast new scientific edifice was to be built. Fleming was working in his laboratory at St Mary's Hospital in London when he noticed, during a particularly damp spell, that a colony of moulds had contaminated a culture of staphylococci that he had prepared on a glass plate. The culture was not discarded

A culture of the mould penicillium.

and when Fleming re-examined it some days later, he observed that where the mould had reached the staphylococci on the dish, the bacteria had almost totally disappeared. Fleming immediately carried out further experiments to investigate this phenomenon. He found that the mould was a well-known fungus of the species *Penicillium notatum*. He observed that this fungus had the ability to inhibit the growth of certain types of bacteria while having no effect on others. His first account was published in 1929, but went unnoticed, and his address to the International Congress of Microbiology had the same negative result. Yet as far back as 1887, the great Pasteur had formulated the concept of antibiosis, that is the possible antagonism between two types of micro-organisms. He had observed that anthrax bacilli, which survived

Alexander Fleming.

Ernst Boris Chain.

A photograph of penicillin taken in polarized light.

and multiplied readily in urine, lost the capacity to reproduce when other types of micro-organisms were added to the urine. Fleming meanwhile unswervingly pursued his studies, adhering to the conviction that the substance produced by the fungi—which he termed *penicillin*—would one day be classified as a drug. At the same time, other research workers succeeded in obtaining a liquid culture medium in which *Penicillium* flourished and survived for long periods. They finally discovered a technique whereby they could extract from this liquid a small quantity of the substance called penicillin. However, it was not until 1938–9 that a group of research workers at Oxford University in England, composed of chemists and doctors, working under the direction of Florey and Chain (later to share with Fleming the Nobel Prize for this research) devoted their energies to the task of identifying the active principle extracted from the culture medium of Fleming's fungus. Chain in particular finally succeeded in recognizing and defining the chemical structure that is common to all penicillins.

The story of the slow and laborious advance in the field of antibiotics is one of obstacles and uncertainties. Yet such a pattern is frequently characteristic of the way that science travels forward, with many halts and stumbles along the way.

Initially, the research worker may be hopeful that he is about to help science take a step forward, but he must always bear in mind the old Hippocratic dictum: "firstly to do no harm". And consequently, the race for progress in the field of medicine is always held in check by long periods of testing the new medication for possible toxicity. These tests are then repeated on a large scale by the drug manufacturing industry, followed finally by a cautious use of the drug by the medical profession.

Despite the sometimes seemingly excessively long trial periods required to establish a drug's safety, it can happen that certain side-effects remain concealed and only reveal themselves very much later, when the drug may already have been in circulation for a number of years. The harm that can result may be serious and widespread, as for instance the tragic consequences of the use of *Thalidomide* towards the

end of the 1960s. This substance had been prescribed as a mild and innocuous sedative, but it proved to have a terrible additional property—when taken by pregnant women at a certain stage of pregnancy, it caused them to give birth to badly deformed babies. The commonest disability affected the limbs, which were in many cases reduced to mere stumps.

However, even without producing such devastating effects, any drug may in addition to its curative properties possess intrinsic characteristics which adversely affect the human organism. Also many drugs that are completely safe for, and well tolerated by the majority of patients, can, in some individual cases, trigger off certain unpleasant and even deadly symptoms that are termed *anaphylactic* or *allergic*. Such reactions can range from a mere sensation of heat or itching, to suffocation, cardial arrest and death. This is one reason why no drug should ever be taken without consulting a doctor, a precaution that cannot be too strongly emphasized.

Naturally, penicillin has not proved exempt from provoking such allergic reactions in certain cases. But not long after its discovery came World War II and there was an urgent need to reduce septic complications as far as possible among wounded soldiers. Britain did not have the resources for producing penicillin in sufficient quantities for it to be available outside a few experimental laboratories. Great technical difficulties still stood in the way of production on an industrial scale, and it was at this time that research on penicillin products was taken over by the United States. But even with this contribution of research and manufacturing facilities it was not until 1943 that the first modest quantities of penicillin were made therapeutically available.

James Salk who discovered the first effective vaccine to counter poliomyelitis.

These were sent to Egypt, and the amount was barely sufficient to treat a few dozen wounded soldiers of the Eighth Army which was in action there at the time. However, the results obtained in the hospital wards were so striking that the U.S. Ministry for Wartime Production took on the organization of penicillin production itself. This operation was so successful that ever increasing and finally sufficient quantities of the antibiotic were able to reach the areas behind the front lines where the need was greatest. From Africa to Europe, from Russia to Asia and the islands of the Pacific Ocean, wherever the troops of the Allied armies were fighting, penicillin proved invaluable. It saved lives, reduced infectious complications, simplified treatment and eased and eliminated the sufferings of millions of men. It can safely be said that many of these soldiers were able to return home alive because a few small bottles of penicillin had been available at their hospital bedside when the men most needed them.

And yet penicillin is also beginning to show limitations. Whereas its activity is invaluable and often curative in the treatment of many diseases (blood-poisoning, abscesses and inflammation, wounds, pneumonia, endocarditis, gonococcal infections, meningitis and even plague), it can, when used indiscriminately, further the development of penicillin-resistant strains of bacteria. Penicillin is not a cure-all either, it does not attack the disease-causing agents of many illnesses.

Penicillin, of course, is not the only antibiotic drug. At the beginning of the 1940s the therapeutic properties of the whole vast range of moulds were still to be explored. In the fervour of the extensive research then in progress, *streptomycin* was obtained in the pure state in 1946 by several teams of investigators. This concluded the research that had been commenced by the American scientist Waksman in 1941, and that had led him in 1944 to isolate an antibiotic produced by a mould called *Streptomyces griseus*. This antibiotic (a name coined by Waksman for therapeutically active substances obtained from moulds) proved to be markedly effective against many bacteria not attacked by penicillin: those of plague, whooping cough, many infections of the digestive tract and the urinary system, as well as others. But above all, streptomycin had the ability to attack the bacterium of *tuberculosis*. In association with two other drugs discovered at about the same period, PAS (*para-aminosalicylic acid*) and *isoniazid*, streptomycin enabled man to wage a decisive and finally victorious battle against tuberculosis, one of man's greatest enemies throughout the ages.

Today, this disease is kept virtually under control in all parts of the world where medical treatment is at a sufficiently high level. But until a few decades ago, tuberculosis was widespread in every continent, striking down countless individuals regardless of class or creed. To give some idea of the severity of the situation, we need only list the variety of forms in which tuberculosis can occur and the different organs it can affect. Apart from tubercular septicaemia, a generalized infection of the blood that was invariably fatal, pulmonary tuberculosis was the commonest and most well known. But there were other widespread tubercular infections, affecting the intestines, lymph glands, larynx, kidneys, liver, spleen, reproductive organs, joints, bones (particularly the vertebrae), skin

Albert Sabin whose polio vaccine is now widely used throughout the world. He made no financial gain out of the vaccine as he refused to patent it "so as not to make a profit from the health of men".

and even the nervous system, where it often led to tubercular meningitis.

Younger people today are fortunate in no longer having to fear this deadly disease. Tuberculosis filled the wards of hospitals and sanatoria all over the world. Today these institutions are for the most part closed or converted to other uses. However, it would not be true to say that modern medicine has completely wiped the danger of tubercular disease from the face of the earth, but only that it is now kept under control. In fact the condition is always latent and ready to explode wherever precautions and prophylaxis are inadequate, wherever living conditions are unhygienic and wherever suitable methods of treatment are unavailable. The disease is still prevalent in certain underprivileged areas of the world, and it is here that the more affluent sections of the community bear a heavy responsibility.

In medicine, as in war, the positions taken up after a victorious battle can never be considered as final. Not long after the discovery that several moulds represented powerful tools in the elimination of many diverse diseases, the bacteria began to strike back. By way of the process previously described for the development of sulpha-resistant strains, a whole range of disease-causing bacteria also developed resistance to the new antibiotics. Numerous strains arose that were practically immune to the active principles of these moulds. Just as the phenomena of *sulphonamide resistance* and *penicillin resistance* had appeared previously, so now *streptomycin resistance* began to appear; indeed certain bacterial cultures became so well adapted to the presence of streptomycin that they actually became streptomycin-dependent and could not survive unless a certain amount of streptomycin was added to their culture medium.

The only course of action that remained was to continue investigating and experimenting in university laboratories and research centres throughout the world. Many other antibiotics have been discovered over the last thirty years, some of them of immense therapeutic value, capable of killing harmful bacteria where the earlier antibiotics had failed to do so. Some examples of antibiotics used throughout the world are *chloromycetin*, especially useful in conquering typhoid, paratyphoid and various intestinal and urinary tract infections; *terramycin, Aureomycin, tetracycline, erythromycin, kanamycin, cephalosporin, oleandomycin, rifamycin* and, among the most recent discoveries, *rifampicin*. It has been possible to produce a wide range of antibiotics with greatly increased bacteriostatic potency against certain micro-organisms and in some cases with a totally destructive effect on bacteria. In order to avoid the useless administration of antibiotics where a particular bacterium might be resistant, a technique was developed some years ago by means of which an *antibiogram* could be rapidly prepared for each patient. Samples of the patient's blood, urine, sputum, etc., are taken and cultured so that any bacteria present will multiply. A number of antibiotics are then tested against these bacteria, to see which is the most active, and it is this antibiotic that is administered to the patient.

Although nearly one thousand antibiotics have been discovered to date, only one hundred or less are in general use. They are sometimes used in conjunction with one another and sometimes combined with another drug in a single preparation in order to attack a wide range of

Crystals of the antibiotic crythromycin which is similar to penicillin. The crystals are shown in polarized light.

diseases under the safest and most favourable conditions.

Lastly, it was discovered some time ago that apart from their characteristic antibacterial action, some of the new antibiotics have the ability to inhibit the multiplication of certain cancerous cells, the type of cell found in malignant tumours, and such antibiotics are therefore used for their anti-tumour action.

In conclusion, it can be said that since the use of antibiotics has spread, many once-fatal diseases have become easily curable. For instance, at the beginning of the century, out of every hundred who fell ill with pneumonia at least thirty people died, whereas today, with the use of antibiotics, fatalities from pneumonia have been virtually eliminated. Similar reductions hold for a great many other diseases. Today's problem is a different one: the danger lies not so much in the risk of exposure to contagion, without the means to combat infection, but rather concerns those areas of the world where hygienic precautions are still inadequate and where these new and effective drugs are not yet readily available.

And yet man's victory over his microscopic opponents cannot be considered complete: a teeming group of micro-organisms known as viruses still remains more or less unassailable, despite the fact that attempts to eradicate them have been going on for many years.

Viruses

Viruses are particles of organic matter, so small that they can only be seen under an electron microscope. It has only been over the last few years that viruses have been isolated and identified. However, it was at the beginning of the century that some research workers deduced that the blood of patients with yellow fever contained disease-causing organisms other than protozoa or bacteria. They called them viruses. Without actually seeing them, cultures of viruses would be made in the decades that followed, and attempts were also undertaken, with some success, to prepare vaccines using viruses with attenuated virulence. But no ready fundamental antiviral discoveries could be made until more was known about the constitution of viruses.

Today the viruses identified number about five hundred, two-thirds of which are capable of causing disease in man. Some attack plants, others attack animals, while a third group is composed of the "orphan" viruses, so called because no one as yet knows whether they are able to cause disease, and if so in which hosts.

Viruses are the smallest organisms isolated to date. They vary in size, depending on the species, from 20 millimicrons (the poliomyelitis virus) to 500 millimicrons (some types of influenza viruses). A millimicron is a linear unit of measurement equal to one-millionth of a millimetre. Under the electron microscope, viruses display many forms: they may resemble small spheres with sharp points, small faceted gems, cylinders like corn cobs, framed pictures, certain kinds of spiders, or else they may be strangely reminiscent of astronautical machines such as lunar modules.

Viruses are composed exclusively of proteins and one or other—or both—of the nucleic acids mentioned earlier, RNA and/or DNA. From what we know of genetic processes they therefore possess the equipment for reproducing themselves by duplication. However, they do not possess the other requisites

The virus represented in this model may look innocent but it is one of the most feared viruses known to mankind—the "infantile polio paralysis" virus.

necessary to maintain an independent existence: they have no enzyme systems or respiratory capacity, and they are incapable of metabolic exchanges. In order to multiply, they have to come into contact with cells into which they can penetrate; here they live by establishing a parasitic relationship at the expense of the invaded host cell. Human viruses, as well as others, make use of the cell's every enzyme and metabolic system, multiplying until the cell is destroyed, then attacking other cells at an increasing rate. Eventually symptoms of the disease of which the virus is the agent show up in the body. The presence of viral nucleoproteins usually triggers off a chemical reaction that results in the production of *antibodies*. These are substances used by the body to defend itself against foreign materials, in this case, the virus. Antibodies can be detected by appropriate analyses; the presence of antiviral antibodies indicates to the doctor that the patient is suffering from a viral disease. In addition, body cells are stimulated by the presence of a virus to produce a substance known as *interferon*. This substance can sometimes block viral multiplication and then the actual disease does not develop. The human body thus has some natural defence mechanisms against viruses.

The different viruses known to be pathogenic to man cause many widespread diseases, particularly since in combination they can bring about complex damaging effects. Again, they may fragment and exchange their genetic material to give rise to new viral hybrids against which the human body has no defences. Recent studies indicate a link between bacterial and viral infection. The respiratory or digestive system for example, frequently contains some pathogenic bacteria that do not produce any symptoms of disease; however, after certain viruses have caused some degree of damage, and have as it were "prepared the ground" by depleting bodily resistance, the bacteria proliferate rapidly and serious infection sets in.

In the respiratory system alone, over a hundred types of viruses have been identified. These are capable of causing illnesses of various degrees of severity ranging from influenza to virus pneumonia. About ten of these are viruses giving rise to the illness commonly termed a "cold". Some ten viruses cause common diseases of childhood, namely *measles*, *scarlet fever*, *chicken pox*, *German measles* and *epidemic parotitis* also known as "mumps". Other widespread virus diseases are *smallpox*, *yellow fever*, the very common *labial herpes* (also known as a "cold sore"), some forms of *encephalitis*, *meningitis* and *conjunctivitis*, and the dangerous disease *viral hepatitis*. But the viral disease which struck tens of thousands of mainly young people throughout the world, and against which doctors were powerless until a few years ago, was *poliomyelitis* or "infantile paralysis".

This terrible disease has raged for centuries in more or less epidemic form, attacking vast numbers of children and adolescents. The symptoms developed within the space of a few days, beginning with a high temperature, together with a sore throat and some intestinal or sometimes nervous disturbances. They were followed by muscular pains and a rapidly ensuing paralysis of the limbs or outright respiratory paralysis with fatal consequences. There was no remedy for any of this, and although there might be some relative improvement among the survivors there were always perma-

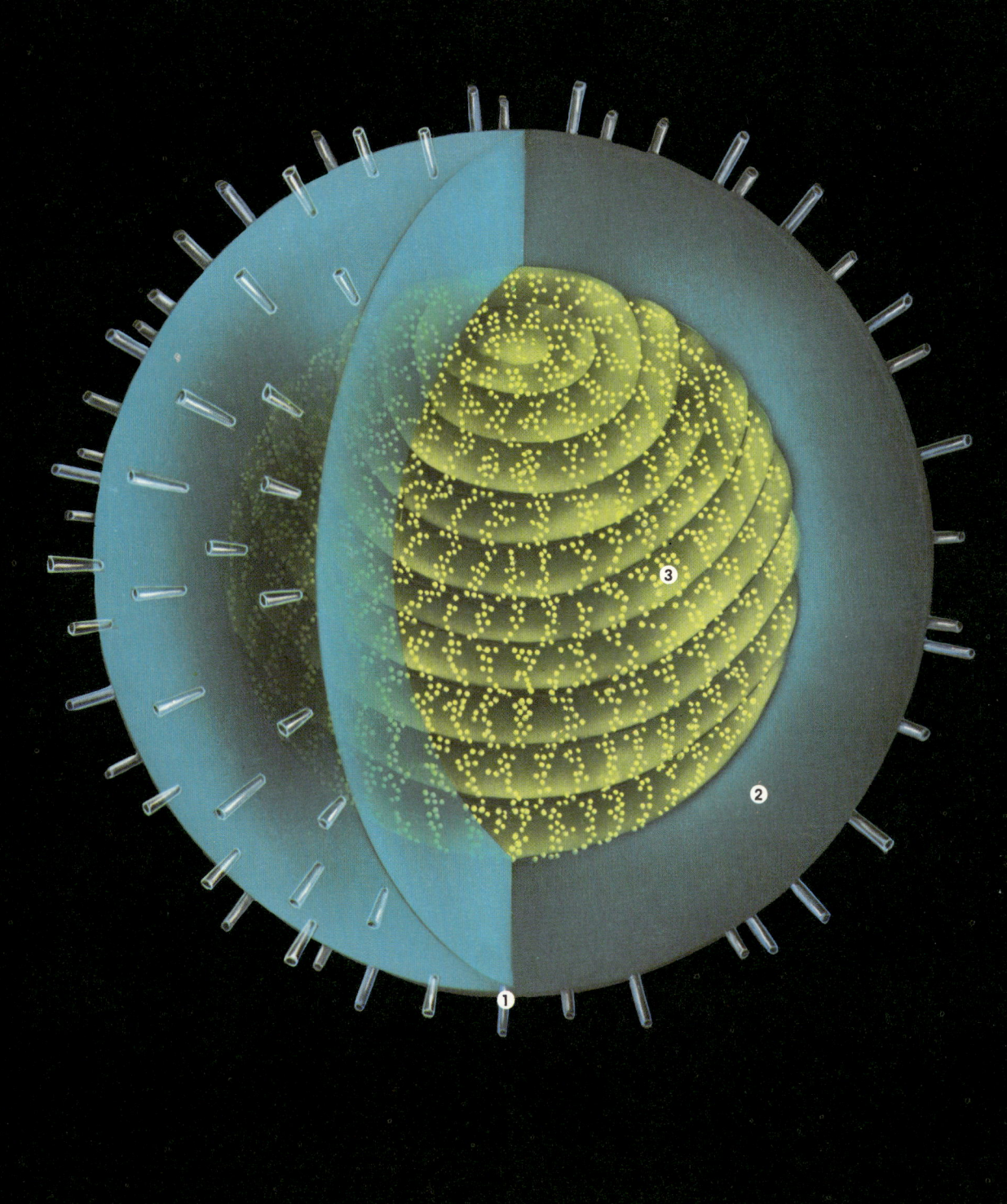

A representation of one of the myxovirus group, the influenza virus. 1. spikes; 2. the external lipoprotein membrane; 3. the RNA-protein core.

nent effects. The arms or legs would be affected with flaccid paralysis, rendering them practically useless, and the limbs damaged in this way did not grow at the same rate as the rest of the body. They remained shorter and emaciated, clearly deprived of a normal blood supply with the nutritional deficiency that this entailed. Any child who survived an attack of this nature would be condemned to remain disabled for the rest of its life.

In 1955, Doctor Jonas Salk perfected a vaccine against poliomyelitis. After carefully testing this vaccine, which was prepared with "killed" poliomyelitis viruses, he found that when administered in five successive injections, it was highly effective as a protection against the disease. Almost at the same time, Doctor Albert B. Sabin, another American researcher, succeeded in developing a somewhat different vaccine against poliomyelitis. His method was to treat live virus with agents that produced mutations, rendering the virus harmless (loss of toxic and paralysing pathogenic effects) while retaining its immunizing potency. An additional advantage of this vaccine was that it could be administered by mouth, as a few drops on a lump of sugar given four times over a period of eight months.

Millions of children throughout the world were vaccinated, and within a few years the spread of poliomyelitis had dwindled to almost nothing. In most countries the cases of poliomyelitis notified and confirmed annually up to 1963 totalled many thousands; but since 1968 there have been only a few dozen.

However, the struggle against viruses is still going on, and in some ways it can be said to have barely begun. As an example, let us look at a discovery that has served to support the suspicions and hypotheses advanced in recent years. In 1969, some English research workers stated that they had succeeded in isolating and identifying a virus which, when injected into dogs, cats and pigs, regularly produced *leukaemia*. Leukaemia is a disease that sometimes occurs in man, and forms part of the vast group of malignant or cancerous diseases. Following this demonstration, there has been a great increase in the research directed towards investigating viruses as a cause of malignant tumours. Many dozens of viruses have been identified to date which induce malignant tumours in various animal species. It has not as yet been possible to demonstrate a direct cause-and-effect link between viruses and tumours in man, but striking evidence is accumulating that suggests that viruses are somehow involved in the formation of certain types of tumours. Various research workers incline to the view that just as an infectious disease cannot exist in a body unless the specific causative organism is also active and present in the body, so there must also be a virus at the basis of every tumour that develops. From America to Europe and Japan, various medical institutes have for some years reported the isolation of viruses from tumour cells, but the definitive answer is as yet unformulated. The role of viruses in cancer and other tumours still remains to be clarified.

Anaesthesia

The field of anaesthesiology has come a long way since 16 October 1846, when William Morton ushered in a new era by administering ether to a patient about to undergo surgery. Today the anaesthesiologist is faced with a number of

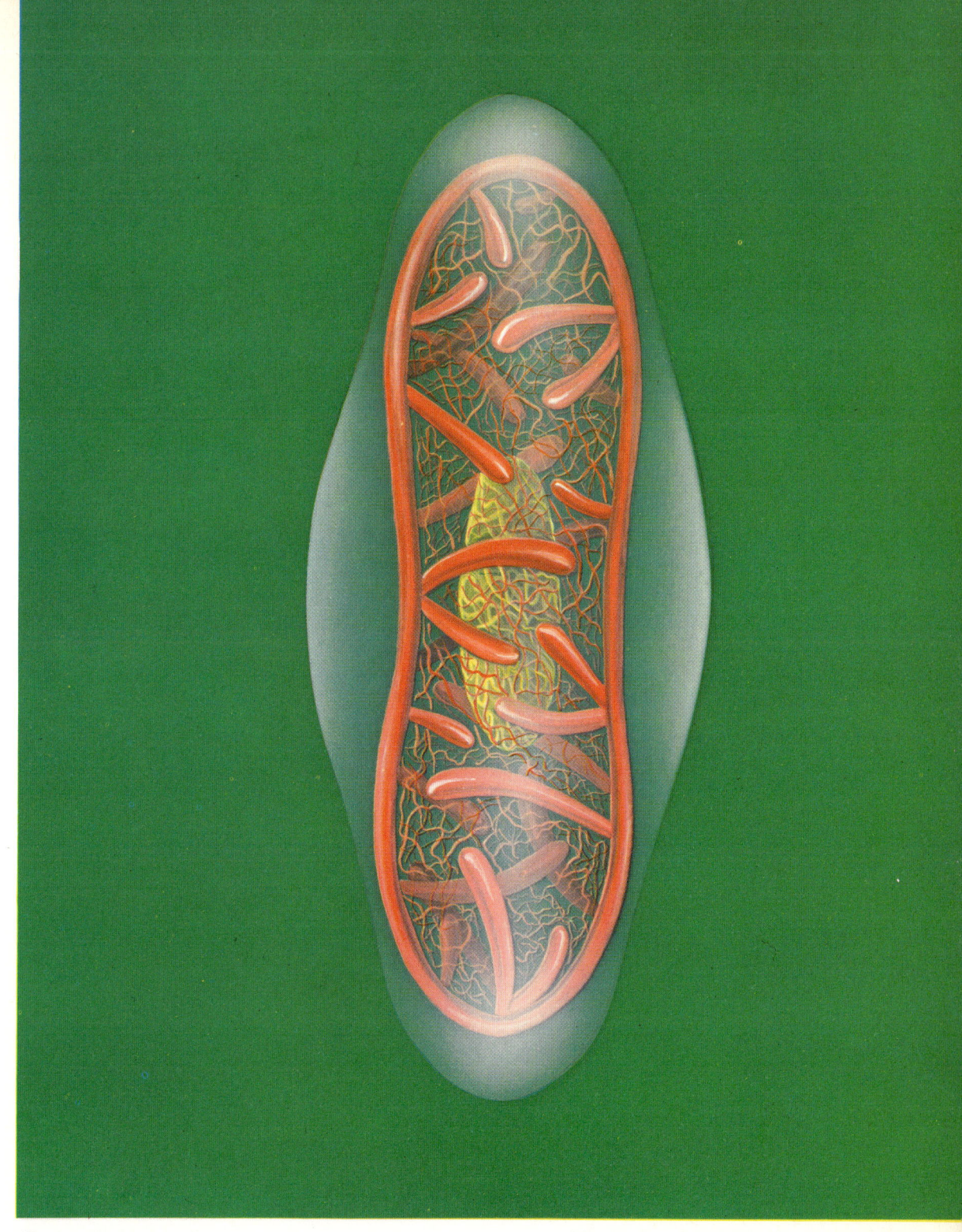

The smallpox virus. The capsule surrounds a biconcave nucleoid. This lateral view of the virus is obtained by incorporating it in a plastic material, of which thin sections are then cut and examined in an electron microscope.

alternatives: he can bring about a state of unconsciousness or eliminate local sensation; he can stop reflexive breathing and substitute artificial means to provide the body's oxygen needs; he can control blood pressure to prevent excessive bleeding, relax the muscles to a point where the body is virtually paralysed and drastically reduce all metabolic processes by cooling.

In medicine, anaesthesia has played a vital part in the development of surgery and initiated the era of treatment of disease with drugs.

During major surgical procedures the surgeon and the anaesthetist comprise a team in the operating theatre; success or failure depends as much on one as on the other. Both may collaborate on the choice of anaesthetic but both will employ the same criteria: the safety and comfort of the patient, and the surgical procedure to be followed. With the recent proliferation of the kinds of anaesthetics available their decision can tailor the chosen drug to the need of the patient.

Generally anaesthetics can be divided into two types: local and general. Under local anaesthesia only one area of the body becomes insensible to pain and there is no alteration of consciousness. The anaesthetics used act directly on the nerves with which they come in contact and paralyse their ability to transmit impulses. The duration of anaesthesia varies from drug to drug or from drugs in combination. Three main classes of local anaesthetics now exist: topical, infiltration and nerve block. Topical anaesthesia is brought about by application of an anaesthetic drug to the surface of skin or membrane. Infiltration anaesthesia is accomplished by injection of an anaesthetic directly into the tissues where it is required. Nerve-block anaesthesia is brought about by injecting the drug of choice close to the nerve trunk which branches into the area where anaesthesia is required: the site of injection may be well away from the operating area.

General anaesthetics render the patient unconscious and without any sensation or movement. The anaesthetic of choice is administered by injection and suppresses various sensory and motor sensors in the brain. This type of anaesthesia, too, is generally administered in one of three ways: by inhalation, intravenously or by rectal absorption.

Anaesthesiology has come a long way since the days of Morton, and current studies in basic and applied research should bring even greater comfort.

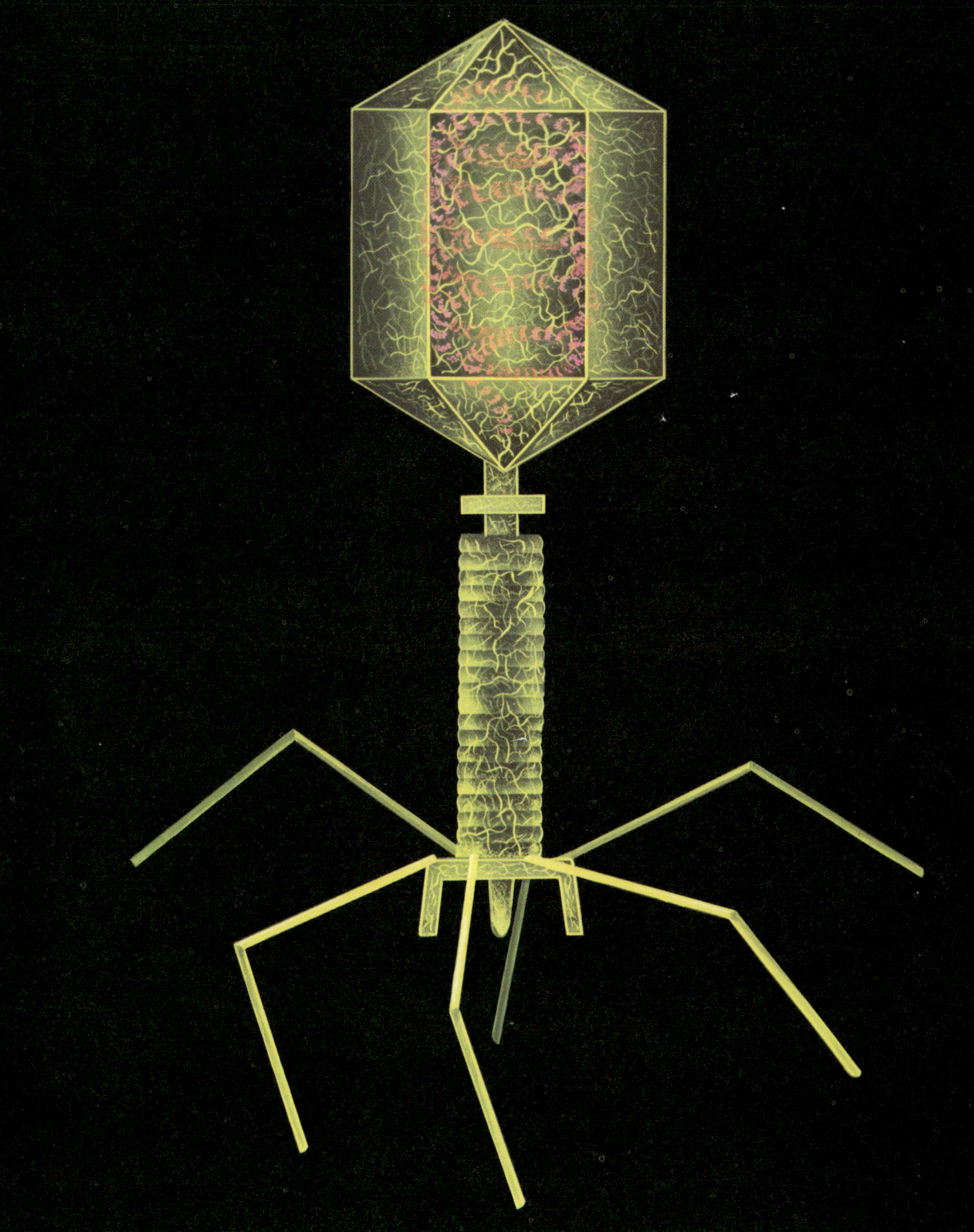

This diagram shows the complex symmetrical formation of the bacteriophage T_2. The "head" is a hexagonal prism, the upper and lower surfaces of which form two hexagonal pyramids. The cylindrical "tail" has a spiral of protein coiling round it, and it terminates in a plate from which six flagellae branch off. These flagellae serve to hook the phage on to the surface of the bacterial cell, which is infected by the phage.

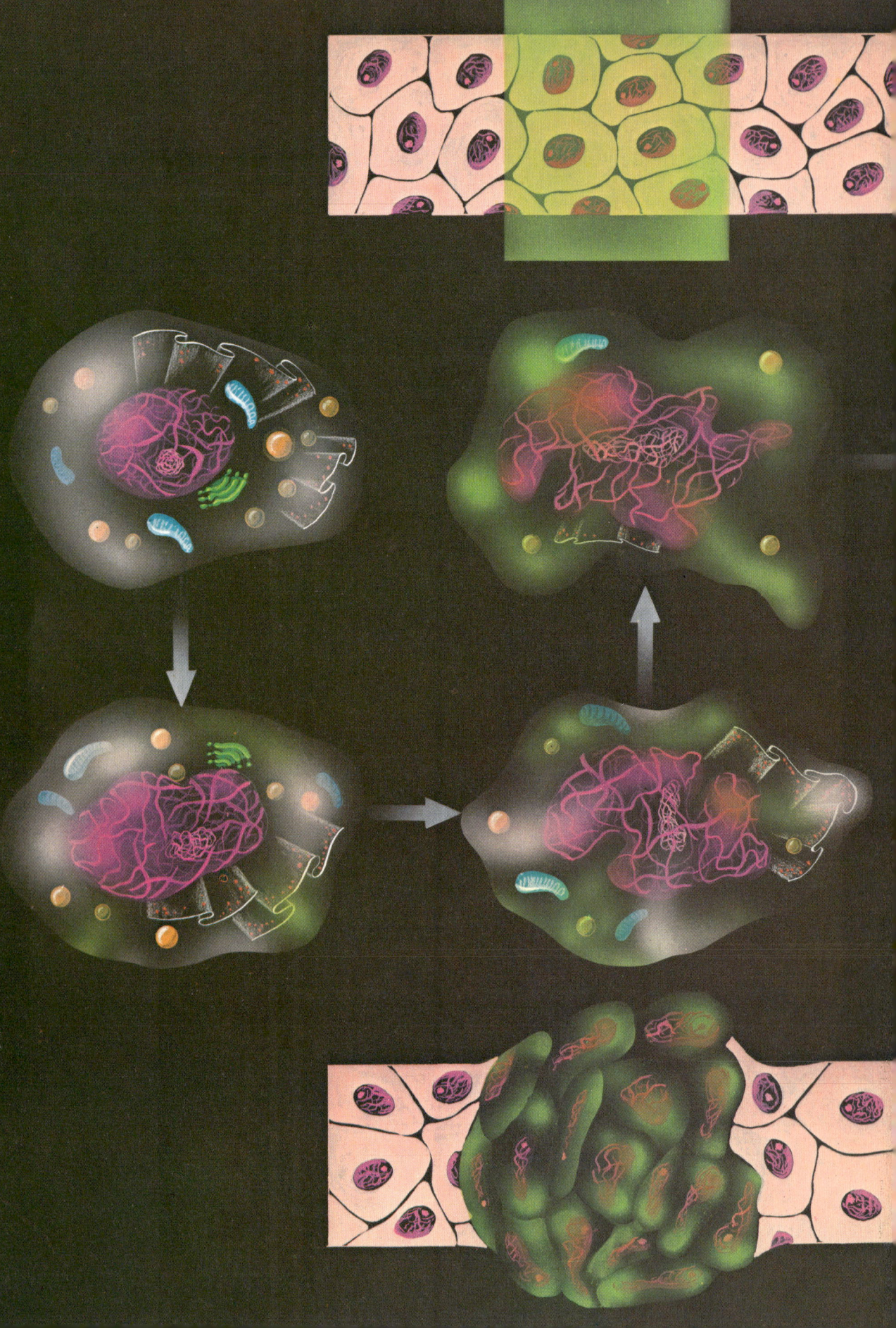

CHAPTER 5

TODAY'S DEATH-DEALING DISEASES

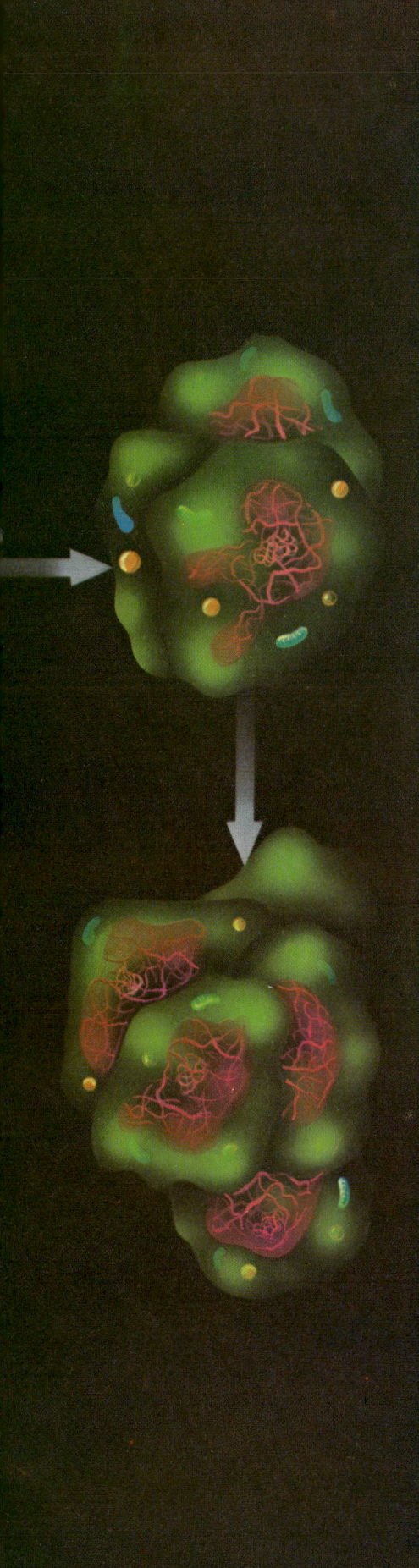

What we have covered so far concerning virus activity leads naturally into a wider field, that of the malignant tumours, commonly grouped together under the term "cancer". Deaths from this cause run into massive figures, and according to the statistics of several investigators, the numbers seem to have increased to a staggering extent in this century, particularly in the more industrialized areas of the world. Others, however, believe that this increase is only apparent, and that it is due to an increase in average life expectancy. There is now a higher percentage of older people, who, in another era, would not have survived the epidemics and infectious diseases of those times long enough to develop cancer. As a consequence of medical science being able to fight infection and cure many functional disorders by surgery, we now have an increased number of persons of advanced age with a greater risk of developing tumours, precisely because these conditions are on the whole most common in late middle age or old age. We say "on the whole" because fatal cancer can strike tragically at young people or even children.

It has not been shown conclusively that environmental factors are necessarily a predisposing cause in the development of cancer. In various semi-primitive areas of the

The formation of a tumour. Various causes (chemical, physical or viral) affect the cells in the green square in such a way that a process of "dedifferentiation" starts; this process is illustrated in the centre sequence. The cells lose their specific characteristics and their rate of multiplication becomes abnormally high. The newly formed cells consolidate around the area of origin and tend to invade the surrounding tissue.

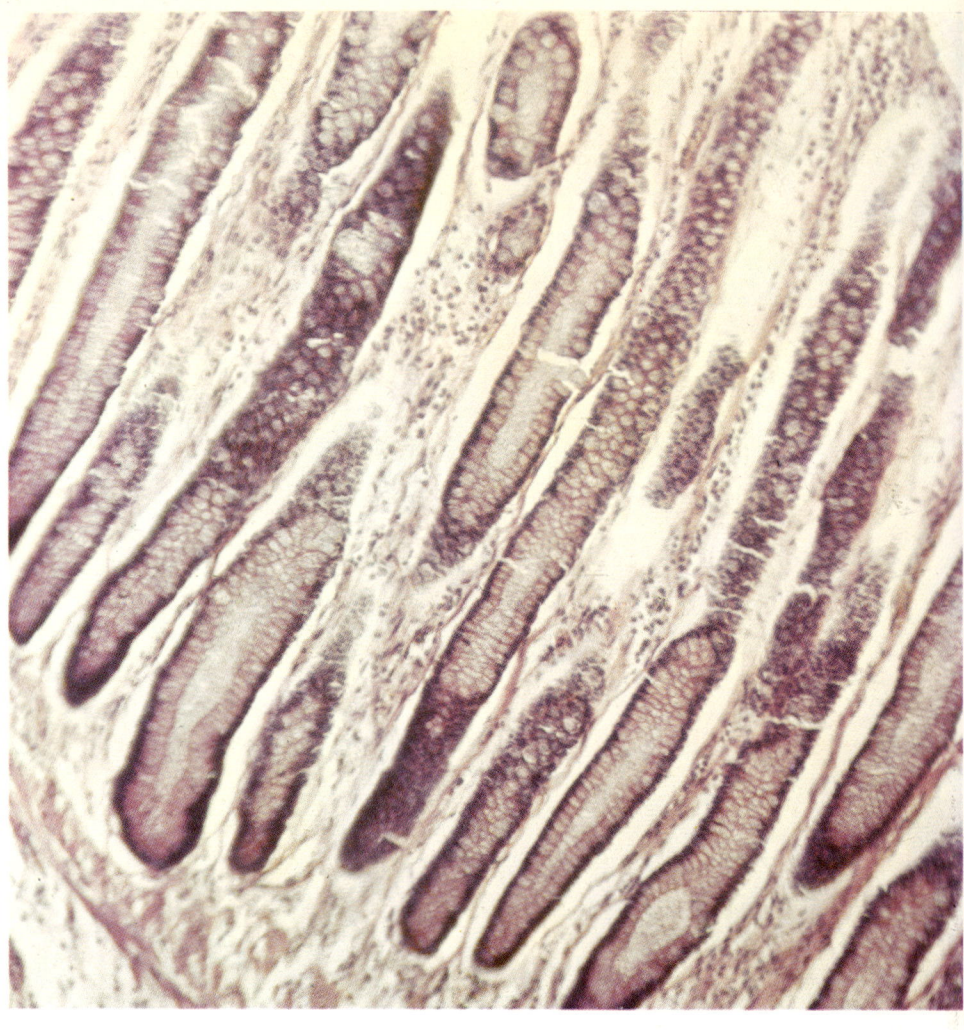

A section of a normal human intestine as seen under a microscope.

world studied from this particular angle, the inhabitants did in fact show a lower incidence of cancer than that observed in more technologically advanced civilizations. However, on closer examination it became clear that the average life span of the former group was shorter, whereas among sections of both populations of the same age, the incidence of tumours was more or less equal. Even so, we must not overlook the finding that groups of Japanese, for example, settled in America, tended to show a higher incidence of the disease than Japanese in their own country.

Tumours are called neoplasms, because they are new (neo) growths developing in one or several different tissues, and whose cellular characteristics differ from those of the original tissue itself. Tumour cells show certain special features, with degenerate characteristics, but they are nevertheless capable of indefinite growth and multiplication with no apparent end-point. Their development is independent of the organ or tissue in which they become established, and they sustain their life processes by taking whatever they need from the host's tissues on which they are virtually parasitic.

Although it has been possible for quite some time to identify tumour cells and describe the morpho-

A microscopic aspect of glandular carcinoma of the rectal intestine.

logical features that distinguish them from all other cells, we do not yet fully understand the physical and chemical mechanisms governing their biological activity. But it can be said that while we still do not know how far we are from the solution, there are good grounds for believing that we may well be quite close to the goal that generations of research workers have striven to reach.

In an attempt to elucidate something of the origins and basic processes of tumours, it should be mentioned that contemporary theory considers the transformation of a normal cell into a tumour cell to be due to a modification of a *gene*. Because of the gene's alteration it is able to confer its aberrant imprint on the successive generations of cells derived from the initially altered cell. This change is thought to arise through the action of particular stimuli, and we are at present seeking to identify just what they may be.

Whatever the nature of the stimulus, it is thought to act at the chromosomal level, and more precisely by bringing about mutations in the nucleic acids DNA and RNA. Once mutations have occurred in the nucleic acids, these create cellular anomalies that are duplicated in every successive generation of cells, so that they multiply in a permanently diseased condition.

When dealing with genetics and the reproductive mechanisms of cells, we saw that DNA has the capacity for self-replication so that when cells divide, each new cell contains DNA that is an identical copy of the original. We also saw how the other nucleic acid, RNA, can carry instructions from the DNA into the cytoplasm and hence to the ribosomes where new proteins are synthesized according to these instructions. Lastly, we have seen that this recurring chain of events in cell reproduction does not necessarily produce an infinite number of cells of the identical pattern, but that spontaneous mutations of varying degrees of importance are always occurring. Mostly these mutations are harmful and only become useful when they happen to be of such a kind as to confer an advantage to the next generation derived from mutated sex cells. There are many possible stimuli that are capable of interfering with DNA and RNA in such a way as to modify the chromosomal entities known as *genes*. When this happens in ordinary tissue cells, then, as growth and replacement occurs, the daughter cells will carry the changed characteristics of the mutated mother cells. Any stimulus then that disrupts the fundamental constitution of DNA and RNA, could result in the reproduction of cells with totally disordered characteristics, no longer responding to the built-in checks and balances of the body, but instead behaving as cells gone biologically "mad". Indeed this is an apt description of the kinds of cells we find in the disordered tissue called *cancer* or a *malignant tumour*. One theory is that a virus injects its DNA into a tissue cell and brings about a duplicating error of the sort that leads to totally unbalanced replication. From that time onwards, the cells derived from this disordered cell will be cancerous in nature.

Causes of tumour development

In 1911, the scientist Rous described a tumour that was named after him, and which could be produced by a totally cell-free filtrate. Because of this, Rous advanced the hypothesis that the tumour was caused by substances smaller than any cell, namely by viruses. It was subsequently demonstrated that these filterable substances were able to cause not merely one type of tumour, but tumours of varying characteristics, for example, *sarcomas*, *lymphomas* and others depending on the tissues into which they were inoculated. Nevertheless, a quarter of a century passed before the theory of a viral cause for tumours overcame the objections and opposition of many other scientists. During recent decades, countless experiments and tests have demonstrated the existence of at least eighty viruses capable of inducing malignant tumours in various animals. As far as man is concerned, there is clearly no possibility of injecting viruses for experimental purposes in an attempt to induce cancer. We cannot, therefore, demonstrate the viral origin of any human tumours, but a good deal of evidence exists to suggest that breast cancer, leukaemia and lymphoma (cancer of the lymph tissue) are due to viral infection. Current opinion inclines to the belief that over fifty per cent of malignant tumours, especially certain forms found in young people, are caused by viruses.

On the other hand, some recent research has shown conclusively that cells made cancerous by the action of a virus can return to a normal state. These results were obtained through careful experiments carried out on frog tadpoles. Numerous tadpoles had their tails amputated, and fragments of malignant tumours (their cells labelled with indestructible and easily recognized radioactive marker substances) were implanted among the cell masses of the tail stumps, at the very point where tissue regeneration would produce the growth of a new tail. As the new tails grew, it was found that all the cells were normal, although some of them contained the radioactive tracers. The absence of abnormal tumour cells in these tails demonstrates conclusively the possibility of obtaining normal regenerated tissue even when some of it is of tumorous origin.

It has recently been demonstrated that a variant of the *polyoma* virus can cause the cells of rat tissue to become cancerous as long as the temperature is around 32 °C (89 °F); if the temperature is raised to 39 °C (102 °F), these cancerous cells return to normal.

There is no doubt that many other causes for cancer exist apart from viruses. Laboratory tests carried out on animals have indicated the existence of more than a thousand chemical substances capable of inducing cancer, and hence termed *carcinogenic*, or at least *co-carcinogenic* because they work in conjunction with other substances in the development of tumours. A good example of this is the now classic experiment with *urethane* and *croton oil* which gives such invariably consistent results that it can be regarded as conclusive. If the skin of rats is painted daily with urethane over a long period, the painted area shows no notable changes, although urethane inhalation produces lung cancer. If, however, this urethane-treated area of skin is then painted with croton oil, a substance capable

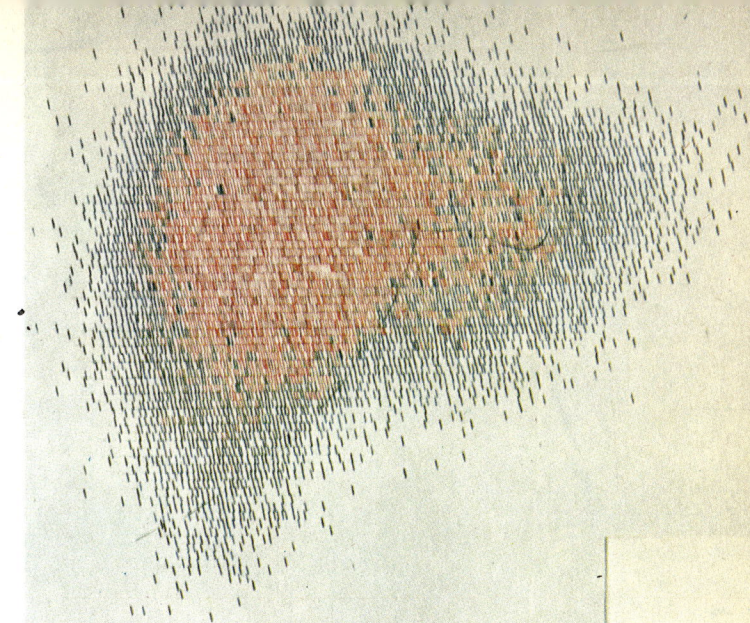

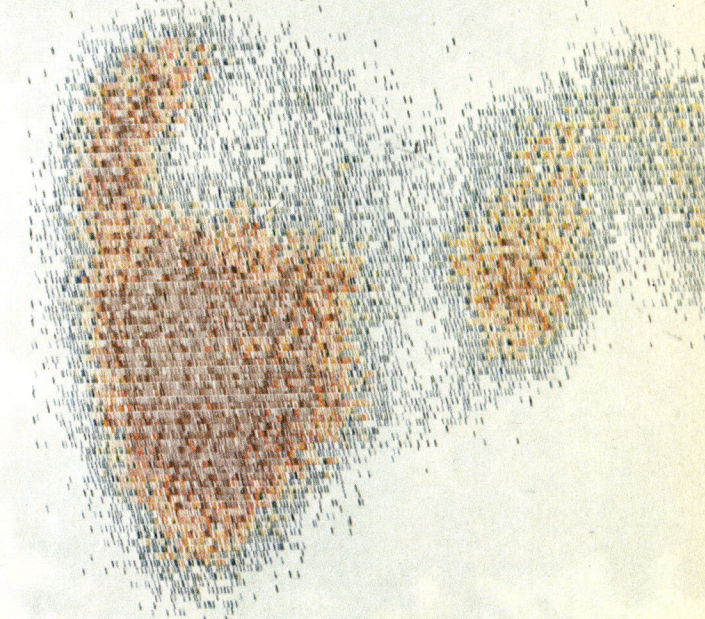

Medicine has now entered the nuclear age. These images of the liver were obtained by a process called "scintigraphy" whereby the patient is given some radioactive gold which is picked up by some cells present in the liver. The intensity of the radioactivity is then measured. Maximum radioactivity corresponds to the red colouring, and the absence of colour represents minimum radioactivity. In the top scintigraph the distribution of the radioactivity is regular and the dimensions of the liver are normal, indicating a healthy organ. In the lower scintigraph, however, the image of the liver is larger, and the distribution of the radioactive gold is quite irregular. The patient was found to have a liver with tumorous metastases from the stomach.

of stimulating cell division but inhibiting cell maturation, many and varied tumours develop at the site of croton-oil application. And yet if the skin is painted with croton oil alone, no malignant change takes place. By a comparison of these and many other findings, a whole host of possible deductions arises which in their turn lead to countless experiments.

It seems reasonable to suppose that cancerous cells arise quite frequently among the tissues of the human body, but that in the light of what we know about immune reactions, only a very small fraction of such cells escapes the body's strict immunological control which probably destroys most of these "unbalanced" cells before they have a chance to spread.

Unlike immunological mechanisms, some of the complex biochemical interactions continually in progress in the human body do not act defensively against cancer. Enzymes, for example, which are essentially "speeding-up" agents, can sometimes, when produced in unbalanced amounts, enhance the development of the disease. The same is true of the hormones: while some of them are important for combating, or at least preventing certain forms of tumours, others (especially those serving specific organs rather than the whole body) have been identified as having carcinogenic activity, when, due to a pathological condition, they are produced in excessive quantities. It is obvious that the effects of an excess of hormone administered from some outside source would be just as harmful—as in the case of certain inappropriate medical treatments.

There are about a dozen chemical substances which have been found to have a carcinogenic action on man. For example, there are the ionizing radiations (X-rays, and atomic radiation); also chromium, nickel, arsenic, soot components and asbestos dust with which asbestos workers come into contact, and which is inhaled by city dwellers every time a car brakes and asbestos dust enters the air. Tobacco and alcohol have also been implicated. In short, man is subjected daily to the introduction of carcinogenic substances into his body, quite involuntarily and sometimes voluntarily, through his respiration, his food and the substances with which he comes into contact. The human body identifies them, isolates them, transforms them and eliminates them as far as it is able—or else it succumbs and becomes a victim of cancer.

For a long time it was believed that in order to successfully transplant a proliferating tumour from one body to another, the transplant had to contain a few thousand tumour cells at least. However, Japanese scientists have recently succeeded in refining a technique whereby a few dozen cells, and finally a single tumour cell can be transferred from one rat to another. Even in the latter case, the recipient rat developed a malignant tumour. Although it is possible to achieve this in the laboratory, it fortunately does not happen under normal conditions of life: the threshold of resistance is higher, though not greatly so, for it has been found that the human body can neutralize and inhibit the further proliferation of some twenty cancer cells but not more. Above this number, the cancerous condition becomes established and the tumour usually spreads in the body with dire consequences. There are thus two obvious goals to be achieved: to reduce the occasions and conditions

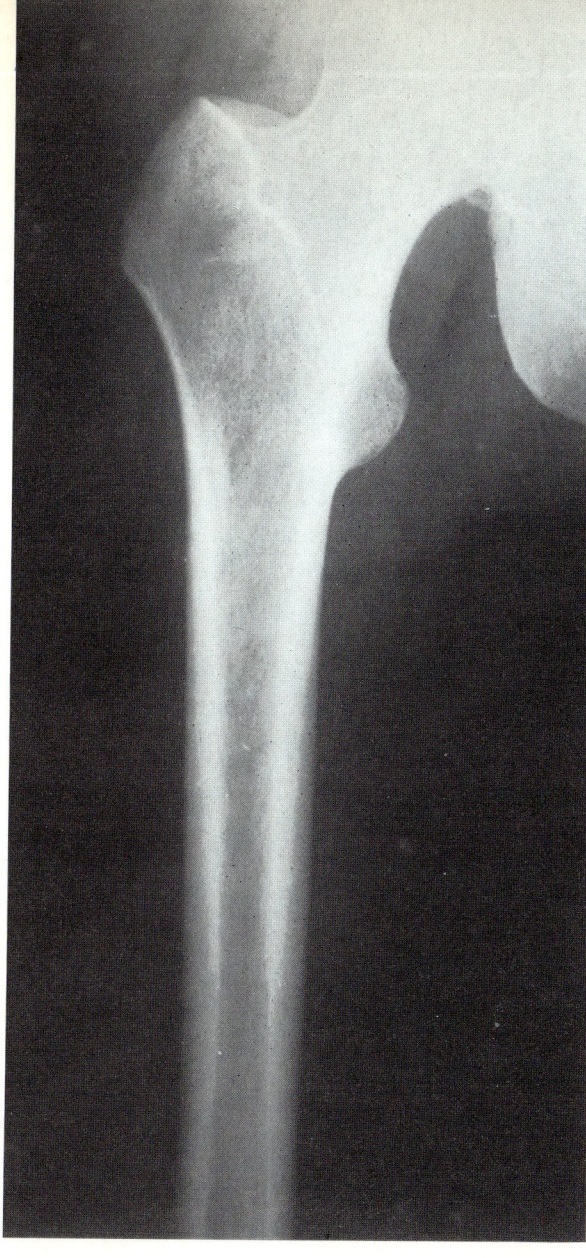 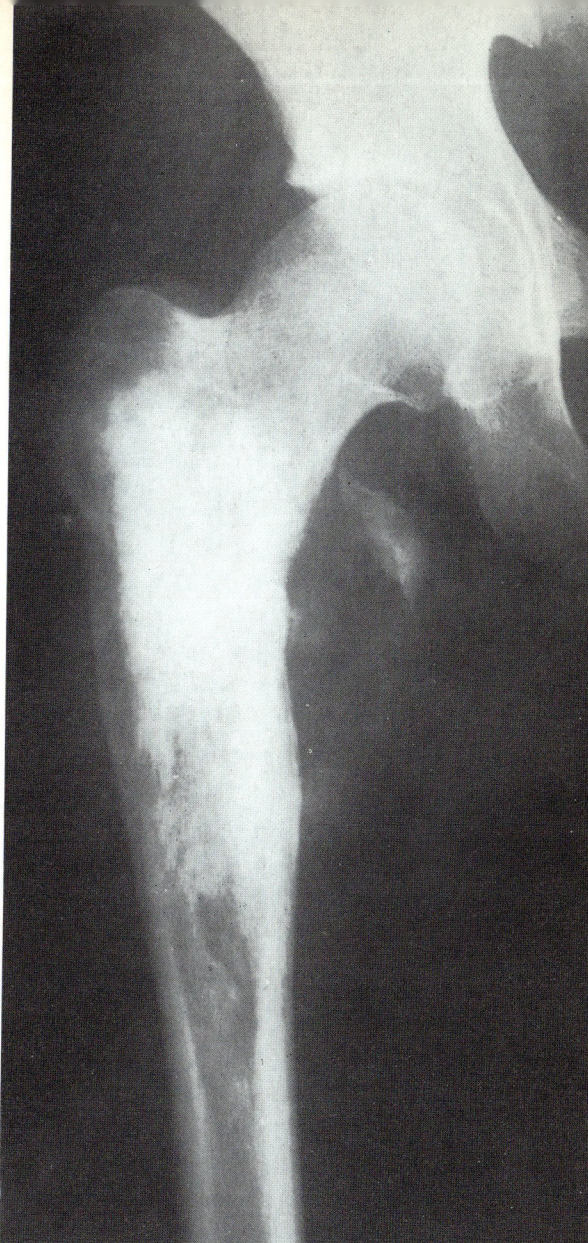

that predispose human beings to the development of cancer and to increase and refine the methods of cancer detection. The disease should be identified as soon as the first indications of its presence appear and before the emergence of obvious clinical symptoms, by means of accurate and specialized examinations.

Among the factors causing cancer that are not inescapably environmental, but under the voluntary control of the individual, is the use of tobacco. This custom has been widespread for some centuries. In recent decades, despite pressures from commercial interests and conflicting reports from various schools of research workers, much evidence has accumulated to support the concept that tobacco smoking is harmful. Over the last few years especially, most of the world's research workers agree that the habitual use of tobacco induces a toxic condition that produces fundamental damage to the organs and systems of the human body. Today smoking is considered to be an

The X-ray on the left shows a normal femur. The femur on the right is affected by a bone tumour (osteosarcoma). The area affected by the tumour appears swollen with the presence of very irregular deposits of calcium salts.

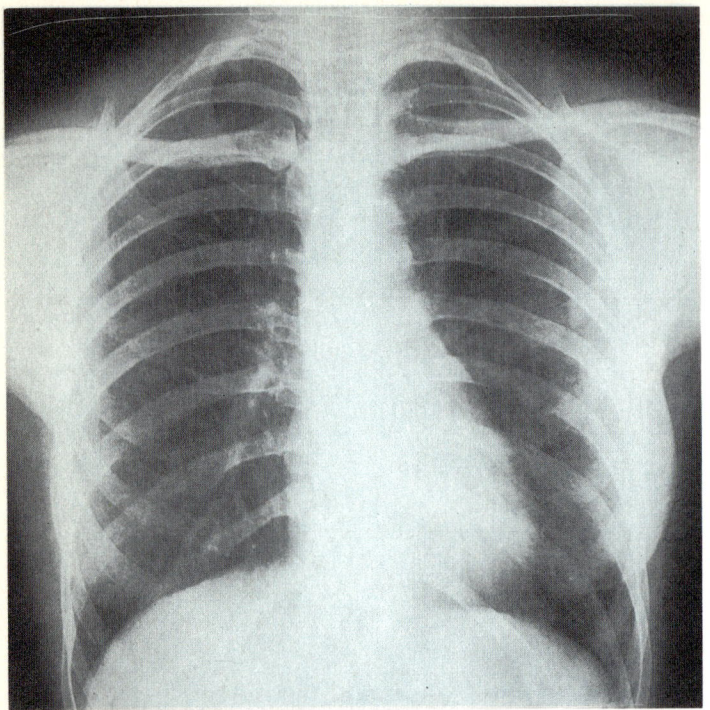

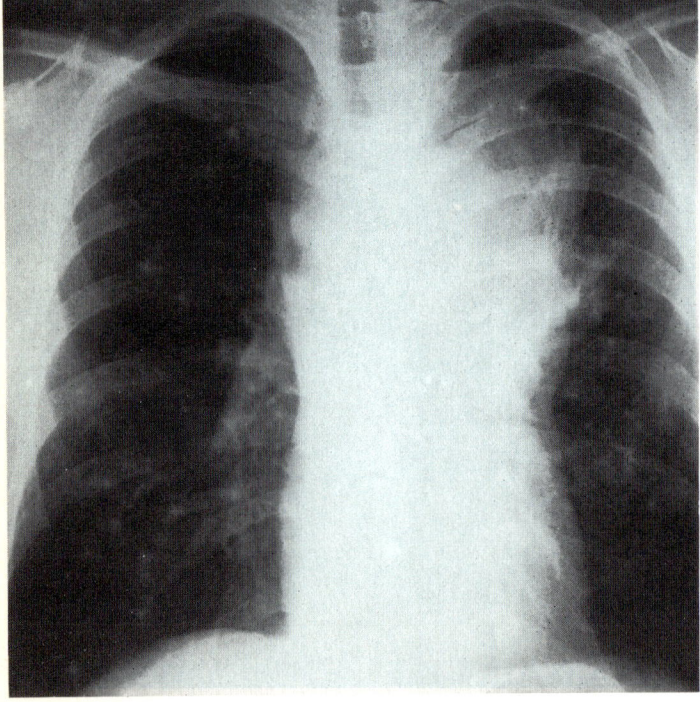

*Above: X-ray of a normal thorax.
Below: an X-ray of the thorax of a patient affected by lymphosarcoma. The shadow of the mediastinum is notably enlarged because of the presence of the enlarged lymph nodes.*

important factor in the process of ageing itself.

It has been statistically calculated that on the average, the inveterate smoker shortens his life about eight years. If we confine our statistics to the sphere of tumours, smoking proves to be one of the main factors responsible for the development of cancerous conditions. Research carried out by international health organizations has shown that a person smoking 40 cigarettes a day is 17 times more likely to develop a malignant tumour than a non-smoker.

Voluntary subjection to the risk of smoking is superimposed on the many unavoidable carcinogenic factors distributed in our environment. These exist in the food we eat and the air we breathe and are a result of inadequately controlled industrial expansion, an expansion from which we all derive benefit but for which we all pay the price.

Defences against cancer

Obviously the first line of defence against the attack of cancer is the reactive power of the individual organism. When carcinogenic agents attack a healthy cell, they begin to disrupt its original reproductive pattern, transforming it into a tiny monster capable of producing an infinity of monsters. To help the body ward off the invasion of cancer-causing agents studies have been in progress for years to prepare a suitable vaccine. But of course, this is only valid if the cancer threatening any particular organism is viral in nature.

Nothing has been left untried in the fight against cancer. It has long been believed that since the problem of cancer comprises so very many different factors, it cannot be resolved by the brilliance of a single research worker isolated in his laboratory. Consequently almost all researchers investigating tumour diseases are working in conjunction with one another and continually exchanging observations and information. At the international level, the United Nations Organization has formed a Centre for Research into Carcinogenic Substances. In the course of technological progress we now invent and create about twenty thousand new chemical products per year, of which some hundreds are put on to the market and used in a great diversity of products. The U.N. group tests these new substances with the object of detecting any carcinogenic side-effects.

Likewise, in the United States, the Bethesda Institute for Cancer Research operates on a huge scale. In its search for anti-cancer drugs, the Institute finances four-fifths of the research carried out annually in this field in the United States and half that carried out throughout the entire world. As part of the vast work of selection and analysis performed at Bethesda, about twenty-five thousand new and old drugs are subjected to the most exacting tests every year, and out of these only one in every thousand is suitable for further experimentation. After all this, there may remain some ten substances worth investigating, perhaps five of which can be tested on man. Finally, there may be one or two out of the original twenty-five thousand that exhibit pharmacological properties justifying their inclusion among the anti-cancer drugs. Today the latter include about forty chemical products that can either slow down the proliferation of tumours or in some cases bring about their regression, particularly in the case of fast-growing tumours where the results are already quite good. The slow-growing

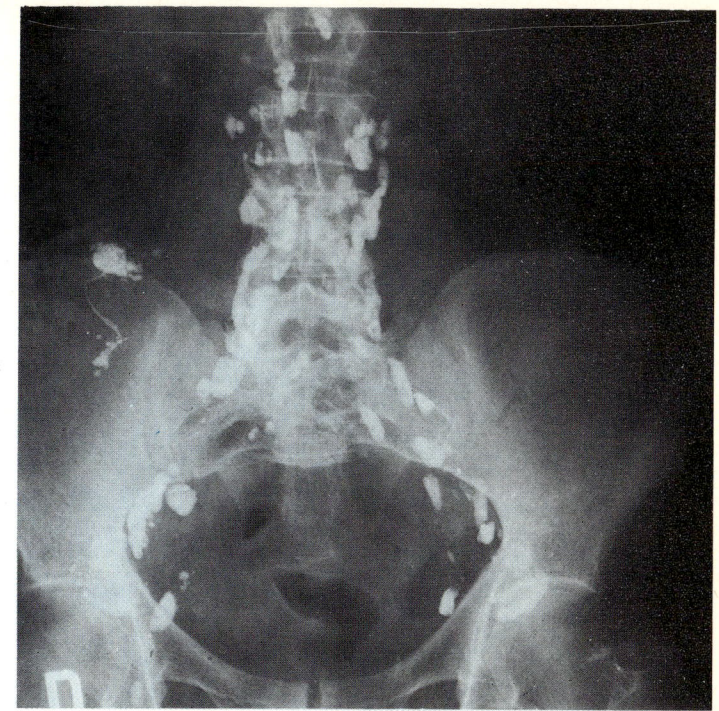

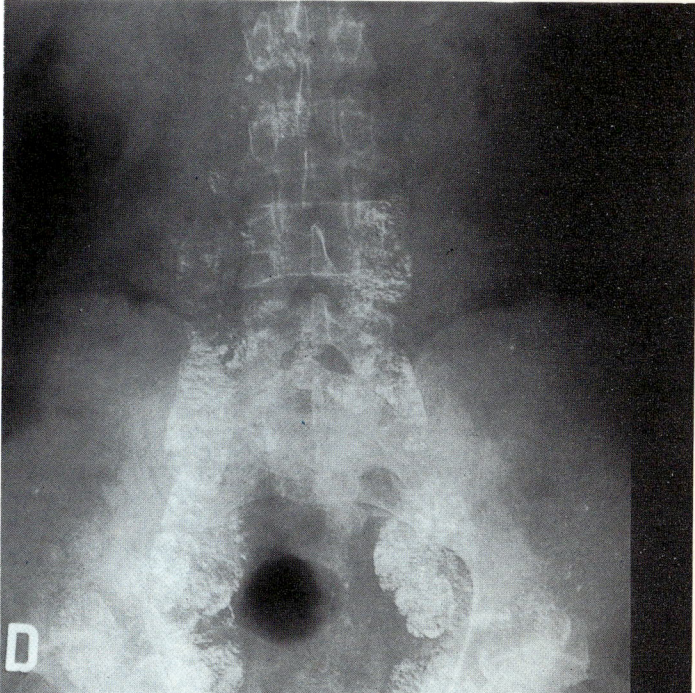

Above: a normal lymphograph. On the X-ray of the abdomen the lymph nodes of the iliac and para-aortic lymphatic chains are observed. These have been made visible by introducing iodine bound with an oily compound into the lymphatic vessels. Below: a lymphograph of a patient affected by lymphosarcoma. The X-ray shows that the lymph nodes are very much enlarged and have a different aspect from those above.

forms of tumours are generally much more resistant to drug therapy; however, it is predicted that new drugs will be found over the next few years that will effectively attack even these tumours.

The fight against cancer has not been confined to drugs, but includes surgery and physical therapy. It can be said that at the present time we are able to cure about forty per cent of cancer sufferers, and that this figure will reach fifty per cent in a relatively short time.

To expunge cancer from the history of mankind, or at least to render it a marginal problem, now seems to be a matter of determination and organization. As has happened with other diseases that once ravaged humanity, the day will undoubtedly come when the battle against cancer will also be won.

Heart disease

If we consider the heart as an organ whose function it is to distribute blood throughout the body, contract and relax about 100,000 times in a day and nearly 500 million times in one's life, and work continuously even when sleeping, it may come as no surprise to learn that more than fifty per cent of all the deaths in the United States and Western Europe are caused directly or indirectly by disease of the heart and blood vessels. Indeed an estimated one in eight of adult Americans have some form of heart disease and another one in eight is suspected of having heart disease. With such statistics at hand it should be obvious that new knowledge in the field of cardiology is greatly needed and that any new finding in the diagnosis and treatment of heart disease should be made available to the public as quickly as possible.

The years following World War I saw the most significant advances in the understanding and treatment of heart disease.

However it was during World War II that our insight into cardiology progressed so far that all other previous advances in this field were surpassed. More precise advances in the fields of biochemistry and physiology have given us clearer insights into our understanding of heart disease. The impact of these studies has made clinical cardiology more of a science than the empirical art it had been in the past.

Along with these studies have come the cardiovascular specialist. As with most specialities it is the size of the community and number of medical facilities which determine the number of cardiovascular specialists and the variety of subspeciality branches in this field. One doctor may be concerned primarily with electrocardiography (that is the making of graphs of electrocurrents emanating from the heart muscle) others may be more interested in studying the techniques of the ballistocardiograph, an apparatus for recording the stroke volume of the heart to enable the doctor to calculate the heart output. As technical advances occur with new and more subtle techniques for studying the action of the heart and its circulation, new subspecialities develop.

New developments in the use of antibiotics and drugs and rapid progress in the field of cardiovascular surgery have favourably affected the course of some forms of heart disease. Emphasis upon preventive aspects of heart disease has stimulated research on many levels. Studies linking a relationship between smoking and cardiovascular disease is one important epidemiological approach to the problem.

The study of heart disease today is dominated by the spectacular results of open-heart surgery, the use of electronic instruments to control heartbeat and advances in vascular surgery. Most exciting are the advances which have been made in attempting to replace a diseased heart with a mechanical heart or a transplanted heart. The concept of a partial or even complete artificial heart is not new. Logically the heart is just a pump. If it should fail to function normally we should be able to replace it with a new pump. The problems in total heart replacement may seem insurmountable because of the phenomenon known as rejection—the body's tendency to reject the grafted organ. However, the use of drugs which suppress the body's immune response and the matching of donor organs to specific recipients (see Chapter 6) have had encouraging results.

Interesting progress is being made on a mechanical assist device, the balloon pump. First used on a patient in 1967, it is employed primarily in patients suffering from an often fatal condition known as myocardial infarction, in which there is occlusion of arteries carrying blood to the heart, and subsequent death of heart-muscle tissue. The balloon pump—a sausage-shaped device manufactured of synthetic fibres—is "snaked" from a distant artery and inserted into the aorta, increasing the blood flow through the coronary arteries. If employed promptly infarction can be reduced considerably.

At present there is much research towards assist pumps and total artificial hearts. Probably many years will elapse before many basic discoveries in cardiovascular research can be put into practice by the clinician, yet our increasing knowledge of basic biological laws is one of the most challenging aspects of medical research today.

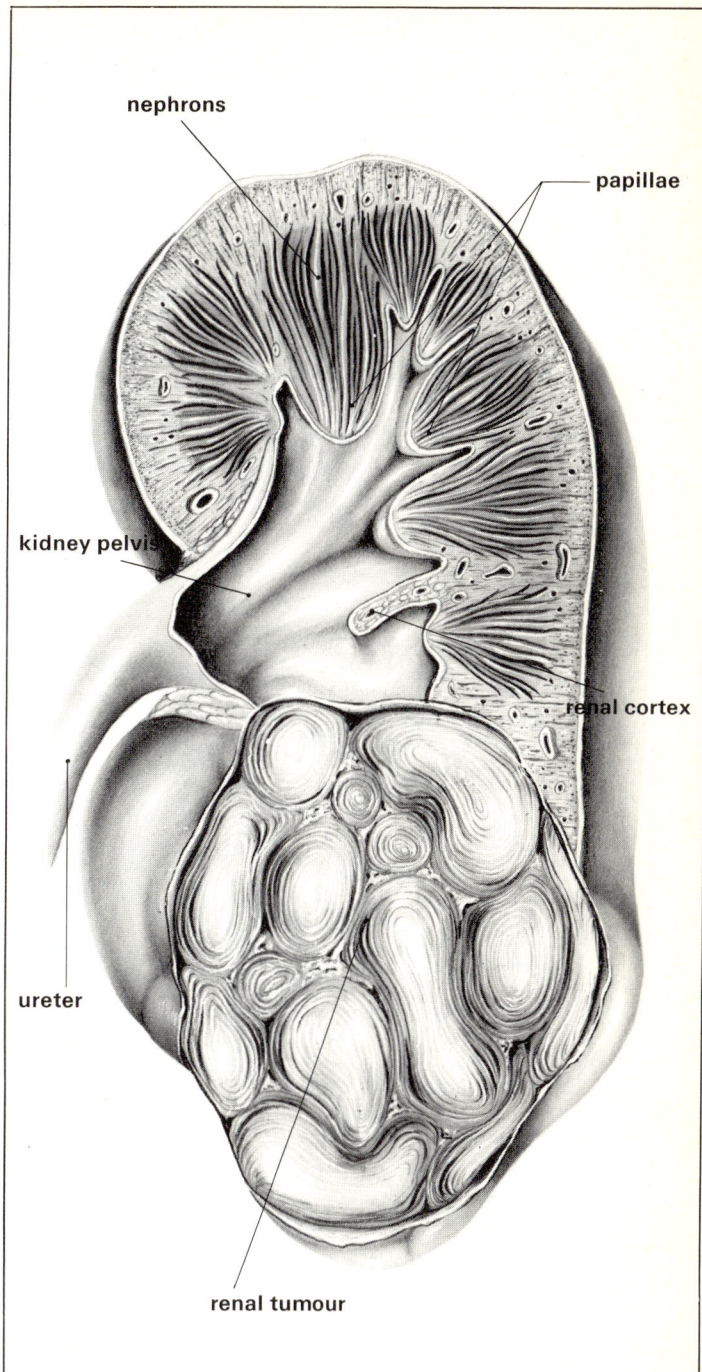

Diagram of a renal tumour localized in the lower half of the kidney, where the normal anatomical entities present in the upper half have disappeared.

Diabetes

Diabetes is a very widespread metabolic disease; about one person in every fifty is a victim. This proportion does not vary greatly from country to country, except that the incidence is higher among populations with an abundant food supply and less frequent where food is scarce. We can see then that this metabolic disorder varies in relation to the nutritional standards of the population under consideration. Diabetes has a profound effect on the work capacity of the affected individual, reducing his output and life expectancy. Consequently, this disease, known as *diabetes mellitus* because it affects sugar metabolism (mellitus=sweet), must be considered as a grave social problem, and here again the World Health Organization is trying to develop a remedy.

Diabetes is due to a reduction in *insulin* secretion by the pancreas, an organ which is part of the gastro-intestinal system. Insulin is the substance which enables the body to absorb and utilize *glucose*, the simple sugar into which all the other sugars and starchy foods we eat (bread, rice, potatoes, etc.) are eventually transformed. The body draws much of its energy from these foods, but it cannot obtain this energy unless the derived glucose can penetrate the cells of the body. In order to do this, glucose has to pass through the membrane surrounding each cell, and it is insulin which enables it to do so. Insulin probably also functions similarly in the case of the amino acids, making it possible for them to enter the cell, for it is only within the cell that these important substances can be utilized. If this mechanism of cell penetration becomes defective, as happens when the supply of insulin is deficient, the glucose continues to circulate in the blood. It gradually accumulates, causing an excessive rise in the blood concentration of glucose, a condition known as *hyperglycaemia*. If such a condition is discovered, it indicates that the body's cells are suffering from a chronic shortage of nourishment. When allowed to persist *hyperglycaemia* will inevitably lead to an intolerable and irreversible degree of deprivation. The extent of this damage, and the rate at which it progresses will depend on just how severe is the deficiency of the insulin supply. The pancreas may still be producing some insulin, and if the amount put into circulation is only slightly lower than normal, the diabetic condition will be mild. However, the deficiency may be considerable or very severe, in which case the diabetes will be proportionately serious. When very severe, the condition used to be fatal, and patients would die within a short space of time. It was only in the 1920s that the mechanism behind the disease was discovered. Soon after this, insulin was produced in the laboratory. It could be injected into the diabetic's bloodstream, thus furnishing a needed substance he could not produce for himself. Insulin is extracted from the pancreas of various animals and it can now also be made synthetically. In recent years, new antidiabetic drugs have been developed which have the same effect as insulin (lowering the blood sugar) but which can be taken by mouth. This is obviously preferable to having to perform insulin injections one or more times a day, but in severe cases these drugs cannot replace insulin completely and are used in conjunction with it.

Now that we possess the appropriate means for treatment, diabetes is an illness that can be given specific therapy under constant

medical supervision. We know that a predisposition to diabetes is definitely hereditary, and that excessive food intake and consequent obesity are likely causes for the onset of the disease. A hypothesis has recently been advanced suggesting that a virus disease of the pancreas might damage the insulin-producing cells giving rise to diabetes, particularly when it affects young people. We also know a great deal about the various consequences of diabetes: the whole metabolism is seriously affected at the cellular level, and the changes produced resemble those seen in ageing. Degenerative changes in the blood vessels are accelerated, involving not only major arteries but especially the smallest vessels called capillaries. Substances are deposited within the capillary walls that narrow and often obstruct the minute channel so that the blood can no longer flow through it. The organs served by these capillaries are thus deprived of their blood supply and develop various disorders. The condition may affect the heart, kidneys or eyes, and even lead to gangrene of the limbs through inadequate circulation. Other common complications of diabetes arise from a greater susceptibility to infections and increased difficulty in curing them. The skin, mouth and particularly the respiratory system and urinary tract are common areas of infection.

Although many tests already exist, everything points to the need for an even more refined system for the early detection of diabetes. Tests must be devised that will reveal the presence of diabetes even when still at a latent stage. This would avoid the deterioration that ensues once the disease gains a foothold.

The Heidelberg IBM scientific centre. The computer is used to determine the exact quantity of radiation to be administered in the treatment of cancer through external application of Roentgen rays, and the analysis of the scintigraphs.

Arteriosclerosis

We now come to a condition of the human body that develops over the course of time as a sign of the ageing process and which affects the cells and tissue of the blood vessels. This deterioration of the blood vessels is called *arteriosclerosis*. Because of it all the organs and systems fed with blood via the circulatory system are also affected. As it gets older, all the body's metabolic processes slow down; on the one hand, the body is losing needed substances, and on the other hand it no longer has the capacity to assimilate other substances and distribute them efficiently to its cells. These cells in turn become increasingly deprived of nourishment, their activity level falls, and they are incapable of sustaining the ceaseless biochemical processes that characterize young tissues. With age this increasing inability to repair and replace used-up materials leads to degenerative changes as part of the normal cycle of living. Today's environmental conditions and way of life, however, have brought about a marked worsening of this situation.

It is still true to say "a man is as old as his arteries", but it has been demonstrated that a young man of twenty can have arteries usually expected in a seventy-year-old.

The pathological picture of arteriosclerosis is fairly consistent: the arteries, or stretches of them, gradually harden and become rigid, losing their initial elasticity. The normal artery dilates as the blood pulses through it with each heartbeat, and its elasticity makes it revert to its normal diameter between pulses. Normally, the increased flow of blood is accommodated by a stretch response of the arterial wall, so that the blood passes easily through it. In the arteriosclerotic artery, the wall cannot respond in this way, so the heart has to work harder to push the blood through. This puts a strain on the heart, and blood pressure consequently rises. Under the microscope, the arterial wall shows cells and fibres that have degenerated through the accumulation of fatty substances, the most important of which is *cholesterol*. Sometimes the inner surface of the artery has deposits of fatty substances, known as *atheromas*, which protrude into the arterial canal, tending to narrow it and sometimes obstruct it. This particular condition is known as *atherosclerosis*.

Below is a list of the most common symptoms and complications that can arise:

Arteriosclerosis of the aorta (the main blood vessel from the heart).

Cerebral arteriosclerosis, which tends to interfere with the mental activity, limiting the power of concentration, the ability to formulate concepts (conceptualization), and the memory. At times this condition can lead to a rupturing of the cerebral vessels causing a fatal stroke or paralysis.

Arteriosclerosis of the coronary arteries, the arteries which carry blood to that tireless muscle the heart. The function of these vessels is so vital that obstruction of even a small section will interrupt the flow of blood to a particular area of the heart and cause what is called a *myocardial infarct*. This is a condition that is becoming increasingly common at the present time.

Renal arteriosclerosis, which causes an increasingly severe insufficiency of the kidneys and which in turn gives rise to a gradual poisoning of the whole system (since the kidneys are largely responsible for purifying the blood of waste products).

Arteriosclerosis of the limbs, especially the legs, with the onset of pains that limit or prevent walking.

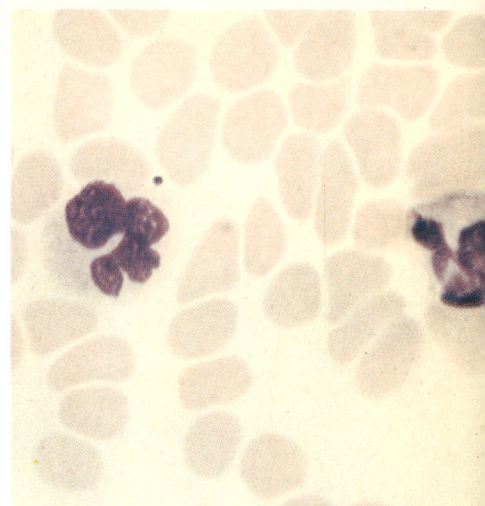

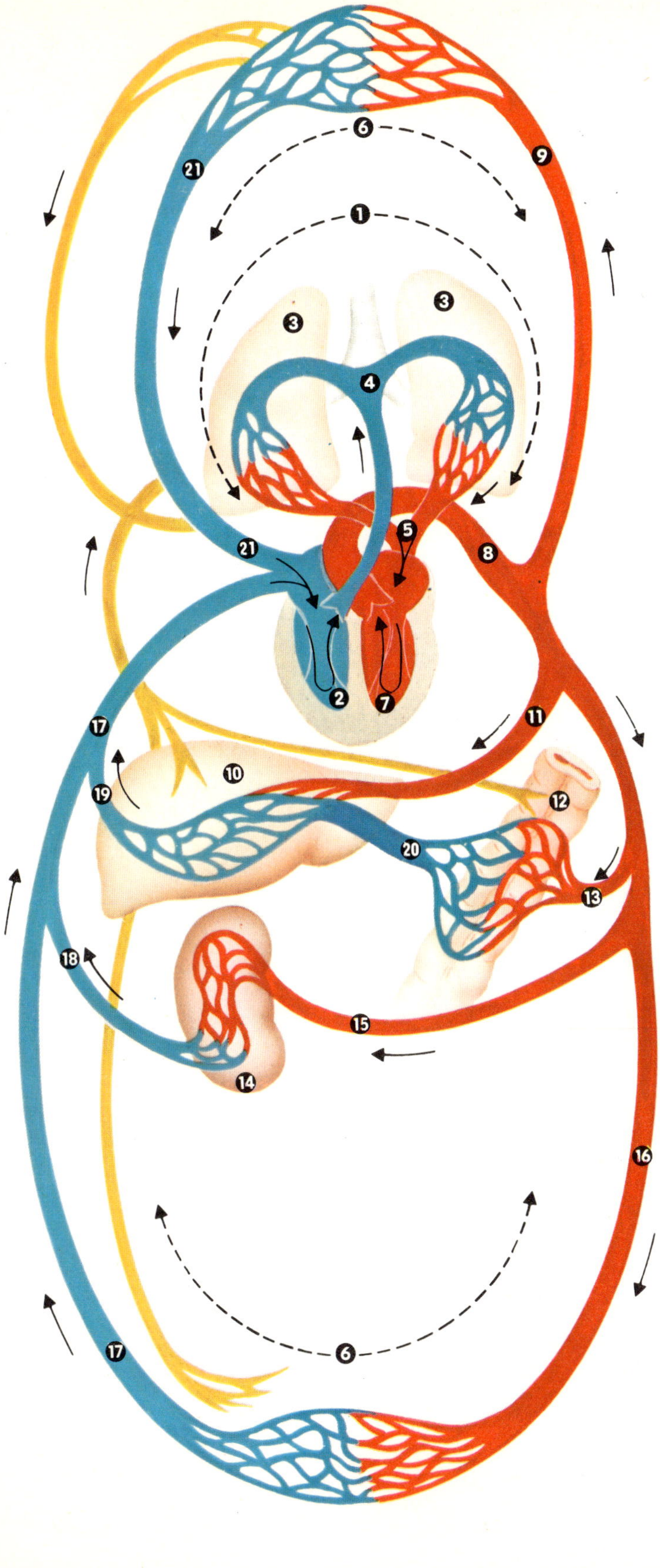

Above: granulocytes present in the human blood.
Left: diagram of the circulation of the blood in the human body.
The small circulation system (1) leaves from the right ventricle of the heart (2) and goes to the lungs (3) carrying venous blood through the pulmonary artery (4). In the pulmonary capillaries the blood gets rid of the carbon dioxide (CO_2), takes in oxygen and returns to the left auricle of the heart through the pulmonary veins (5). The large circulation system (6) leaves from the left ventricle of the heart (7) by the large artery (aorta) (8) which sends a sizeable amount of blood to the head and upper limbs (9) and also provides nourishment for the abdominal viscera, the liver (10) by means of the hepatic artery (11), the intestine (12) by means of the mesenteric artery (13), the kidneys (14) by way of the renal arteries (15); finally the aorta subdivides into the iliac arteries which provide nourishment for the lower limbs (16). The venous blood returns to the heart through the lower vena cava (17) that collects the blood coming from the renal (18) and hepatic (19) veins. It also indirectly collects the intestinal blood which passes first through the portal circle (20) and then through the liver. The venous blood of the cephalic areas returns by means of the upper vena cava (21) to the right auricle of the heart and from there to the right ventricle to go back finally to the small circulation system.

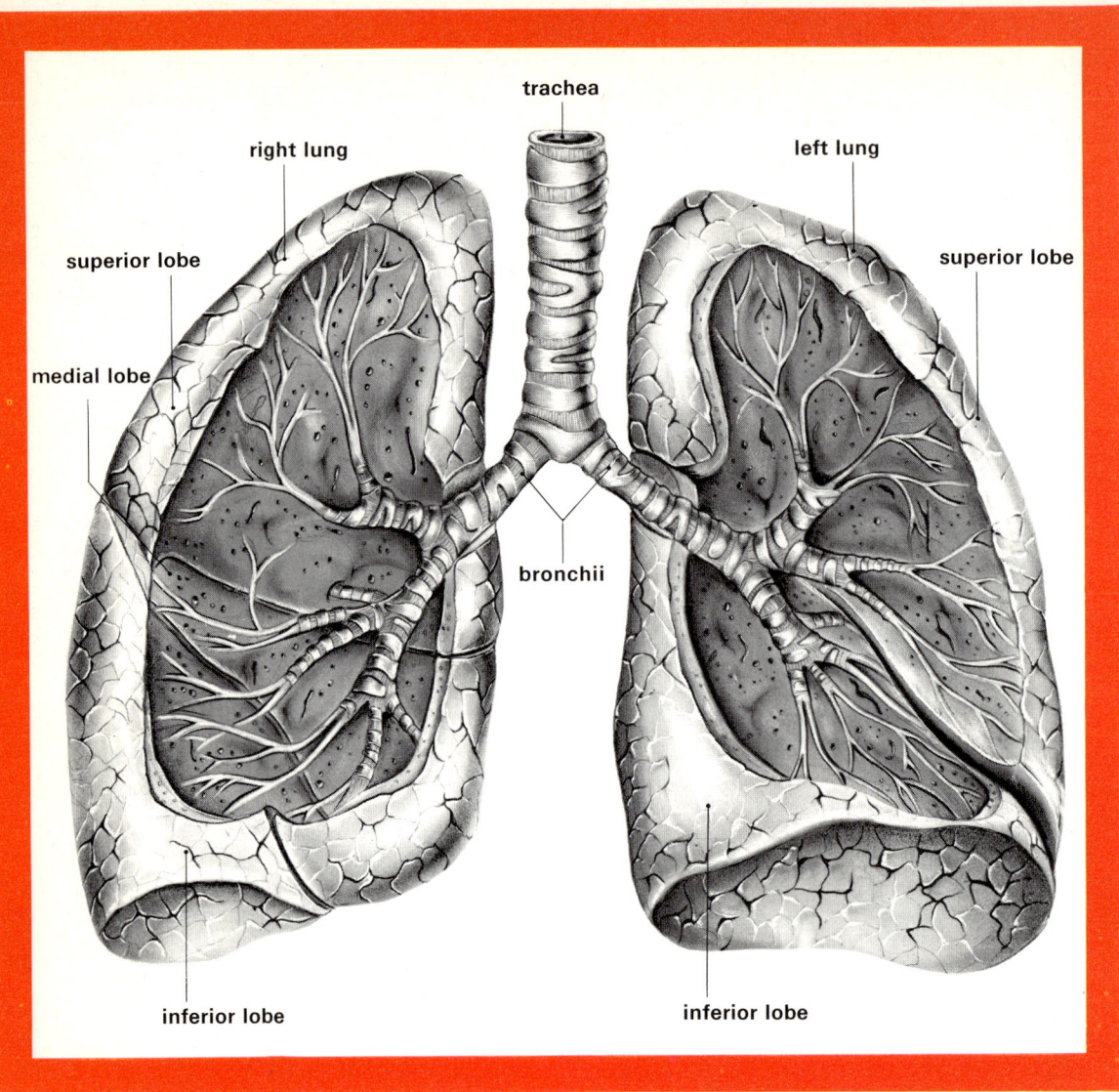

The human respiratory system apparatus: trachea, bronchi, lungs.

During recent decades, all these severe pathological manifestations have become increasingly common, and begin to show up at increasingly earlier ages. In fact, in this century cardiovascular (or circulatory system) diseases have increased proportionately more than any other category of disorder. It must be stressed that factors other than ageing and hereditary predisposition undoubtedly play some part, and are to some extent under our voluntary control. There is the problem of excessive eating, particularly the indiscriminate consumption of fats. Other factors probably involve our obsessive work pace alternating with equally strenuous holidays, atmospheric pollution, the nervous tension to which we are subjected, and our continuously sedentary life whereby we exchange a seat at the workbench or office desk for a seat in the car. We are not getting the necessary muscular exercise to burn up excess calories and rid our body of waste substances that get stored up and impair cell function.

By living under these conditions

and allowing arteriosclerosis to set in and take its toll, it is reckoned that on the average, we are depriving ourselves of ten years of active life and of a healthy and useful old age.

Psychosomatic illnesses—the brain—psychiatry

Contemporary psychiatry is one of the most active fields of modern medical research. These studies are based on the conviction that an understanding of the psyche, or human behaviour, can only be firmly based if it rests on solid biological facts concerning the functioning of the brain and the whole nervous system.

At the beginning of the century, the Italian Camillo Golgi introduced new techniques for studying the structure of the nervous system, and clarified certain details of nerve-cell structure. The Spaniard Ramon y Cajal perfected these methods and concluded that the single cells, called *neurons*, which when taken all together constitute the nervous system, are not joined to one another in the same manner as most cells whose surfaces all touch. Neurons are connected through a system of branching extensions (called *dendrites*) issuing from each cell body. These extensions come into very close proximity but do not actually touch. The nerve impulse flows along the dendrites, passes through the cell body and is carried by way of another extension into near contact with the dendrites of a neighbouring neuron.

During the years which followed, research by the German biologist Loewi led to the conclusion that the transmission of nerve impulses (or waves of nerve excitation, which can be measured electronically) came about through the release of chemical substances, one of which is *acetylcholine*. These substances are released from the endings of the conducting nerve extension and act like a chemical bridge in establishing contact with the surface membrane of the dendrites of an adjacent cell. The nerve impulse is thus passed along even though there is no actual physical touching between the various branches of the neurons. During the last few decades, brilliant experiments by Eccles, Huxley and Hodgkin, show conclusively that this chemical transmission of the electrical wave of nervous excitation is related to variations in the concentration of sodium and potassium *ions* (electrically charged particles) at the *synapse*, the name

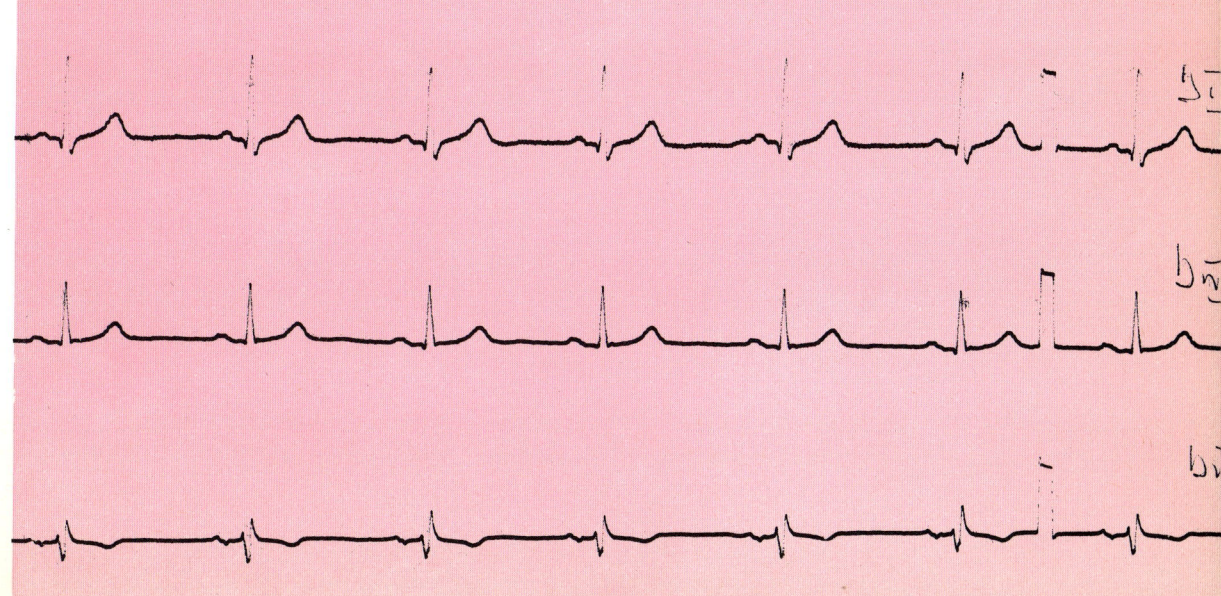

A typical electrocardiograph.

for the point of near contact between nerve endings. These scientists recorded the ion exchange taking place across the cell membrane of the nerve ending that is being excited. It is interesting to note that when the nerve is in a resting state, sodium ions cannot traverse the membrane. However, the membrane remains permeable to potassium ions which become concentrated inside the cell. In a state of excitation, when the appropriate chemical is released and in an infinitesimal space of time, the membrane becomes permeable to sodium ions which now penetrate the cell. Immediately afterwards, the permeability characteristics become modified again, and the cell returns to the resting state. Such acute observations of the physiochemical processes that underlie the production and transmission of nervous stimuli are the starting point of contemporary studies on the human brain and nervous system.

If we consider the brain not only from the angle of its delicate anatomical structure or its complex bioelectric function, but as the mediator between substance and spirit, or mind and matter in man, we are still in a kind of no man's land, where modern psychiatry must proceed with the greatest caution. None the less, psychiatry is advancing, with a sense of commitment, into the complex field of mental illness. It used to be thought that mental disease was due to a disturbance of the anatomical and functional mechanism of the central nervous system at some point. This view was contradicted at the beginning of the century by Freud, who introduced a new conception of the problems involving man's mental health. He wrote: "The human being produces pathological symptoms as a projection of his conflicts which he is unable consciously to resolve and hence pushes them away into the unconscious." The way thus opened for modern psychotherapy, which seeks to produce an integration and balance of the conscious and unconscious in man's own "ego": if this balance is not achieved, there is disorder with mental deterioration and disturbance.

Another area that straddles the threshold between mind and body is the field of *psychosomatic illnesses*. These are conditions in which there is a deterioration in the relationship between a subject's mental and physical functions. Protracted and habitual states of tension can profoundly affect the autonomic nervous system controlling the workings of the internal organs by stimulating or inhibiting the output of hormones produced by the pituitary or adrenal glands. States of anxiety or tension can cause various forms of illness from bronchial asthma to colitis, from hyperthyroidism to gastric ulcers.

As a result of these discoveries, a new group of drugs has been developed call *psychopharmaceuticals* or *psychotropic drugs*. After suitable testing, these drugs are now used alongside the traditional medicines designed to treat physical illnesses. They have the capacity to alter mental function in various ways, acting at conscious and unconscious levels. They may bring about a lowering of excessive and continuous nervous tension, induce a beneficial tranquillizing effect to promote sleep, or cause relaxation of the internal organs. Alternatively, they may induce wakefulness and promote good moods, as in the case of drugs known as anti-depressants. The type of action required, and hence the drug to be prescribed, has to be selected by the doctor according to the needs of the individual.

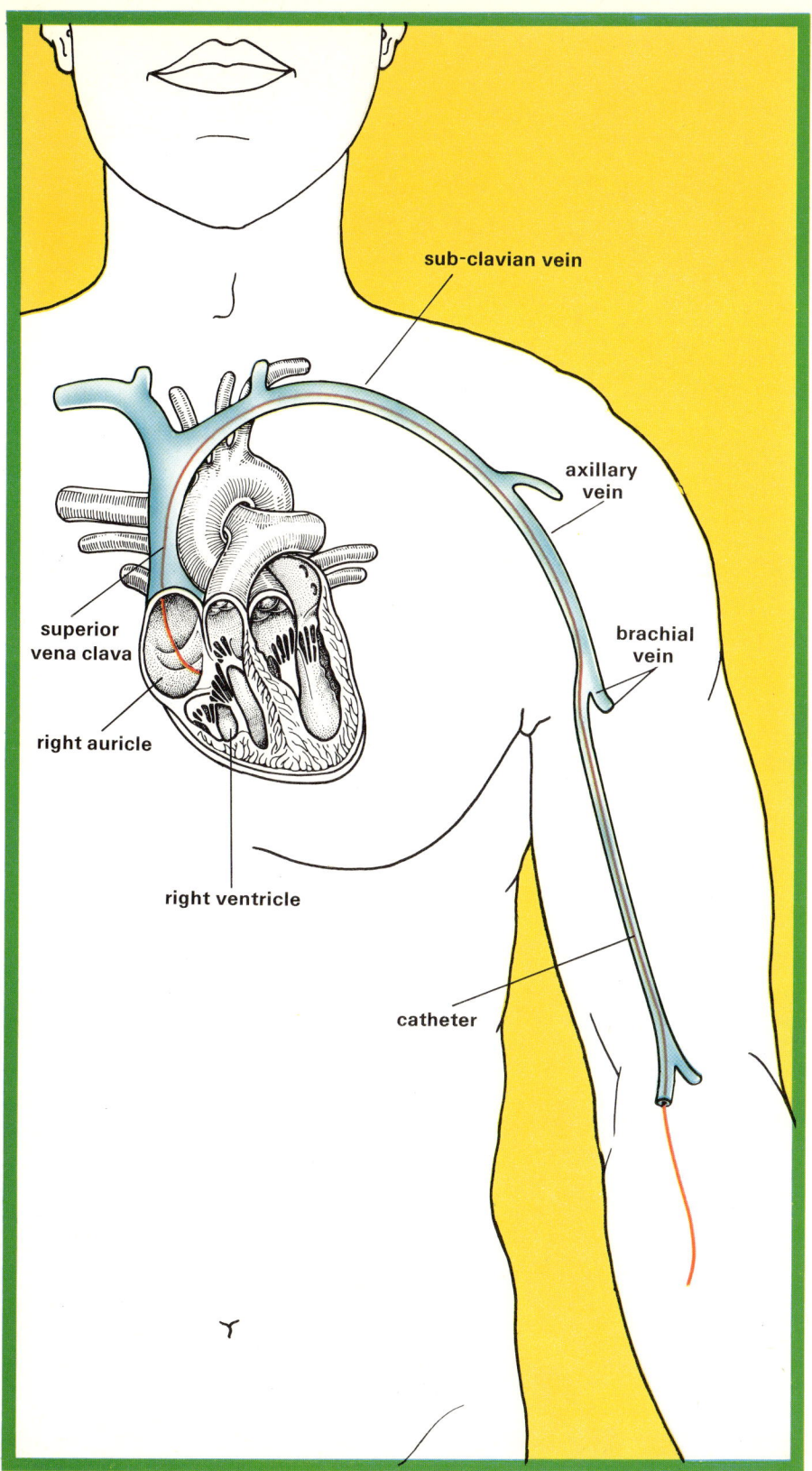

A cardiac catheterization. The catheter is passed into the blood vessel at the left elbow, and carefully pushed along it until it reaches the heart.

Earl Sutherland.

The hormones

We have already mentioned one of the hormones when we discussed the role of insulin in diabetes. Hormones are internally secreted substances produced by specialized cells present in anatomical structures known as the *endocrine glands*. Hormones are effective in minute quantities, being released into the bloodstream as required, and carried to all parts of the body where hormonal activity occurs. The main functions of the hormones are those of enhancing or stimulating enzyme synthesis and influencing the permeability of cell membranes. All the glands are interrelated in a complex and harmonious balance which governs the regulation of countless fundamental processes in our bodies.

The turn of the century saw the first steps in the biochemical analysis of the previously invisible workings of hormones: first came the preparation of *adrenaline* in the pure state, followed by that of *thyroxine*. These are the hormones secreted by the adrenal and thyroid glands respectively. In 1929 the female sex hormones were isolated and active principles (called *cortisone*) were extracted from another part of the adrenals, the adrenal cortex. The male sex hormones in turn were isolated during the 1930s. The discovery of hormones naturally led to their utilization, so that it was finally possible to combat many disorders against which medicine had hitherto been completely powerless.

In 1942, the Chinese professor Choh Hao Li of the University of San Francisco in California, isolated another important hormone, ACTH. In 1949 he isolated crystalline somatotrophic hormone (growth hormone) from the complex *pituitary gland* or *hypophysis*;

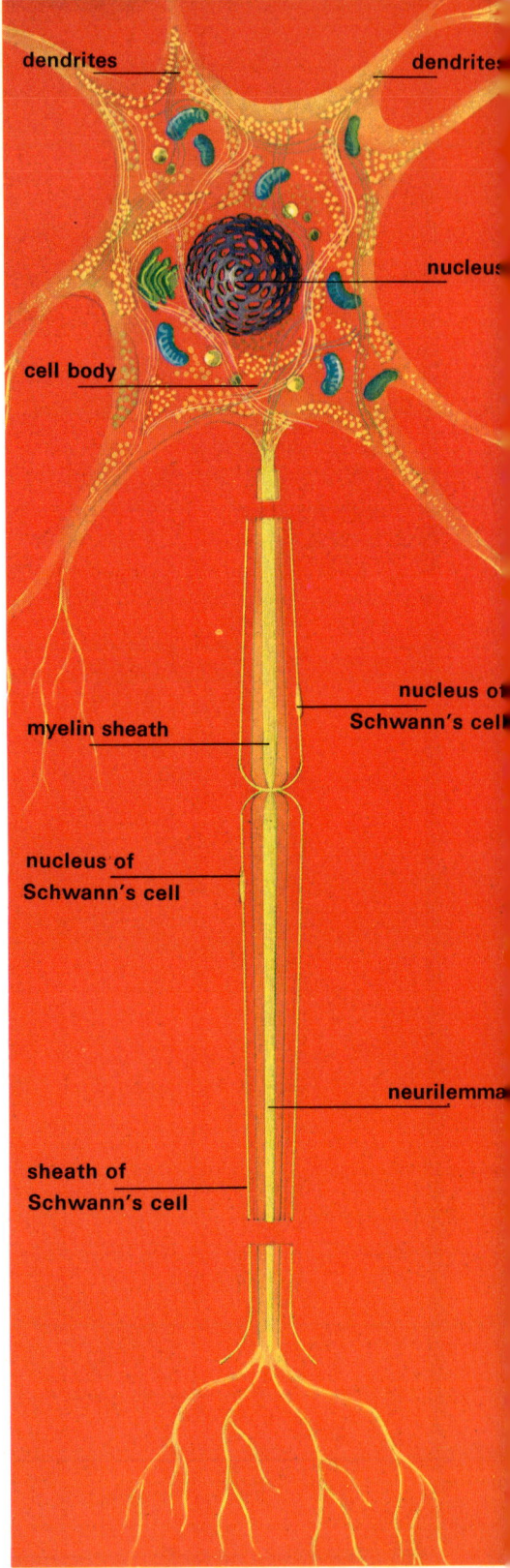

A nerve cell.

the main function of this hormone is to regulate and hence determine the development and growth of the human body. From then on, Professor Li devoted his efforts to furthering our knowledge of this hormone. Some idea of the difficulties he progressively surmounted during his research is given by recalling that it took until 1956 for him to purify growth hormone completely, and another ten years' research was required to determine its chemical structure; finally, in 1970, he announced its synthesis in the laboratory. This meant that he had artificially reproduced its long chain of no less than 190 amino-acid molecules linked in their precise order, although this synthetic hormone probably still requires some refinements for it to be identical to the naturally occurring substance.

We have cited these details concerning growth hormone because they provide a good opportunity to illustrate the sometimes unexpected developments and interconnected findings that open up new possibilities in science. Growth hormone is useful not only in correcting causes of dwarfism by increasing stature; but through the discovery and investigation of its properties, Dr Li was able to extend his studies to another field of application, starting from the following "working hypothesis": Given that growth hormone increases cell growth, and knowing its chemical composition, it ought to be possible to produce its opposite, namely a hormone that can block cell growth. This line of research clearly has a specific aim: to block the growth of cancer cells which are in fact the result of uncontrolled proliferation.

The 1971 Nobel Prize for Medicine was awarded to the American scientist Sutherland who had a few years previously identified a chemical substance in the body known as *cyclic adenosine monophosphate*. The fundamental property of this material is to stabilize biochemical interactions whenever a particle of hormone makes contact with any cell that has to be sensitized. This discovery of a new previously unsuspected chemical bridge opens up the possibility of countless interpretations and applications. It is generally considered to herald a new and major breakthrough for future understanding of what basically causes the living body to become diseased.

Rheumatic diseases

The treatment of rheumatic disease, or at least those conditions where an inflammation of the joints with its attendant pain and limitation of

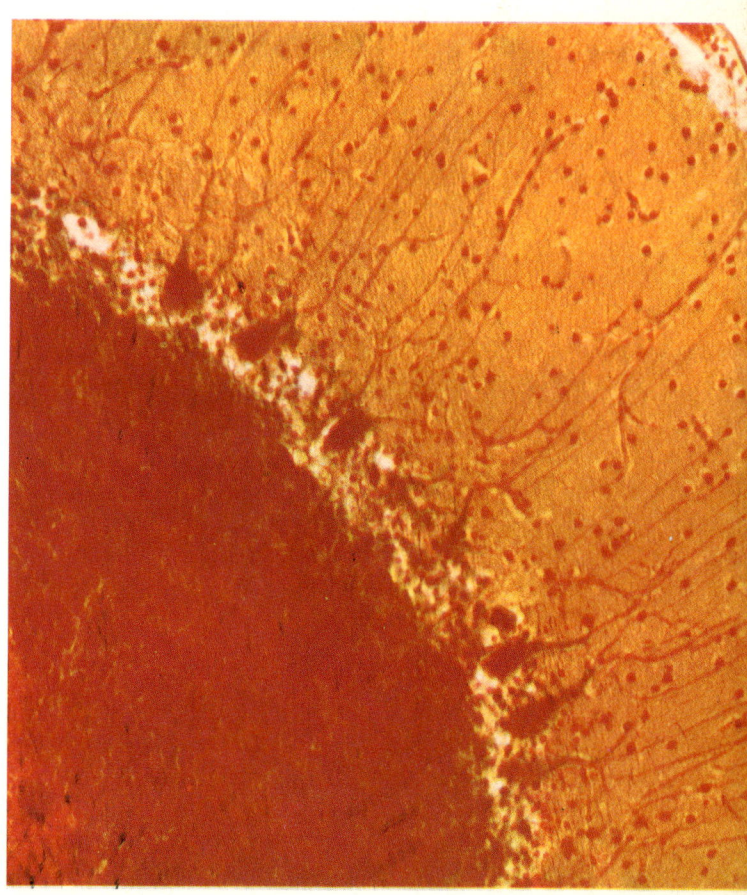

A histological section of the human cerebellum.

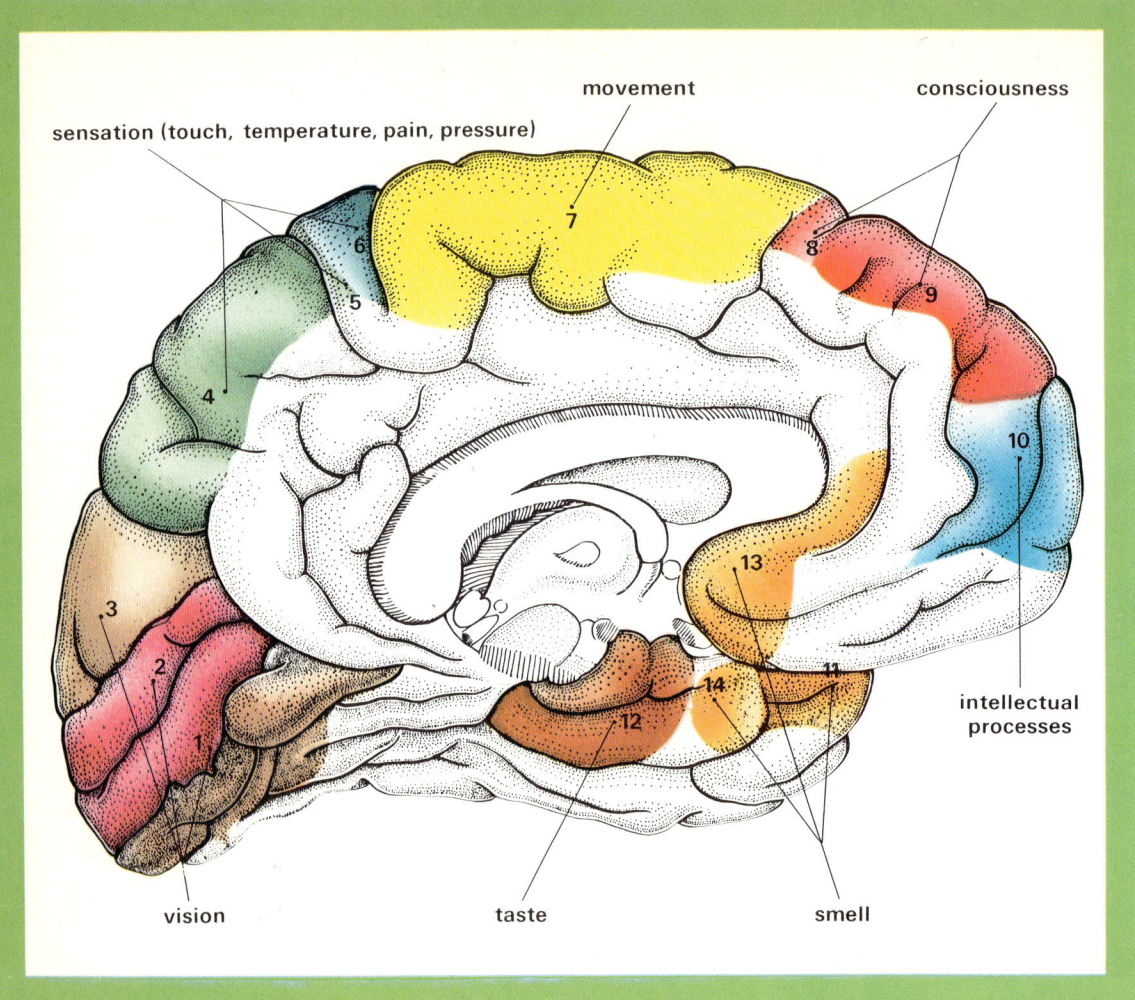

Central nervous system. Plan of the functional localizations of the medial side of the left cerebral hemisphere. 1, 2 and 3: the areas of vision; 4, 5 and 6: the areas of general sensitivity; 7: the motor area; 8 and 9: the area of consciousness; 10: the area of high mental activities. 11, 13 and 14: olfactory area; 12: area of taste.

movement is present, was greatly helped by the discovery of *cortisone*. This is a hormone secreted by the adrenal cortex, which soon after its isolation was produced synthetically. In addition, the recent development of numerous corticoids, very much more active and less toxic than the parent substance, have markedly increased the possibilities for safe therapy.

For decades, *sodium salicylate* and *acetylsalicylic acid* (better known as aspirin, and admittedly of considerable value), were the only treatments available for these diseases. In this century the medical profession was confronted with such an increase in arthritic and rheumatic disease that these ailments were finally recognized as being of social significance. These diseases were responsible for a high percentage of absenteeism, and were chronically incapacitating to the point where they often made quite young persons unproductive and a burden on society. Fortunately, by now at least some of the principal factors causing rheumatic diseases have been discovered and it has become possible to treat and prevent many of the symptoms.

Among the various kinds of rheumatic disease that exist, we can distinguish a first group characterized by the presence of inflammatory processes. This group in-

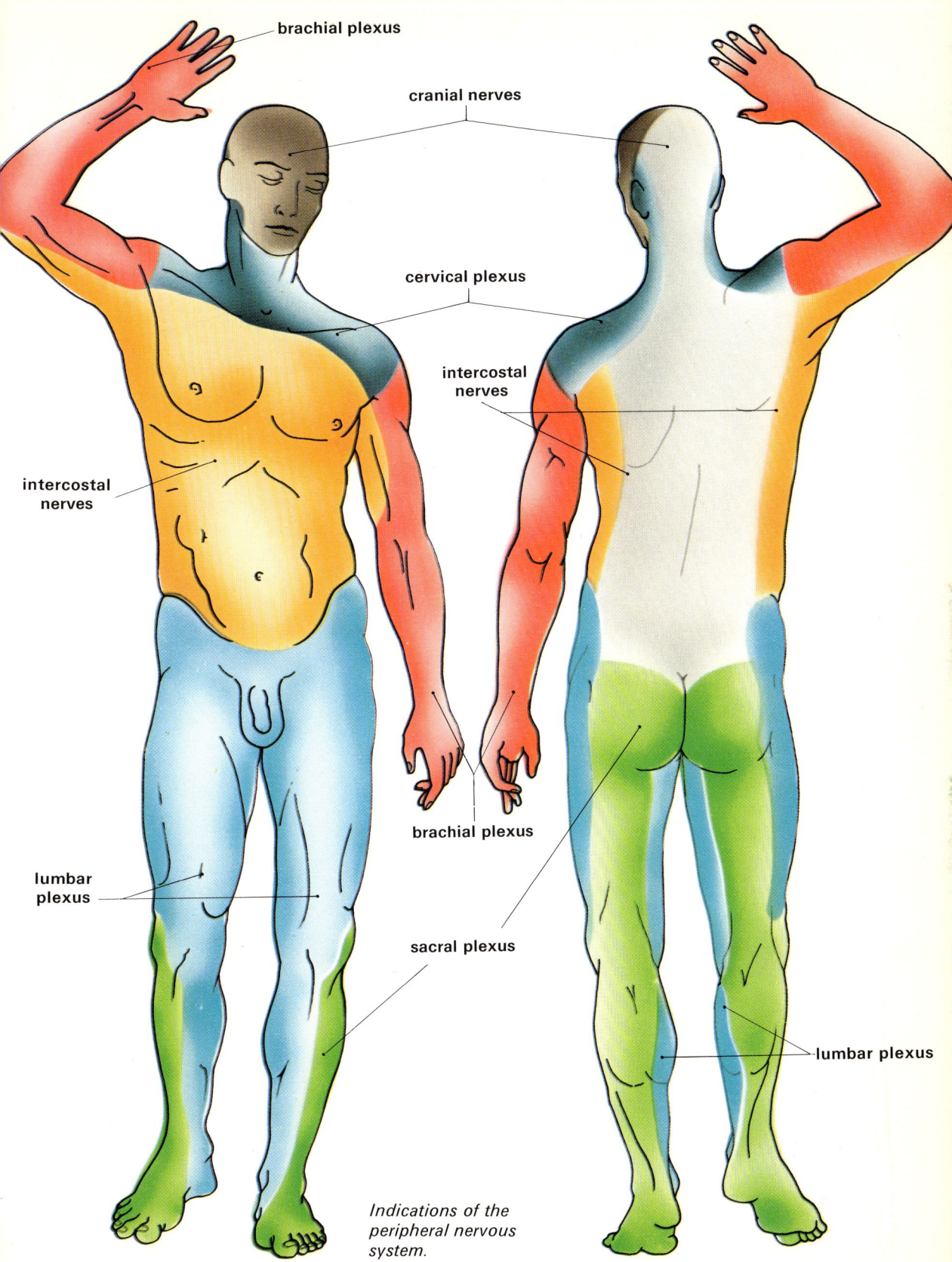
Indications of the peripheral nervous system.

81

cludes *rheumatic fever*, *rheumatoid arthritis* and *ankylosing spondylitis*.

A second group consists of those rheumatic manifestations which arise as a sequel to, or complication of, an infectious disease caused by a well-defined pathogenic agent, a *haemolytic streptococcus* or more rarely a *staphylococcus*.

Generally the infection enters and spreads from the upper respiratory tract; it very often starts as tonsillitis which is so common in infancy. Sometimes this infection does not completely die out but takes an insidious course. Over a period of time which may be as long as three to ten years, the streptococci diffuse by way of the bloodstream and become established

Doctor Witt of the Department of Mental Health of North Carolina carrying out an experiment into behaviour patterns and the effect of environmental conditions upon them. The experiments consist of administering various drugs to separate groups of spiders and observing the differences between the patterns of webs woven while under the influence of the drugs and those woven under normal conditions.

elsewhere. The heart is frequently affected, leading to a deterioration of the heart muscle (myocardium) or heart valves. This serious illness is called *rheumatic endocarditis*.

Such an alarming situation develops only if young patients are not given the necessary treatment in time. Formerly there was no way of treating these infections but with the advent of penicillin it is possible to effect a satisfactory and often total cure. It is essential that the penicillin be given immediately and continuously (sometimes for as long as five years) when such infections first set in. Treatment should not be discontinued on the grounds of an apparent recovery merely because the more obvious aggravating symptoms have disappeared. Here again we must remember that medical progress cannot be truly effective unless accompanied by a degree of awareness and responsibility on the part of the public who stand to benefit from it.

Allergies

In this century we have been able to understand the underlying causes of a whole group of symptoms that were previously completely inexplicable. These are the *allergies*. An allergy is an alteration in bodily sensitivity and reaction when exposed to certain foreign substances.

With the preparation of a chemical substance known as *histamine* came

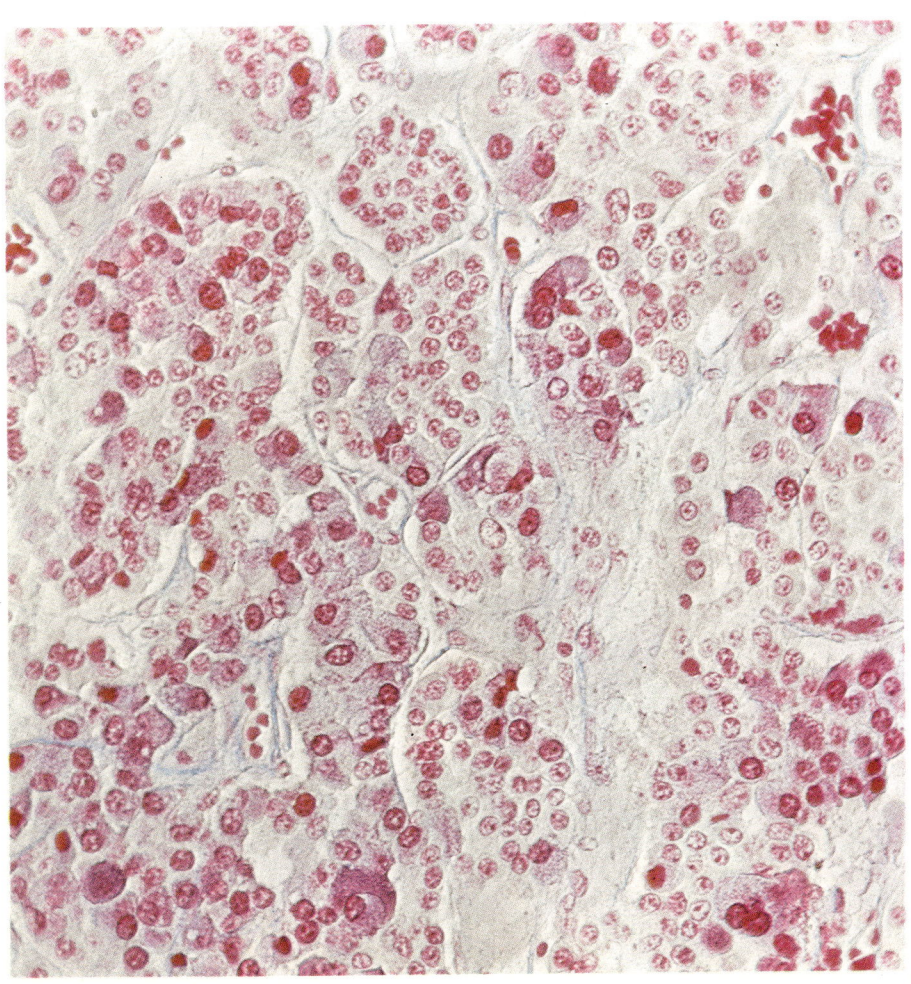

Human hypophysial gland cells.

the discovery that there was a close analogy between the effects of administering doses of histamine and the allergic symptoms called *anaphylactic reactions* that had been accidentally produced in patients when inoculating certain sera. In 1932, significant quantities of histamine were identified in the blood of dogs in which anaphylactic shock reactions had been artificially induced. In 1937, the scientist Bovet prepared a substance which, when injected into guinea-pigs protected them so that they survived massive inoculations of histamine five times greater than the lethal dose. He called this substance *antihistamine*.

On the basis of these experiments, antihistamines began to be used to combat allergic diseases in man. They were first widely used in the 1940s and since then they have been increasingly perfected.

These illnesses cover a vast spectrum of human ills for it is now recognized that organic allergic reactions can stem from contact with almost any kind of external stimulus, be it of a physical, chemical, biochemical or bacterial nature. Alongside these external causes, numerous internal factors have also been found. There are cases when the body finds itself in the strange situation of reacting abnormally to its own immunological processes, and certain individuals can become allergic to themselves so to speak.

On the whole, however, the causative agents of allergy are external in nature, usually bringing about their reaction when brought into contact with the skin. Alternatively, they cause symptoms when inhaled or ingested, in which cases the reaction is usually more serious and far-reaching.

The very presence of light, cold, heat, X-rays, can all give rise to allergic symptoms; perfumes, creams, the pigments in cosmetics, and soaps can cause skin irritation, ranging from a mere redness and slight itching, to much more intense and sometimes serious manifestations. Various drugs and medicines—and this applies to practically all of them—can cause unforeseen reactions. A sleeping pill that normally induces only a few hours' sleep can have a ten times greater effect on individuals.

Similarly, an injection of antibiotic can in some cases lead to death within a few minutes, due to an allergic reaction. It is very important, therefore, for doctors to make initial tests when allergic reactions are suspected. It is also thought that acute rheumatism of the joints, gout, gastric ulcer and many common migraines may be partly allergic in origin.

But the commonest forms of allergy affecting millions of people throughout the world, especially at certain seasons, are those referred to as *allergic rhinitis*, the symptoms of which are sneezing and a runny nose. This often develops into *hay fever*, or may affect the respiratory tract more extensively giving rise to the much more serious condition of *bronchial asthma*. All these allergies are grouped under the name of *pollinoses* when they are caused by the inhalation of flower pollens. They can also be brought on by contact with other plant substances such as leaves, roots, seeds, horse-hair in mattresses, cotton, hemp and various kinds of atmospheric dust.

Allergy can also arise from substances of animal origin: the fur, feathers and fragments of dry skin from domestic and farmyard animals, such as dogs, cats, rabbits, hens, pigeons, sheep and horses.

Among foodstuffs, the most common causes of allergy are fish and shellfish, but individuals can also be

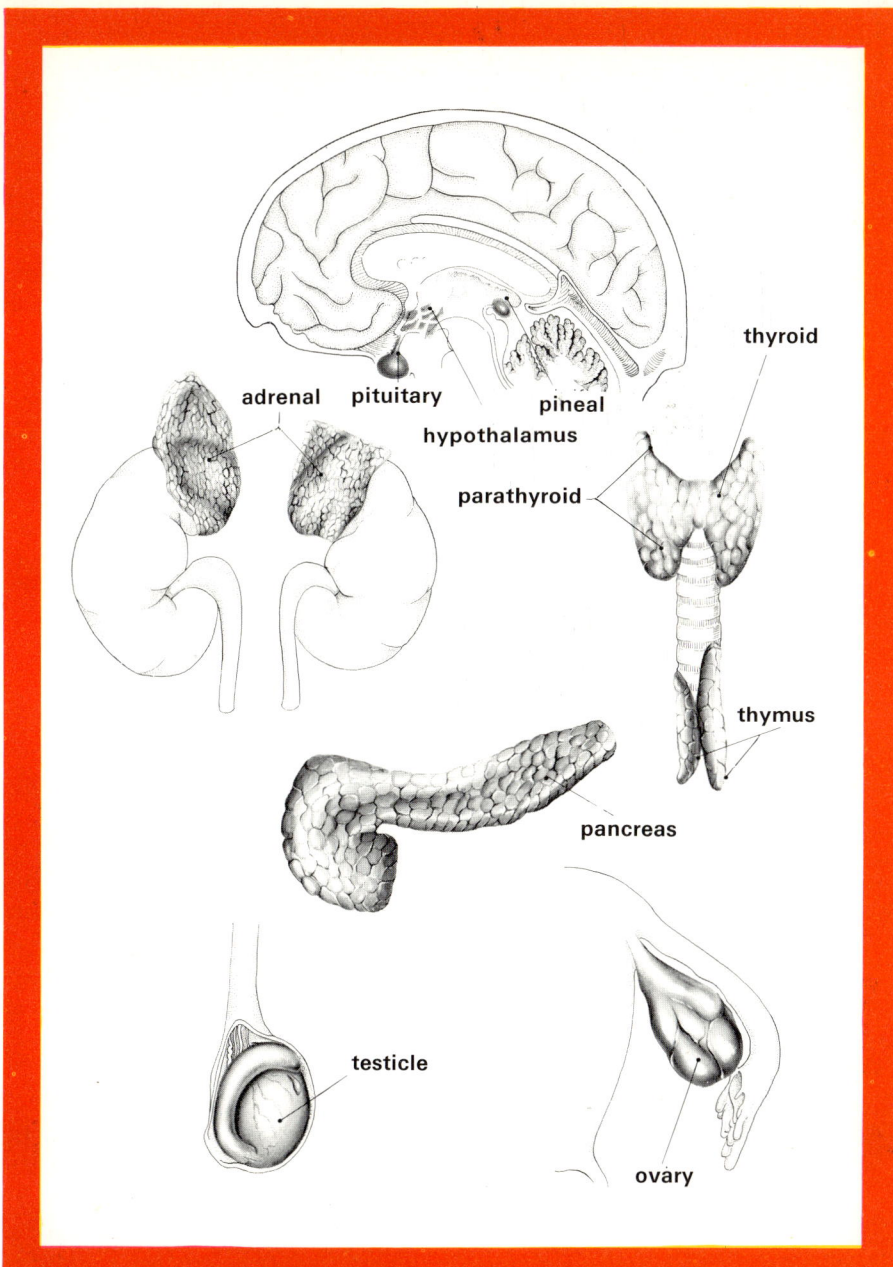

Glands of the endocrine system.

allergic to milk, eggs, certain vegetables, certain fruits (such as strawberries or peaches), chocolate and alcoholic beverages. These allergies most commonly affect the digestive apparatus and the skin, though they can sometimes be manifested as *conjunctivitis* or inflammation of the eye membranes. This condition can also arise by contact with pollens, dusts and various fluids.

It is apparent then, that almost anything in our environment can prove unexpectedly hostile, and unleash a complex of symptoms that was once incurable but which today can be controlled by an effective range of anti-allergy drugs.

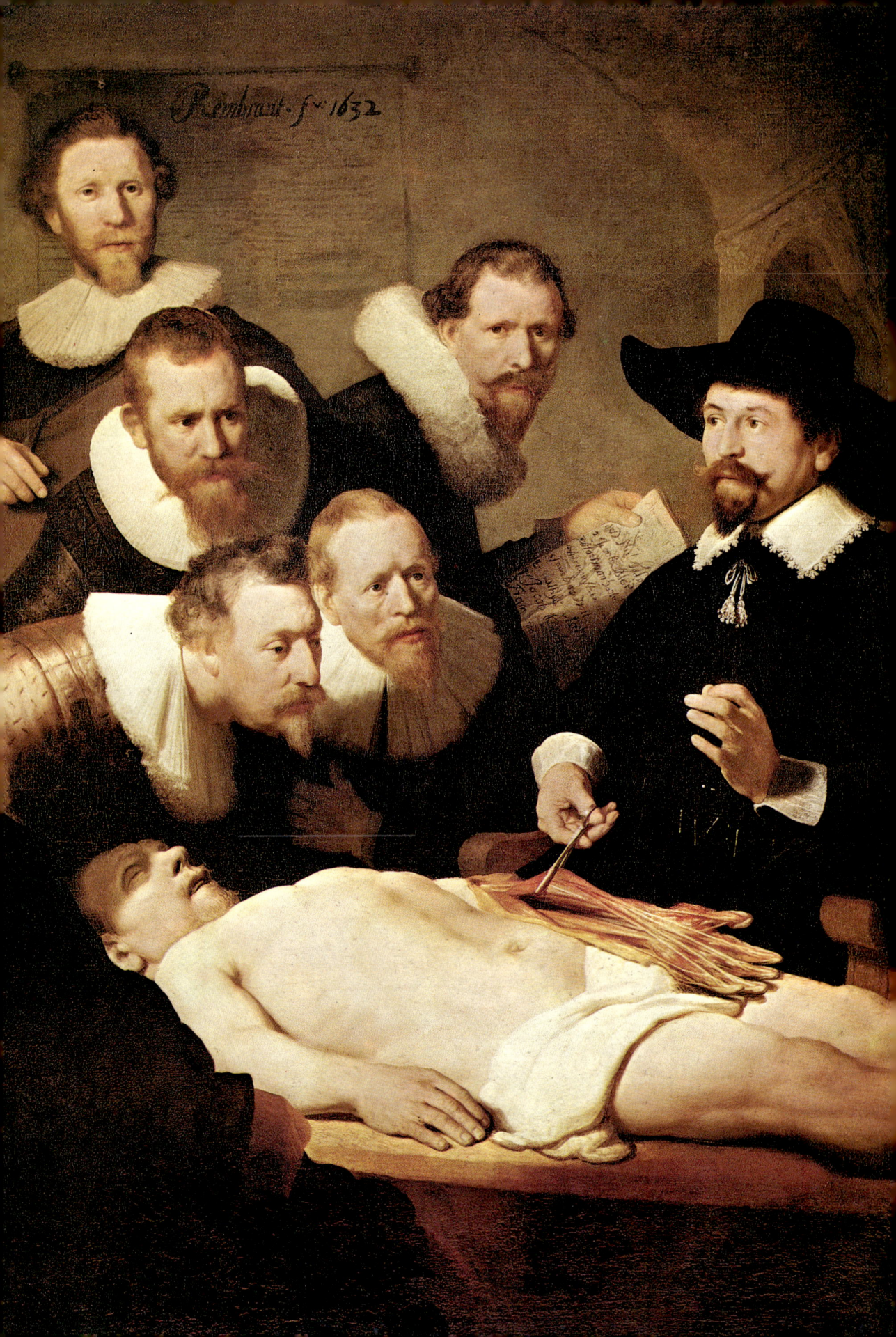

CHAPTER 6

SURGERY AS A MEDICAL TOOL

The practice of surgery was scorned by doctors for many centuries, and was entrusted to barbers and bloodletters. As time went on, and as medical knowledge increased, especially over the last 150 years, the roles of doctor and surgeon grew steadily closer until by the middle of the 19th century they were virtually indistinguishable. Today the surgeon is regarded as a doctor who treats patients by surgical means, following a thorough medical diagnosis of the patient's disease.

The advance of surgical technique was at one time seriously impeded by the fact that patients could not withstand the protracted pain involved in lengthy operations. Such pain could cause fatal collapse and, in any case, prevented the relaxation and immobility necessary for a surgeon to gain access to the internal organs. Only in the last few decades has a new medical figure come to stand alongside the surgeon: the *anaesthetist*. Anaesthesia has now been established as a field in its own right, and every surgical patient is assured of an accurate programme that is adapted not only to the various stages of the operation, but also to his particular cardiovascular and respiratory condition and his metabolic rate. In short, the anaesthetic technique used takes into account the complete medical picture of each patient.

The anaesthetist has at his disposal many mixtures of gases and chemical solutions that he can administer in accordance with the successive stages of the operation, inducing varying degrees of anaesthesia depending on the surgeon's needs. Using non-toxic substances, he can influence the patient's mental state to reduce over-excitment. He can choose from a vast range of analgesics (pain-killers) which, as their name implies, simply block the perception of pain. Lastly, he can induce deep sleep under the most favourable conditions and maintain it for hours without the risk of causing any unpleasant side-effects. In this way the anaesthetist spares the surgeon a great deal of tension and frees him from a sense of urgency so that he can devote all his skill to the operation itself.

However, the anaesthetist is only one of the technicians who assist the surgeon. The operating theatre now has access to many new kinds of aids. Developments have occurred and are still taking place from both the scientific side—with the detailed clarification of anatomy, histology, immunology, the biochemical and physical constitution of the blood—and from the technological side—with the perfection and invention of instruments and apparatus. Surgical tools have flourished under the impetus of technological progress in

The Anatomy Lesson *by Rembrandt.*

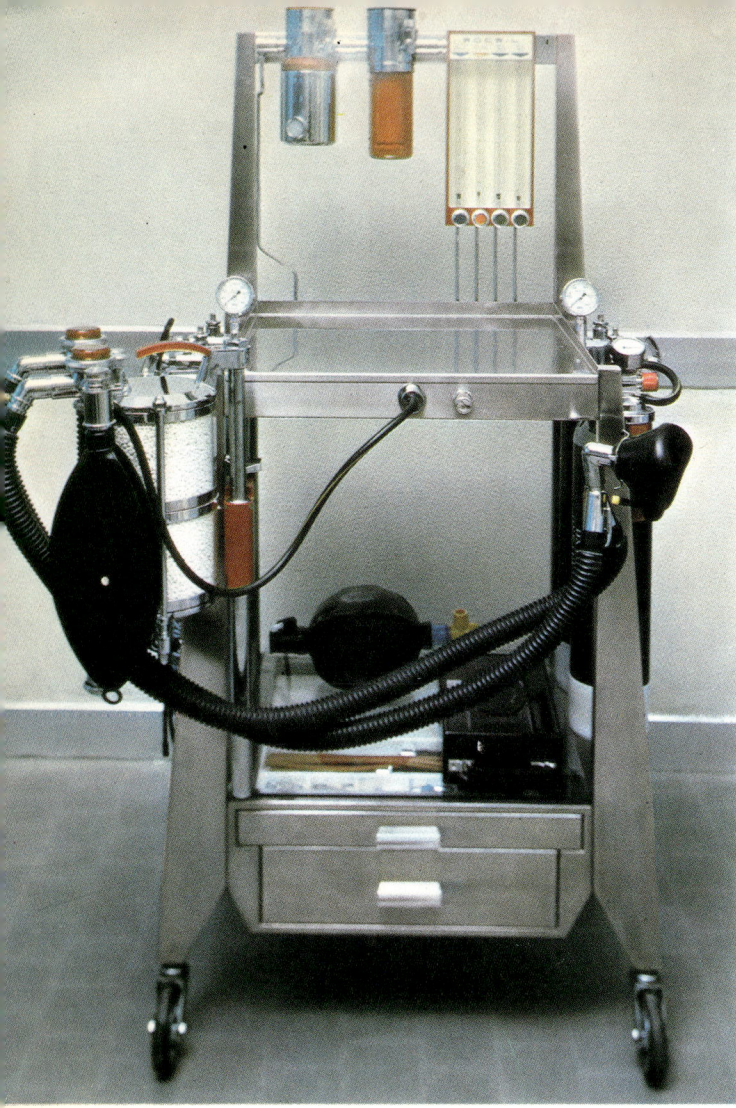

the area of new metal alloys and other new materials. Mechanics, mathematics, engineering and electronics throng the ante-room to the modern operating theatre, vying with one another to offer the best that the human mind has conceived and produced. Thus, the surgeon of today, while still retaining full responsibility for the operation in progress, can count not only on the active collaboration of his surgical assistants but also on the great help provided by the anaesthetist, and the various technicians who keep the patient under constant observation. There are specialists and machines that control and activate respiration and blood circulation or even artificially replace them while the patient is on the operating table.

Modern surgery, therefore, is not the product solely of the skill of a single man but of the co-ordinated efforts of many individuals: the so-called surgical *team*, specialists in many fields who unite their talents within the confines of the operating theatre.

A whole range of surgical instruments has come down to us from

An anaesthetist's apparatus.

An automatic respiratory apparatus which, by a process called intubation, uses nasotracheal tubes in the nose and throat to assist the breathing of people who otherwise cannot obtain enough air on their own.

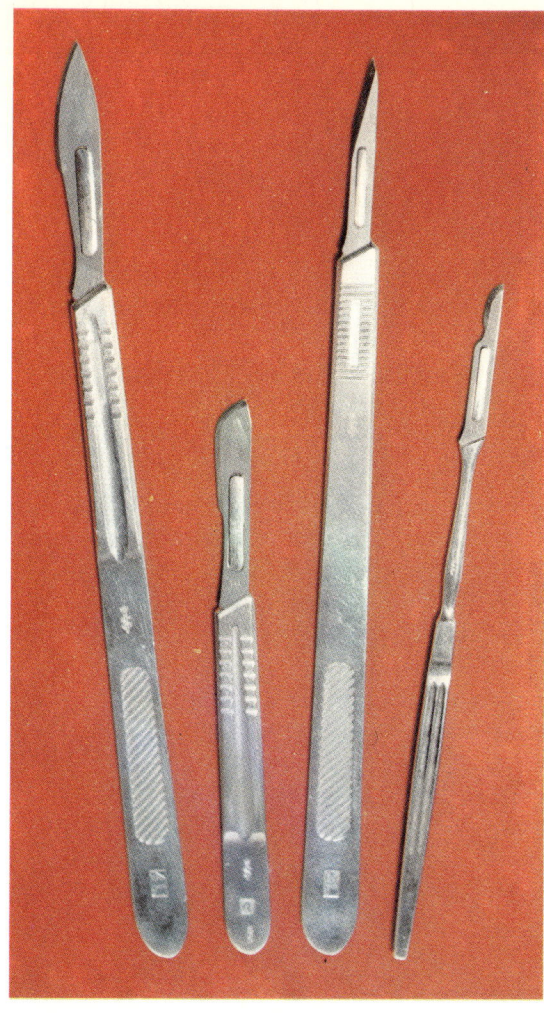 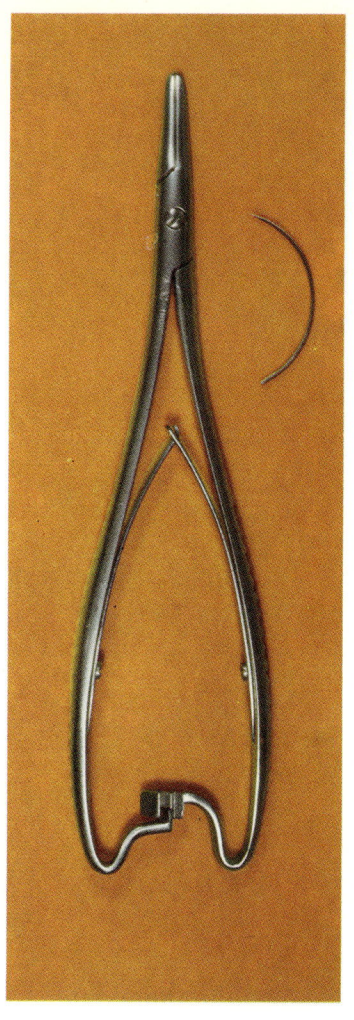

Surgical instruments. Left, scalpels. Right, a needleholder.

ancient times and the Middle Ages. The sight of them makes one shudder to think of their being used on human beings who were, moreover, fully conscious, or at best only mildly unconscious from alcohol. Today with the use of special metal alloys and the innovations made by surgeons, instruments are both highly efficient and minimally injurious. Loss of blood is reduced to a minimum. Haemorrhage resulting from small blood vessels being cut is stemmed by the use of special clamps which keep the vessels closed until they are tied up with ligatures. An alternative technique, known as electrothermal cauterization has also been developed. For some years now the surgeon has also had at his disposal certain kinds of gauzes and sponges made of materials that not only stop the flow of blood, but also disintegrate on their own within the body. A plastic substance has been developed which can be painted on like varnish, or even sprayed over the raw surface of operated tissues to arrest bleeding.

Also, the procedure of suturing which often takes up considerable time during an operation, has been speeded up with the help of mechanical stitchers that are now beginning to come into general use.

But it is above all to those machines that are capable of temporarily taking over the interrupted functions of certain organs, that the surgeon owes his opportunity to take bold operative measures never possible before. Of these machines, one of the most impressive is the *automatic respirator* which allows continuous control of respiration during an operation, and even replaces the respiratory function entirely during chest surgery.

Chest and blood vessel surgery

By constructing a special operating theatre in which the pressure was below atmospheric levels, the German surgeon Sauerbruch took the first step towards solving the problem of intrathoracic (within the chest cavity) surgery. Once it had been shown that lung operations of various kinds could be performed, it was not long before medical men could envisage taking the ultimate risk: a direct operation on the heart for therapeutic purposes.

The precedents for such an operation took place during the first half of this century. The Frenchman Alexis Carrel laid down the first technical foundations for surgery on the blood vessels, and also performed animal transplants of various organs including the heart and kidneys. He was assisted in these studies by the French surgeon Leriche, and the techniques were perfected to the point that by mid-century the first arterial transplant was successfully performed on man.

Several years later, the Frenchman Dubost succeeded in performing the first resection of a large aneurysm of the abdominal aorta. He replaced the defective portion of this large artery with a healthy piece taken from another vessel. Barely two years later, in 1953, the tenacious and brilliant research of the American surgeon, De Bakey, an ardent champion of the use of artificial materials in vascular surgery, was brought to a satisfactory conclusion on the operating table. The first vascular transplant with a synthetic substance called Vinyon was performed successfully. These first results were followed by other successes in Europe and America. They opened the way to the great expansion of *cardiovascular* (the heart and its associated vessels) surgery that has dominated the last decades of our century.

The rapid progress of vascular surgery has naturally been helped along by contemporary advances in every other sector of medical science. One example worth quoting is the production of *heparin*, a substance that decreases the blood's ability of coagulation, and consequently lessens and prevents the risk of fatal clots both during and after surgery.

Above all, however, we should stress the enormous value of another technique, that of *blood transfusion*. As is so often the case, this practice, too, has its roots in much earlier research. In 1901, the various *blood groups* that characterize human blood were identified. It was discovered that transfusions could be given harmlessly, provided that the donor and recipient were of the same blood group. In the following decades, transfusion became ever more widely used especially because of the enormous increase in haemorrhages due to the growing number of motor-car accidents and other modern risks. It has become necessary to set up, wherever possible, blood-collection centres, where people donate blood, and *blood banks*, where this precious element is treated and preserved for as long as possible to be readily available when needed. Blood transfusions are given not only in cases of acute haemorrhage, or when required during operations. They are also used

An automatic respirator which can take over the function of physiological respiration during surgery involving the chest cavity.

for therapeutic purposes in many blood diseases (from severe anaemia to leukaemia and haemophilia), in some forms of cancer, and in certain blood conditions in newborn babies whose blood must be totally replaced immediately after birth.

Heart surgery

The advent of heart or cardiac surgery was brought a step nearer by information gathered from a study of the electric currents produced during contraction of the heart muscle. These currents are due to changes in electric potential and can be measured and recorded on a chart by an *electrocardiograph*, an instrument first constructed at the beginning of this century and perfected around the 1930s. This was made possible by the introduction of electric leads with special valves that permit a thousandfold amplification of the voltage variations arising during heart activity. The electrocardiograph provides the doctor with a tracing, the *electrocardiogram*, from which he can assess the strength or the irregularity of the heart's bioelectric activity.

91

The same system coupled up to a television circuit provides a continuous visual record of the patient's heart condition so that it can be monitored throughout an operation.

However, an operation, especially one performed on the heart, entails a great number of preliminary tests of all kinds. When the diagnostic symptoms indicate a serious heart malfunction, as many preliminary checks as possible must be carried out to ensure the greatest possible degree of safety. A very great help in this respect is *cardiac catheterization*, which is common practice today in every centre for cardiac surgery, but which was used for the first time under very unusual circumstances. Around 1930, in a small German hospital, a recently qualified young doctor, Werner Forsmann, decided to demonstrate once and for all that it was possible to gain access to the heart chambers by starting from a point outside the human body. Shutting himself in a room in the hospital, alone and unaided, he made an incision in the

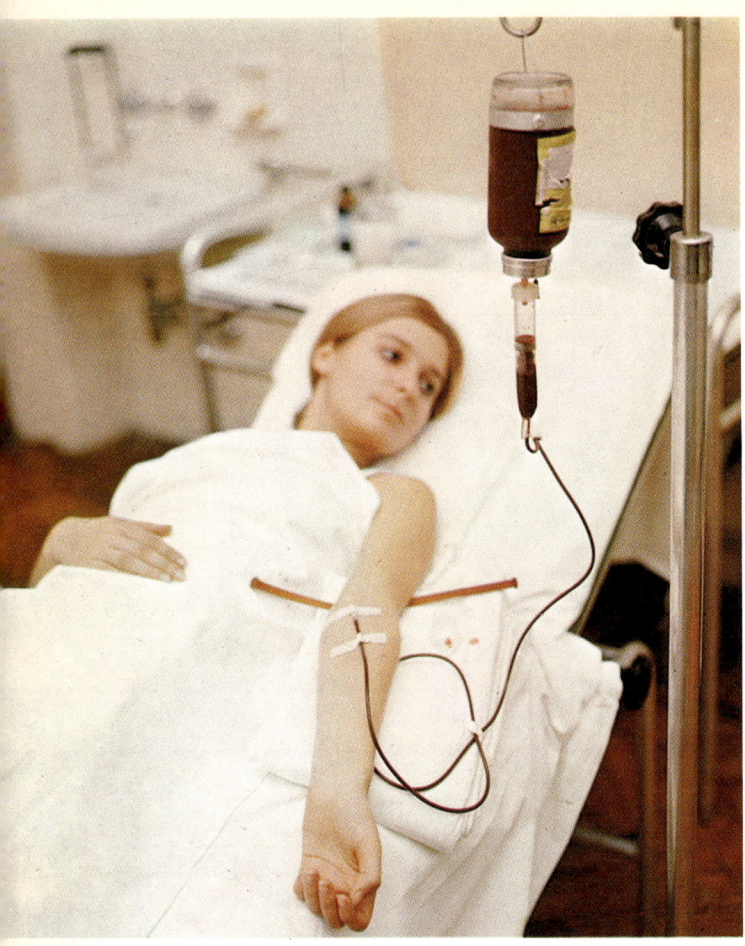

A patient receiving a blood transfusion. Donating blood is one way in which ordinary people can help save lives which would otherwise have been lost.

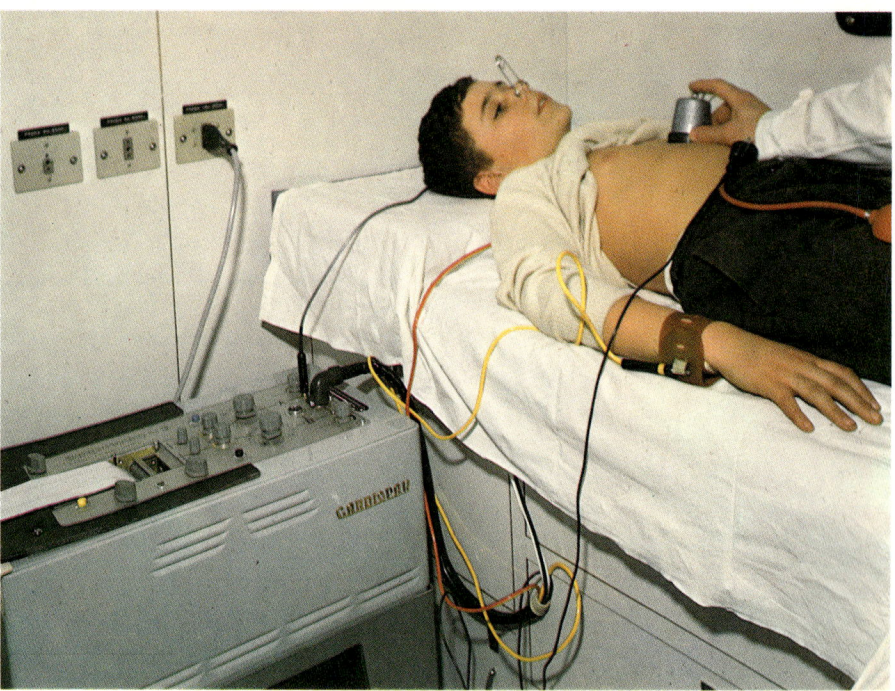

The making of an electrocardiogram.

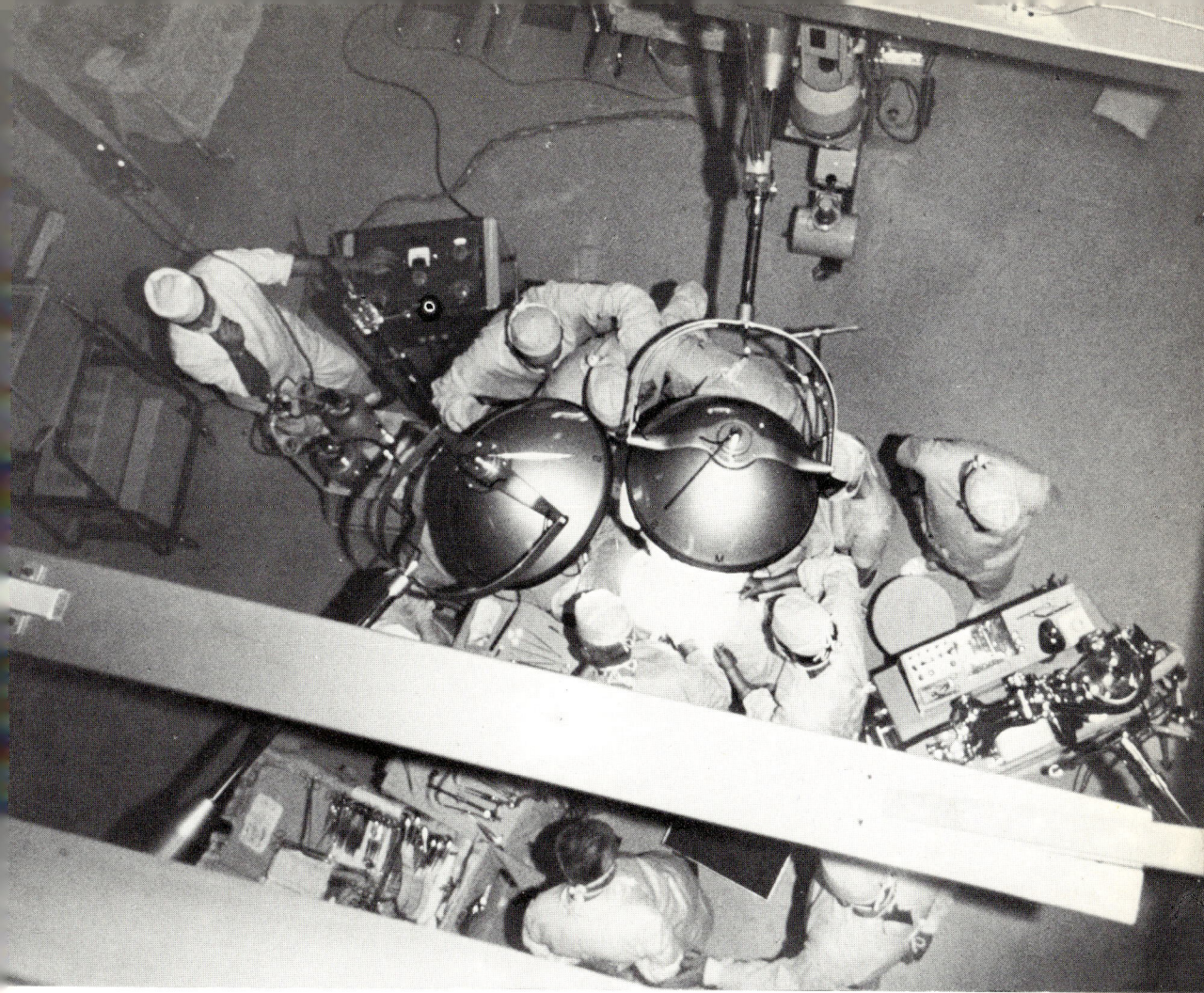

skin in the hollow of the left elbow (the inner side of the arm). Having located the vein under the skin, he carefully inserted the tip of a flexible tube (the same type that is used as a bladder catheter) into the vein, trying to lose as little blood as possible. He then slowly pushed the catheter along the vein, and when he estimated that it had penetrated some 30 inches, Forsmann judged that the tip should now have reached the heart region. Pressing down on the incision in his arm, he made his way excitedly to the X-ray department where he instructed the astonished radiologist to X-ray his chest immediately, in order to confirm that the catheter tip had entered his heart. Using a mirror, Forsmann was able to see from the position of the catheter on the X-ray screen that this was indeed the case. Forsmann's venture may have seemed foolhardy, but it began the era of cardiac catheterization (using somewhat more perfected instruments) as a routine diagnostic measure. It also paved the way for the use of the modern device called a *pacemaker* or *cardiac stimulator*.

Normally the heart of an adult pumps about 2,500 gallons of blood around the body in the course of twenty-four hours. This enormous work output comes about by repeated and regular contractions of the heart chambers, the auricles and the ventricles. The muscle fibres of these chambers contract in response to a bioelectric impulse that originates in a nerve centre within the

A typical surgical operation being performed by Professor Stefanini's team at the Surgical Hospital of Rome University.

heart itself, called the *sinus node*, or pacemaker. The impulses are transmitted at a certain rate, which varies according to whether the subject is active or at rest. A healthy heart varies within definite limits and excessive irregularity usually only occurs in various diseased states. Then there are changes in heart muscle contractibility and the consequences may lead to a condition known as *heart block* which can end in stoppage of the heart (cardiac arrest) and death. Cardiologists had the idea of introducing a probe into the heart via Forsmann's route, monitoring the procedure by X-rays, so that a wire could reach the tip of the right ventricle. This wire could carry an electric current which would initiate the cardiac impulse, so that the heart could beat normally as it would with a normally functioning pacemaker. A great many subsequent variations were based on this idea. In one, the electric current was carried to the outer surface of the heart through the chest cavity. But the most difficult problem was that of providing a source of electricity that an individual could carry about his person, together with the necessary apparatus for transforming it appropriately, since he clearly could not remain permanently wired up to an electric outlet. During the last twenty years this problem has been resolved by the development of increasingly sophisticated and lighter equipment, up to the miniaturized versions of the present day which can either function continuously, day and night, or intermittently when a warning system indicates an irregularity in the heartbeat that requires immediate artificial aid. The supply batteries have been reduced to the smallest dimensions and have a charge that lasts for several years. Today, the very first miniature atomic pile pacemakers are in use: these convert the heat given off by plutonium 238 into electrical energy, and ensure that the pacemaker works at maximum efficiency for ten or twenty years.

Another important aid in cardiac surgery is *hypothermia*, a technique in which the body temperature is lowered so that the metabolism is slowed down and there is less need for oxygenated blood to be carried to all parts of the body, including the heart. The patient is cooled in a bath of water at 32 °C, and is then enveloped in a special double-walled container which has a system of pipes running between the inner and outer casings. Water is pumped through these pipes as required, either at a low temperature when the patient's body has to be cooled further, or at a higher temperature when the patient is rewarmed to bring his temperature to normal.

For the first half of this century, all heart operations were carried out "blind"; the decisive step that made "open-heart" surgery possible was the invention and perfection of the *heart-lung machine*. This apparatus is based on the principle whereby all the patient's blood is withdrawn through a vein and pumped through an oxygenating apparatus, after which it is returned into the patient and circulates normally while by-passing the heart. The patient's heart and lungs are thus relieved of performing their usual functions.

In 1953, the American surgeon Gibbon performed the first operation on a heart through which no blood was circulating, the work of the heart being taken care of outside the body. In the following year, the American Lillihei perfected the heart-lung apparatus even further: venous blood, withdrawn from the patient and full of toxic substances, was mixed in the oxygenator with countless little bubbles of oxygen.

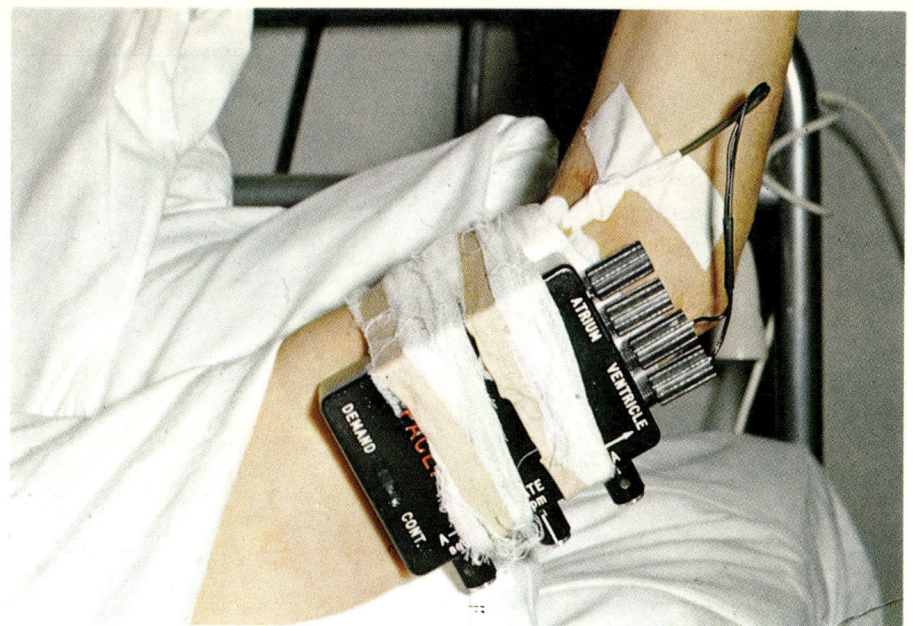

One type of heart pacemaker. These devices are now in increasing use, saving more and more lives.

By employing these techniques—which are still in the process of being improved—the motionless open heart can be surgically operated on for whatever length of time is required. Especially in cases of heart valve defects, whether congenital or acquired—conditions which either severely restrict a patient's life or make it downright impossible—surgery can today substantially improve the condition. Countless persons can now be saved by surgery from a painful future or even from imminent death. Such patients may range from days-old babies to the very old.

This field of medical science has grown even more advanced in recent years, since the onset of surgical removal of faulty auricular-ventricular heart valves and their replacement with artificial valves of metal or plastic. Such devices were developed through the co-operative endeavours of many kinds of research workers, including doctors, biologists and technologists. By pooling their ideas and professional expertise these workers can create materials that have to fulfil particular requirements and possess entirely unique characteristics. Ours is the era that has seen the birth of the bio-engineer, working closely with the surgeon.

There are various types of artificial heart valves, but nothing can alter the fact that these are all foreign bodies, with the disadvantages that this entails. Problems may range from breakdown in function to clot formation, or excessive damage to the red blood corpuscles which are easily bruised and ruptured. Research is being done on possible improvements.

Organ transplants

It can be seen how surgery, having come this far, was now ready to tackle actual transplants. By transplants, we mean the transfer of a tissue or whole organ from one site to another, while retaining intact its vascular system, so that the tissue or organ is able to resume its function in the new site and maintain a normal and regular flow of blood.

Transplants can be performed from one part of an individual's body to another, from one individual to another of the same species, and lastly, from an individual of one species to an individual of a different species. It becomes progressively more difficult for a transplant to become established, depending on the biochemical and cellular differences between the transplanted tissue and the surrounding host tissues. The success of a graft depends not only on the techniques but also on the laws governing the body as a whole.

Dubious reports of limb transplants, or at least partial limb transplants have been received in past centuries. What is certain is that for the first half of this century thousands of research workers concentrated on the problem of transplants, and tens of thousands of experiments on animals finslly enabled surgery to realize its age-old aspiration. Around 1950, several surgeons in America and Europe succeeded first in transplanting a kidney from a corpse to a living person and next from one living person to another, with a longer survival period each time. Since that time, several thousand patients have undergone such operations.

During recent decades, human transplants of liver, lungs, segments of intestine, ovaries and larynxes have been attempted with varying degrees of success. In the experimental field, increased efforts are being made to extend possibilities to the limit by probing into still hidden natural processes. To take an example, as significant as it was sensational, the Russian scientist Demikov succeeded in transplanting a second head on to dogs and keeping these two-headed dogs alive for long periods. Scientists throughout the world are aiming at being able to transplant any organ. Organizations have already been set up for receiving and preserving donated organs against the time when it will be feasible to transplant them with complete success.

But the really sensational achievement that excited the entire world and gave rise to endless debates, came in December 1967. Radios and TV sets in every country gave out the news that in the hospital of Groote Schuur, in Cape Town, South Africa, the young surgeon Christiaan Barnard had transplanted the heart of a young woman into a dentist named Louis Washkansky, who would otherwise have died from cardiac insufficiency within a very short time. Such an undertaking fired everyone's imagination, mostly because it seemed like an on-the-spot decision. In reality, however, it was a step that had long been in preparation and had matured over the course of time. Barnard himself had long been a visitor at the operating theatre of De Bakey, Shumway and Cooley, the three leading heart surgeons of America. By this time other surgeons were also ready to perform such an operation; but Barnard was favoured by circumstances in that the necessary human material was available at the right time. Then, too, he had the courage to attempt what had never been tried before.

More than a hundred similar operations have since been performed in other parts of the world, particularly in the United States and France. The majority of patients have survived for a few weeks, some for several months and a few, who are still alive, for several years.

The initial enthusiasm gave place to the criticism and disapproval that inevitably follow any new enterprise. But the first step had nevertheless been taken and from then on accumulated experience was gradually to take this branch of medical science out of the pioneering stage. At the

present time, the major difficulty—as with all transplants—is the problem of *rejection*, namely the crisis of biochemical incompatibility that arises within a year at most when a body is compelled to act as host to an artificially introduced foreign tissue.

The body's defence mechanisms are triggered by the appearance in the body of chemical entities that the body recognizes as foreign substances. These entities may take various forms: living bacterial cells; toxins secreted by bacterial cells; foreign particles that may enter by an open wound or transplants from one body to another. In all such cases the body's defence mechanisms recognize their presence and set about fighting the invaders. The gross symptoms of this fight may be manifested by fever, swelling, irritation, blisters, rashes, vomiting and so on. These reactions stress how violently the body strives to maintain its integrity. It is a fight to the end, the end either of the body or of the invader. In only very few

The heart-lung machine enables blood to pass out of the body and then re-enter the blood stream, thus by-passing the normal circulatory system.

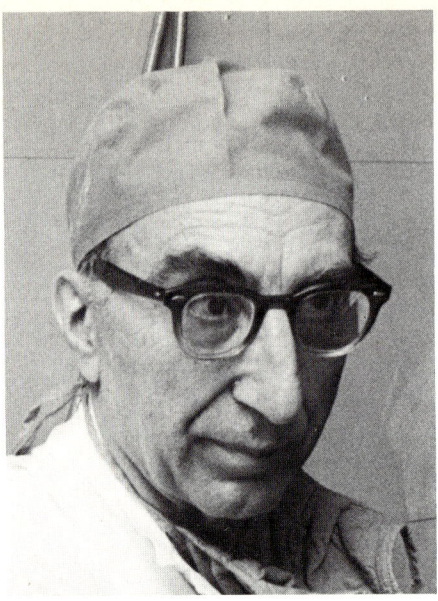 

Left: Michael De Bakey. Right: the French surgeon, Dubost.

instances will the defence mechanisms tolerate the foreign tissues. However, not only may the body reject a foreign substance such as a graft, but a graft may reject a body. When an organ from one body is placed in the body of another the immunological defence systems of each work against the other.

The defence mechanisms' initial attack is carried out by *lymphocytes*, scavenging white cells that circulate freely in the blood. Like free-living organisms they are capable of movement and can engulf and digest small invading particles and even whole cells of invading organisms. Once a lymphocyte has dealt with an invader in this fashion it becomes sensitized to all the cells of that species. If the lymphocyte should again contact such a cell it can release, and can cause other lymphocytes to release, chemical substances that may neutralize or destroy the invading particles. It is for this reason that our first contact with a particular infectious disease may produce unpleasant or severe symptoms; future encounters with the same infectious organism may proceed with few or no symptoms.

It is this ability of our defence mechanisms to recognize and take action against an invading substance that we call immunity. We can say that the immediate overpowering rejection of an invading substance by the lymphocytes is an immune reaction. Unfortunately the immune reaction may not always work to our advantage. In most transplant procedures in which a surgeon wishes to replace a defective organ with a good one from another body the immune response is not advantageous, for it usually causes the recipient to reject the organ.

Promising research is in progress on the establishment of compatibility between donor and recipient by using the latest findings in immunology and genetics. The ideal combination occurs between identical twins, whose bio-chemistry is also identical. Organ transplants have been performed in which host and donor were identical twins with no immunological reaction or complications. However, when dealing with people of different genetic make-up, close genetic match between donor and host becomes unimportant. Instead, compatibility depends on a relatively small number of genes known as *histocompatibility genes*. As with other genes, these are to be found at different points on the chromosomes, but the most important are found at one point on one chromosome. While incompatibility among other genes may have little effect on the survival of a transplant the histocompatibility genes must be compatible for the transplant to take. Although only identical twins have identical genes many people have compatible genes on that one chromosome.

Although the use of tissues with genetically similar make-up is most promising there is the other extreme: the use of tissues so different genetically from those of the host that the defence mechanisms of the host are unable to cope.

Since the science of sorting out and typing of compatible genes is still young, we cannot often depend upon finding suitable donors, but this problem may be overcome through the use of a group of drugs called *immunosuppressive drugs* which inhibit the immune reaction.

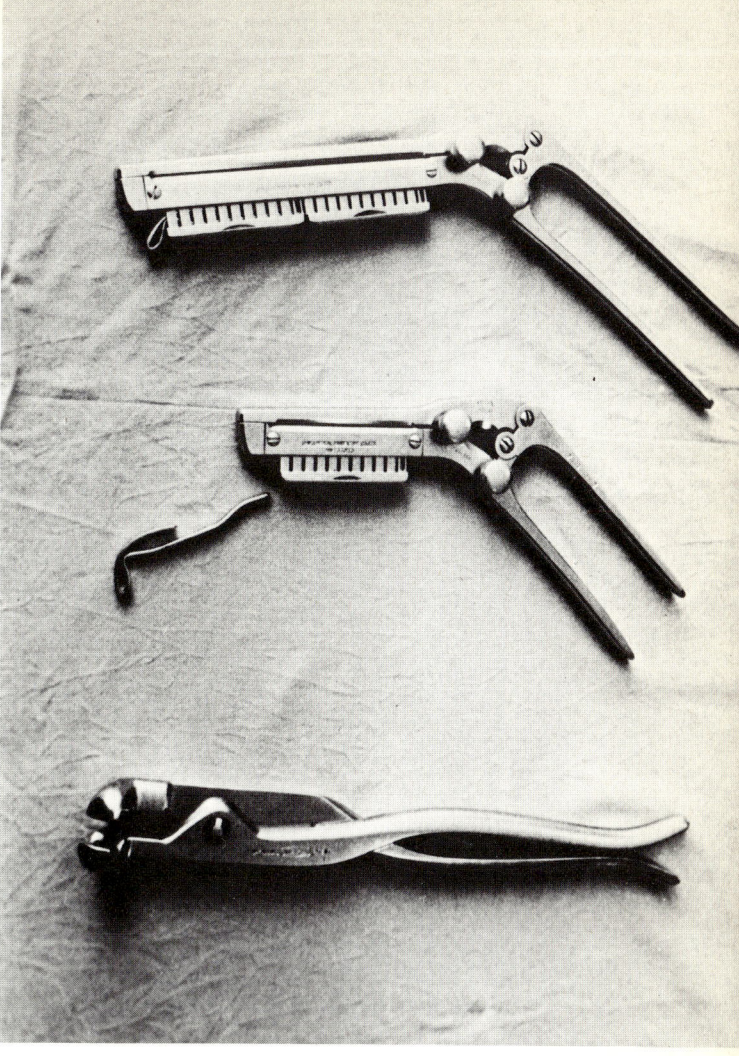

Surgical "sewing machines" used for mechanical suturing.

A. Denton Cooley

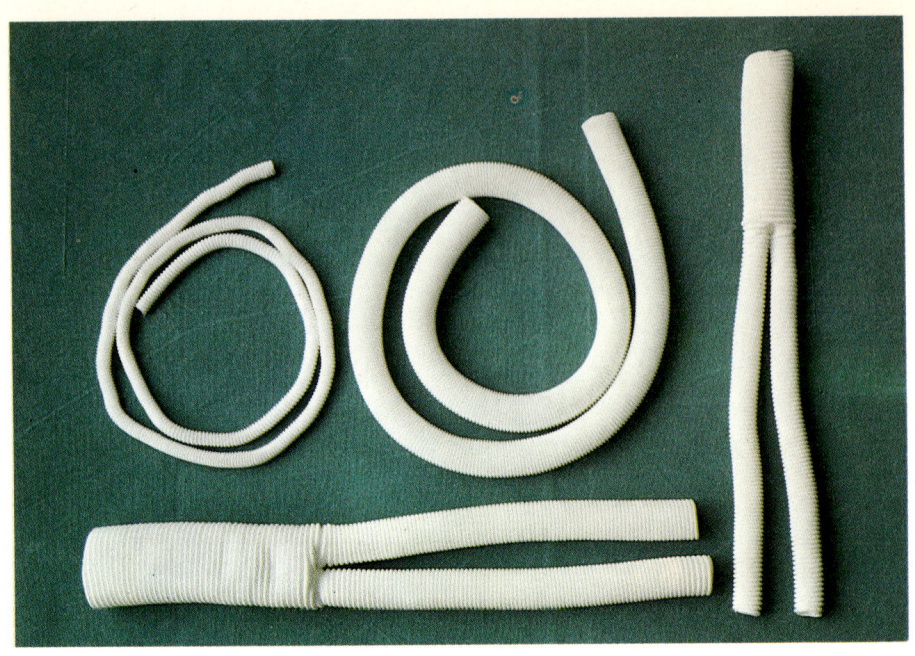

Above: artificial arteries made of Dacron.

Below: an electronic heart battery.
Opposite: a range of cardiac valves: in the foreground the Edmark-KAY Schiley Hufmagel; in the background the Beall-Barnard valve; the top valve is the KAY Schiley, MG Series developed by the Bosa Company in Milan, Italy.

The combination of these immuno-suppressive drugs with hormone-like substances called steroids, curtails the division of lymphocytes to a greater degree than other cells; so replacing them becomes futile. Unfortunately the patient must always rely upon these drugs to suppress the immune reaction, leaving him defenceless against all other infectious diseases. The development and use of broad-spectrum antibiotics has helped reduce this risk.

There are many grounds for believing that the problem of rejection may be conquered in the near future. Promising research is in progress on the establishment of compatibility between donor and recipient, by using the latest findings in immunology and genetics. A whole new horizon is opening up before mankind, involving a revised definition of what constitutes the moment of death. Strict criteria will have to be established to enable the removal of organs at the earliest possible moment. Also, a reappraisal of moral and religious scruples concerning the exploitation of the human body for these purposes will have to be made. Science, with its problems and its demands is thus gradually modifying man's very way of thinking, in anticipation of a near future when things will come to pass that only yesterday were considered impossible.

Prostheses

A *prosthesis* (plural "prostheses") is an artificial substitute for a missing or defective part. Examples are the artificial heart valves mentioned earlier. The technique or science of replacing missing or defective body parts by such artificial devices is known as *prosthetics*.

The availability of corrosion-resistant metal alloys, and above all of plastics—materials which are light, elastic, strong, resistant to deformation, relatively easily joined to living tissues and compatible with them—has increased the use of prostheses during recent decades. Commonly used materials in this field are nylon, teflon, dacron, certain silicones and plexiglass. For many years, sections of veins and arteries have been replaced by small lengths of plastic tubing. Some surgeons have prepared models of a complete artificial heart and are now ready to proceed to the stage of implanting such a model into man.

There are many organs and systems that can benefit from the installation of prostheses following disabling diseases or injuries. For many decades it has been customary to replace even very extensive bony areas of the top of the skull, lost through injury, by suitable plates of precious metal or metal alloys of recent origin. Prosthetic replacement of the jaw-bones, and the larynx, can in some measure restore the functions of chewing and talking when these are lost. Acoustic electronic prostheses can greatly enhance the hearing faculty in those suffering from deafness.

Great progress has been made in the field of artificial limbs. Apart from being able to supply limbs closely resembling the real limb in outward appearance, it is now possible to provide the artificial limb with many functional abilities. The bioelectric impulses emitted by the central nervous system can be used to enable artificial limbs to perform a range of movements. The central nervous system sends out signals via the motor nerves to reach the muscles; electrodes are inserted at the correct levels to pick up these electrical impulses, and other electrodes are connected to these muscles whose contractions control various

An artificial hip joint, the development of which has rescued many sufferers from permanent pain and confinement to a wheelchair.

An X-ray showing articular prosthesis of the hip.

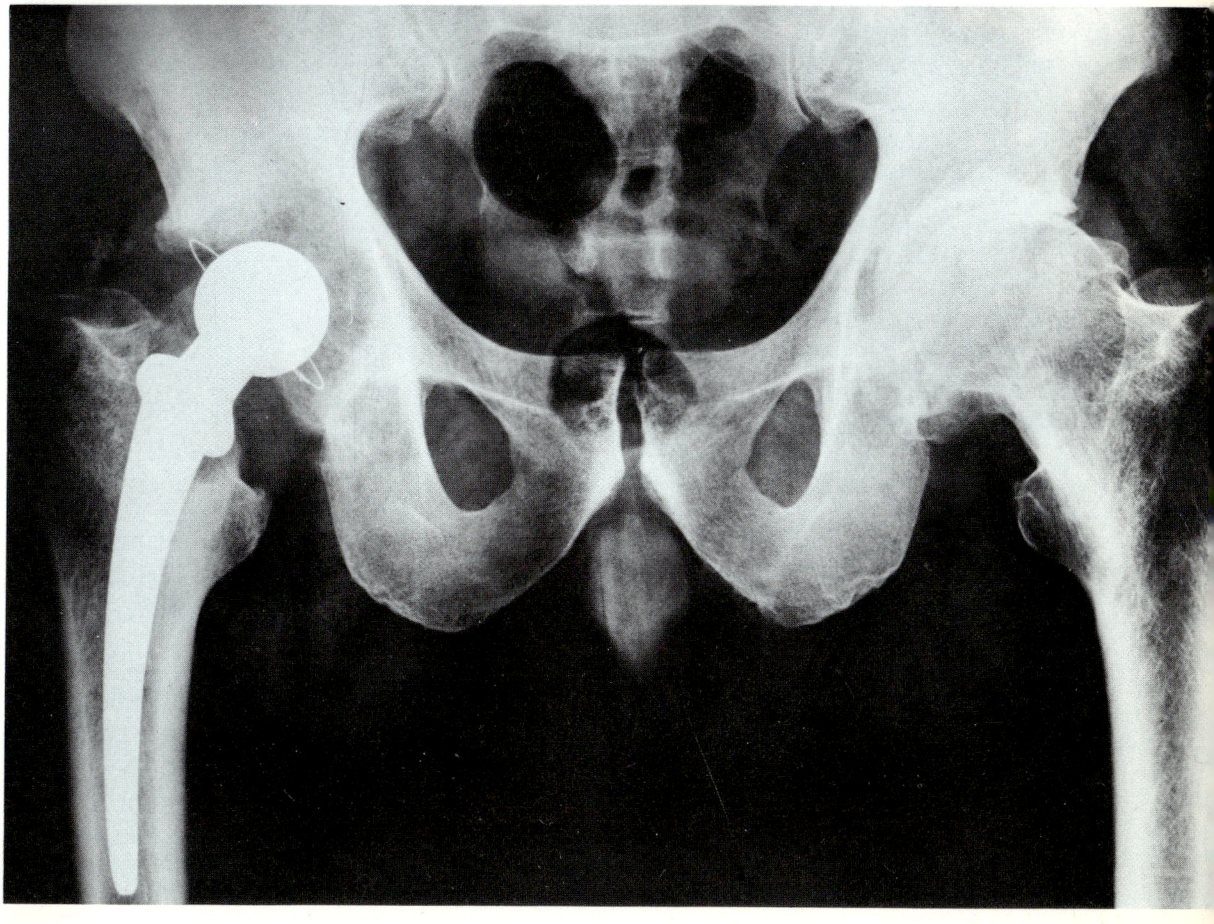

movements. In this fashion, even the most complex and minute movements such as those of the hands, can be duplicated. A transistor system amplifies these signals, which are conveyed to a micrometer that transforms the impulses into mechanical motion. All this is under the patient's control and the motion is translated into movements of separate parts of the artificial hand—co-ordinated efficient movements, impressively similar to the natural movements of the real hand.

In the field of prosthetics, we should also mention the successes achieved over a period of years with *arthroplasty*, the artificial reconstruction of joints so seriously damaged by arthritis, injury, fractures or ageing as to need replacing. Total prosthetic replacements are also performed on highly complex joints, such as the knee and even the entire hip joint. In the latter case, the head of the femur is reconstructed in stainless steel and the hemispherical socket into which it fits is reshaped in plastic. The problem of attaching these artificial parts to the respective bones of the operated individual has been solved by using a substance whose cementing properties have given satisfactory results. This very modern technique not only eliminates pain but also restores almost complete mobility of the joint.

The American Cardiology Association has recently been informed of the development of an "artificial muscle" composed of a special nickel-titanium alloy called Nitinol. This substance is so sensitive to temperature variations that it alternatively expands and contracts dozens of times per minute. Since the human heart contracts on average seventy times per minute, considerable research has already been done towards constructing a heart substitute which, unlike the plastic models, would be able to pulsate due to the intrinsic nature of its make-up.

This successful attempt to imitate faithfully and to reproduce artificially that which only yesterday was considered the exclusive province of nature herself, has led to the urge to study nature even more deeply. The aim of such studies is to apply the knowledge gained in the living world to new devices and techniques in the world of machines, in other words a whole new branch of science: *bionics*.

Neurosurgery

Neurosurgery and the marvels it has accomplished also came about after several research workers had discovered how to gain access to the brain and spinal cord for diagnostic purposes.

It was in the early 1920s that the first results were obtained, through X-ray examinations of the *cerebral ventricles* (natural cavities inside the brain) and the brain as a whole. At the same time, it was found that by injecting a contrast medium into the carotid artery (one of the blood vessels in the neck) the arterial branches in the brain originating from this artery would show up. This made it possible to recognize any intracranial anomalies such as aneurysms or even indications of tumours, that might be present.

The same years saw the successful application of electrodes directly to the surface of the brain, first performed by cutting an opening through the skull. This operation was done in order to record the electrical impulses associated with brain activity. After years of research, the German scientist Berger was able to identify and record these impulses without having to open up

Herbert Olivecrona, the famous Swedish neurosurgeon.

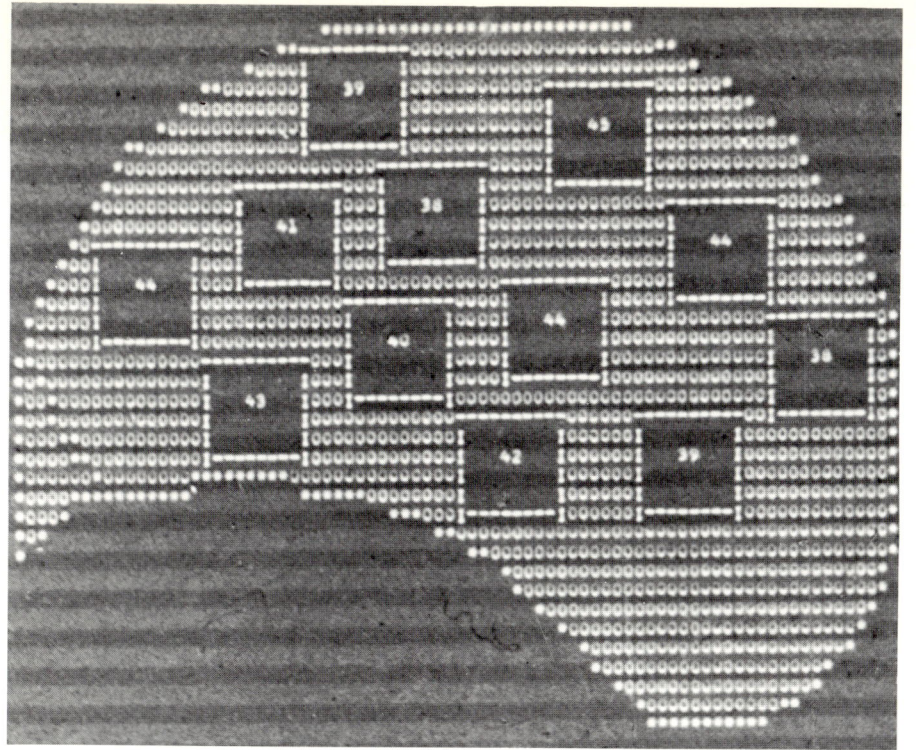

Cerebro-vascular insufficiency is due to obstructive lesions of the cervical arteries in their extracranial passage. Before the condition can be treated surgically it is necessary to estimate the progress of the flux in the different centres, in an extremely short time. The time taken has been cut by 70% by using a special apparatus, incorporating photoscintillators, and an IBM system. The cerebral plan opposite has been printed by a computer and summarizes the values of flux for each separate area.

the skull. In 1929, he finally announced: "I believe I have found and presented for the first time, the electroencephalogram of man."

In the second half of this century, a method of brain investigation known as the *echo-encephalograph*, based on the principle of echo-scanning, was perfected and made available. A more recent method for detecting intracranial anomalies is *scintiscanning*, in which radioactive substances introduced into the vascular system are dispersed through the brain. Changes in the distribution pattern of the radioactive isotopes provide the surgeon with sufficient diagnostic information to operate on structures deep within the brain tissue.

Cushing was the first skilled neurosurgeon to tackle the removal of endocranial tumours. With more precise methods of diagnosis and improved surgical techniques, the mortality rate fell from an initial ninety per cent to ten per cent. From then on, many famous surgeons such as Olivecrona of Sweden and Cooper of the United States, have made such important contributions to the field of brain surgery that patients, who only a few decades ago were considered inoperable and fated to die, now recover.

There are some cases where it is not necessary to destroy or remove large tumour masses, and where instead neural pathways deep within the brain need to be selectively interrupted. This is achieved by a technique known as *electrocoagulation*, where minute sections of tissue are destroyed by the application of an electric current. Here the use of *stereotaxic* (meaning oriented in three dimensions) apparatus, placed around and attached to the patient's skull like cap, enables the surgeon to exactly calculate the direction and depth of penetration of the electrocoagulation needle, necessary if the operation is to be 100 per cent successful.

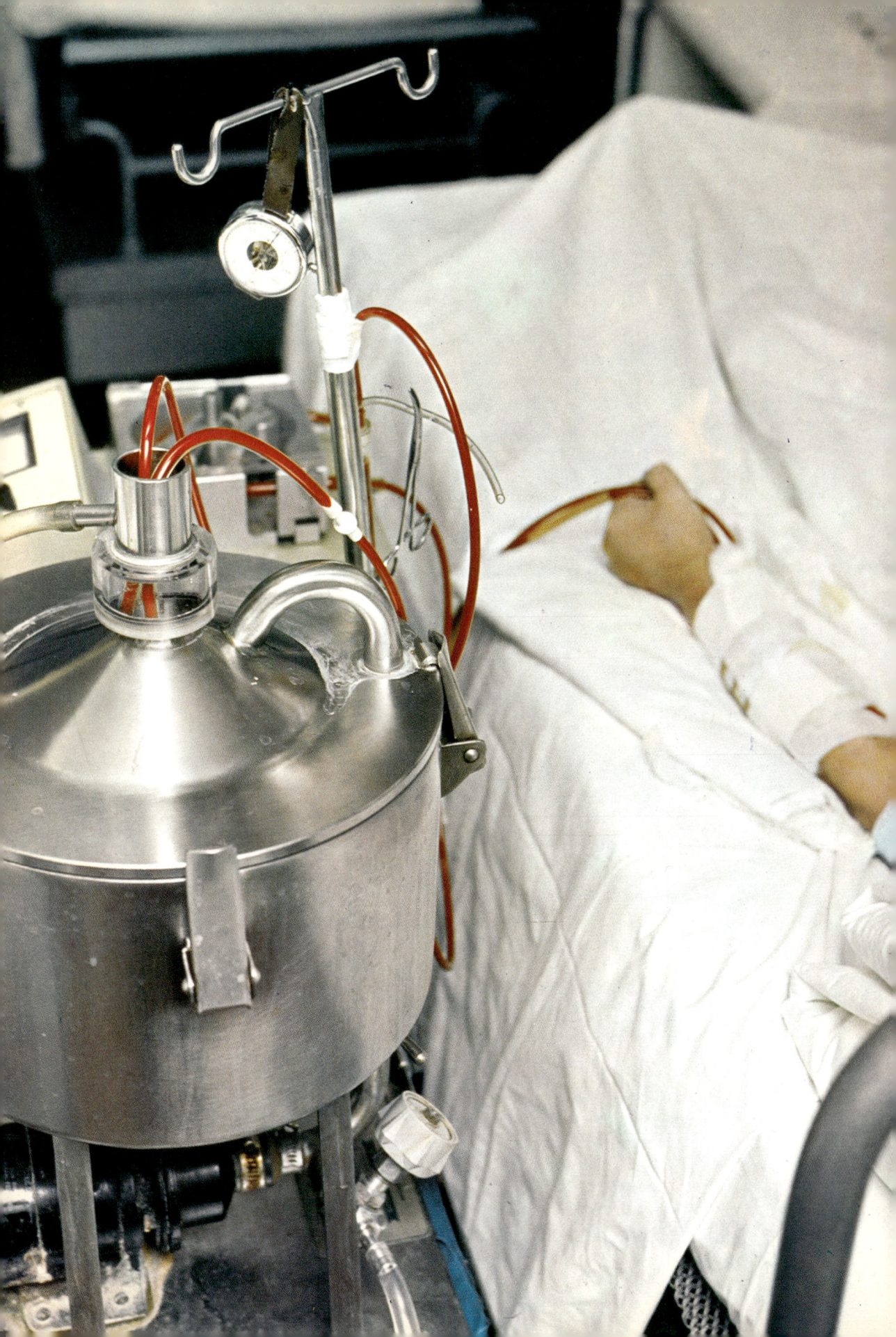

CHAPTER 7

HEALTH SERVICES

The earliest ways of caring for the sick involved magic and primitive remedies. Then followed the founding of medieval-type hospitals, based on the principle of helping the sick in accordance with the standards of Christian charity. Gradually this has evolved into our present attitude, and governments throughout the world now work towards a goal when all citizens will have the right to complete and assured health care, although the development of such services is at a different stage in every country.

Today we begin protecting the health of the individual by giving advice to young prospective parents, and by regular examinations of expectant mothers, followed by medical care during childbirth and the succeeding nine months.

The baby is vaccinated against infectious diseases during the first months of life and examinations to assure normal development are conducted regularly.

When the child leaves the immediate family environment and starts attending school, he comes under the care of some sort of school health service that renders various kinds of medical care depending on the state of medical advance in the country.

When the individual enters the world of work, new and more complex problems arise in protecting him from the potential toxicity of the environment, a highly varied and manifold source of danger brought about through the growth of industry. Many types of work carry a risk of exposure to *occupational diseases*. Routine checks and special regulations to control these risks exist to some extent everywhere. Special preventive measures are taken to protect workers exposed to radiation or factors likely to cause skin diseases and damage to the respiratory system. Sickness and accident insurance is tending to become obligatory everywhere.

Many of the so-called social maladjustments are being seen in a new light because of changing attitudes due to recent advances made in the fields of biochemistry, physiology and genetics. The stresses of contemporary living may have compounded the age-old problems of alcoholism and drug-abuse, but fortunately new insights into the physical nature of these ailments have convinced many practitioners that their origins are physical as well as psychological, although many physicians are still prejudiced in their attitude to these diseases.

Although many industries and other organizations have become acutely aware and now encourage treatment of these diseases because of the great loss of money annually in decreased productivity, the in-

Haemodialysis. The patient lies on a bed while his blood passes through the dialysis machine and is regenerated.

cidence of recovery remains low. Organizations such as the National Family Council on Drug Abuse, United States Public Health Service, Alcoholics Anonymous, Addicts Anonymous and the President's Advisory Commission on Narcotic and Drug Abuse, seem to hold the most promise through their programmes in education, research and therapy on an individual and community level.

For old persons, a new branch of medical science known as *gerontology* has developed, which studies the problems of ageing in all its aspects. The aged individual, even when not ill, still faces problems of a psychological nature, deficiencies due to slower metabolism, and a functional decrease in the cardiovascular, respiratory, digestive and urinary systems. Again, depending on the country in question, there may be visiting nurse services and day centres where a specially qualified staff co-operate in various ways to maintain the proper functioning of failing organs or systems of the ageing person.

When the individual's health deteriorates and disease sets in, nursing homes, geriatric wards or hospitals are available, variously organized according to the patient's needs and the place or country in which he happens to live.

The modern hospital

The organization of modern health services has led to the creation of hospital institutions of such size and complexity that they virtually resemble whole cities. The hospital and university complex at Houston in the United States, for example, can provide accommodation and the most up-to-date treatment for almost fifteen thousand patients.

However, these gigantic complexes with their centralized services (kitchens and food distribution, laundry, transportation, etc.), create burdensome administrative problems, so that the optimal size for a modern hospital is now considered to be about a thousand beds.

Innumerable problems have to be overcome before a hospital can be run satisfactorily and efficiently. Needs can sometimes be contradictory, as in the case of emergency treatment where speed may conflict with high standards of medical quality.

Apart from the administrative offices, and the maintenance supply systems whose auxiliary generators ensure heat and electricity under all circumstances, the hospital is in direct connection with the world outside through its out-patient department and emergency services. Ideally the latter should be staffed around the clock by specialist personnel (physicians, surgeons and

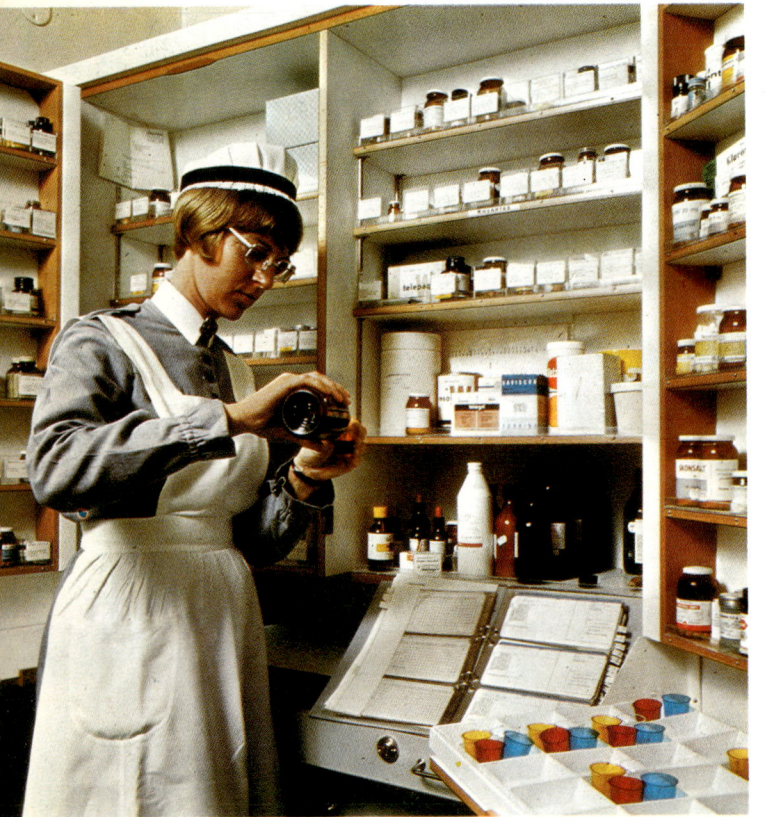

A typical modern hospital pharmacy.

Hospital laboratories can now be administered by electronic computers linked directly to the analytical instruments.

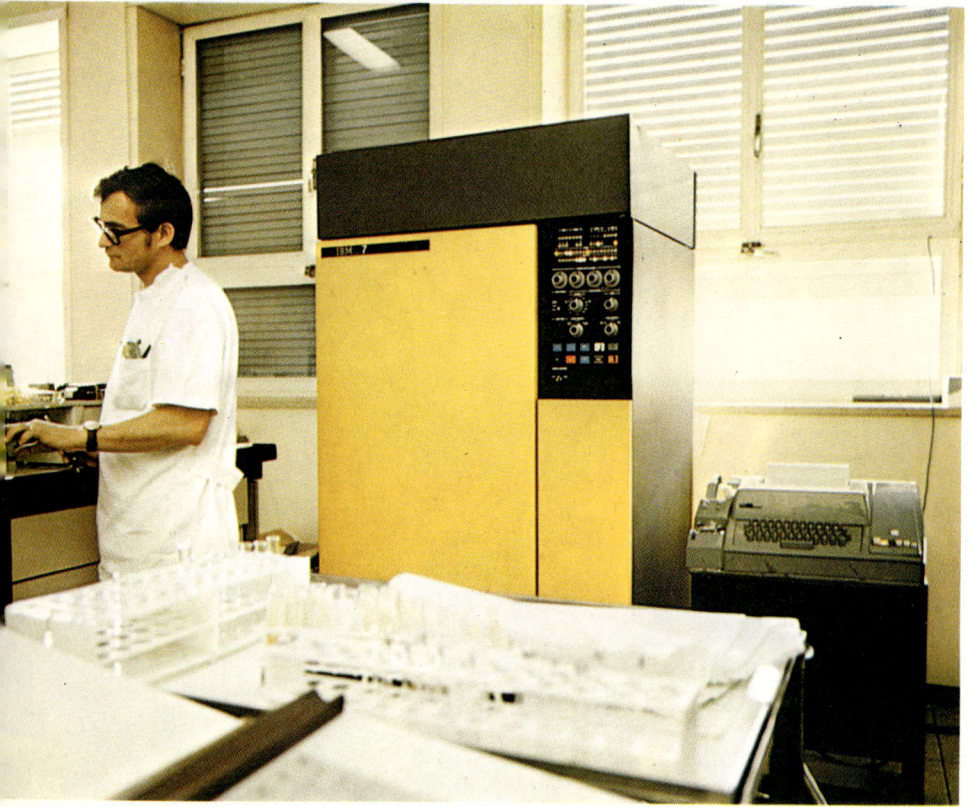

Results of research are centralized and transmitted to the electronic centre which proceeds to organize the work of the laboratory.

Defibrillatory apparatus.

anaesthetists), while an *emergency operating theatre* and an *intensive care unit* should be in constant readiness. The intensive care unit is the most recent addition to the modern hospital. This is where the most seriously injured victims of car accidents are brought, as well as those emergency cases where the immediate problem is to ward off imminent death by using the most modern equipment and techniques.

Alongside the intensive care unit is another highly specialized department, equipped with *coronary units*. These include continuously running *electrocardiographs*, *defibrillators*, oxygen tents and everything else the cardiologist needs to give immediate and maximum assistance during the first decisive hours or days of a heart attack. It has been statistically proved that the rapid use of these technical devices, combined with constant supervision, markedly reduces the mortality rate of the victims of this increasingly widespread disease.

In addition to the *chemical pathology laboratory* and the *pathological anatomy* department, which perform all the necessary biochemical and anatomical investigations for the whole hospital, a new department has been established in a growing number of institutions. This is the department of *extrarenal haemodialysis*, which makes use of the *artificial kidney* machine, designed by the scientist Kolff. In healthy persons, the kidneys' main function is to excrete those waste products which are soluble in water. The kidneys also regulate electrolyte and water balance by varying the concentration of the urine. If the kidney function is defective (a condition known as renal insufficiency, or, in severe cases, renal failure), waste products accumulate in the blood. The artificial kidney is an extremely valuable piece of equipment which can take over the function of purifying the blood by a mechanism known as dialysis. The patient's blood passes through the machine and is returned to the circulation with the waste products removed, relieving the kidney of all work. This treatment can be repeated at regular intervals in cases of chronic renal insufficiency, and is extremely useful in cases of kidney transplant. It can also be used in any cases of renal insufficiency which develop unexpectedly after surgical operations.

A new type of artificial kidney has recently been developed in the United States. It is very much smaller than the usual apparatus, but has a much greater dialysing capacity. This represents another step towards the goal of the future: a machine small enough to be permanently installed inside the patient, in much the same way as

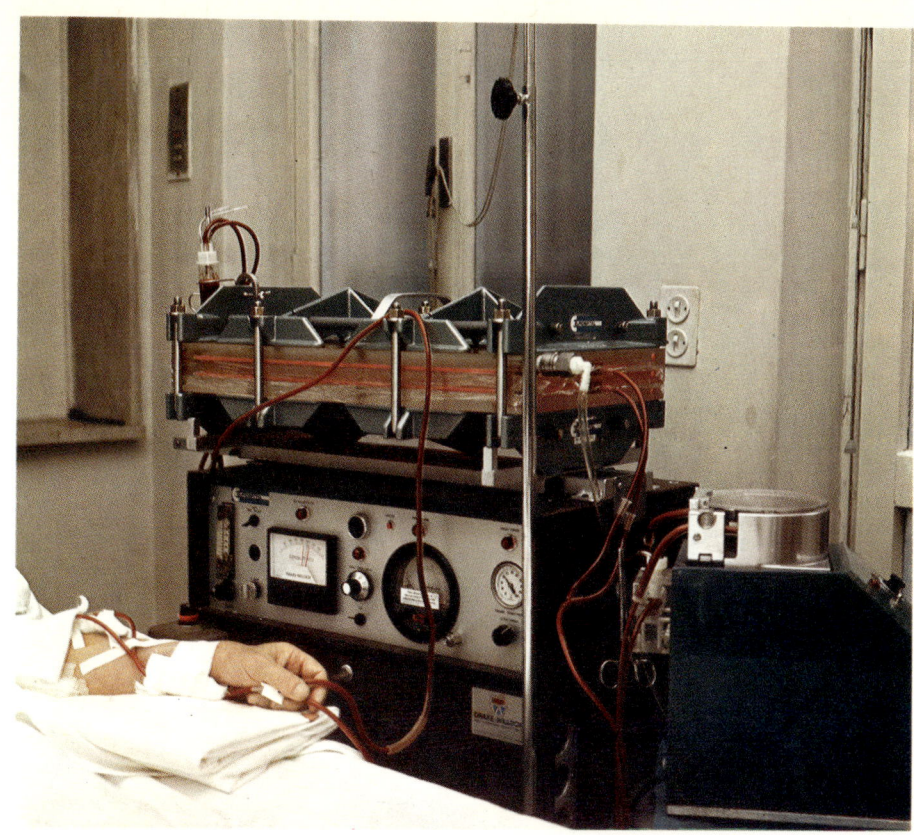

The Drake-Willock artificial kidney, adapted for domiciliary haemodialysis.

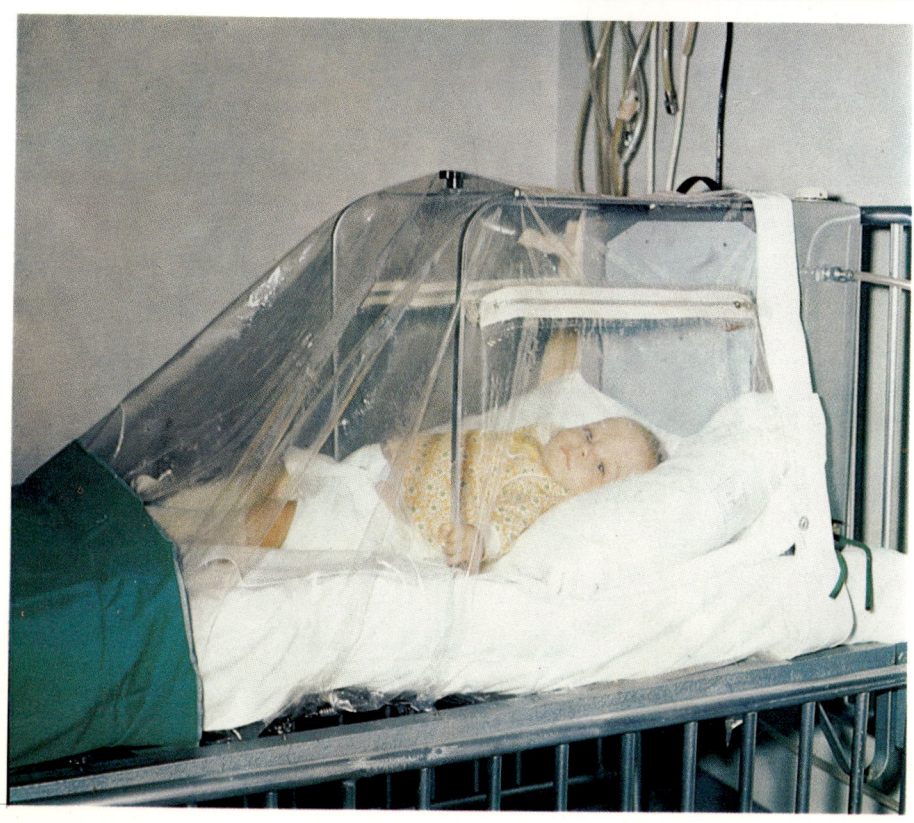

An oxygen tent.

any other prosthetic apparatus.

The hospital is thus a combination of various departments, each specializing in a particular field, from internal medicine to general surgery, from paediatrics to obstetrics and gynaecology, cardiology, orthopaedics and traumatology, ophthalmology and otorhinolaryngology (also ear-nose-throat or ENT for short). There is a department for cancer diseases, and special departments for skin, venereal and contagious diseases. Other departments are being added as other medical fields gradually acquire autonomy through the expansion of specialized knowledge and the development of new treatments. The doctor's sphere of action is becoming narrower. Within the framework of the medical profession, there is in fact a tendency to encourage doctors to concentrate as far as possible on learning everything there is to know on a single area of the body. This specialist approach makes group work even more necessary.

Collaboration in work leads to new undertakings that extend into the field of preventive medicine, for example medical check-ups. A check-up consists of a complete series of examinations and tests carried out by a group of specialists on one person, designed to obtain an accurate picture of the state of health at regular intervals.

Other facilities are available to meet the needs of all the hospital departments, such as the *blood bank* where large quantities of blood types are stored.

The radiology (X-ray) department uses equipment and techniques that are constantly being improved. A recent innovation is the installation of television circuits which afford greater protection for the doctor. The physiotherapy depart-

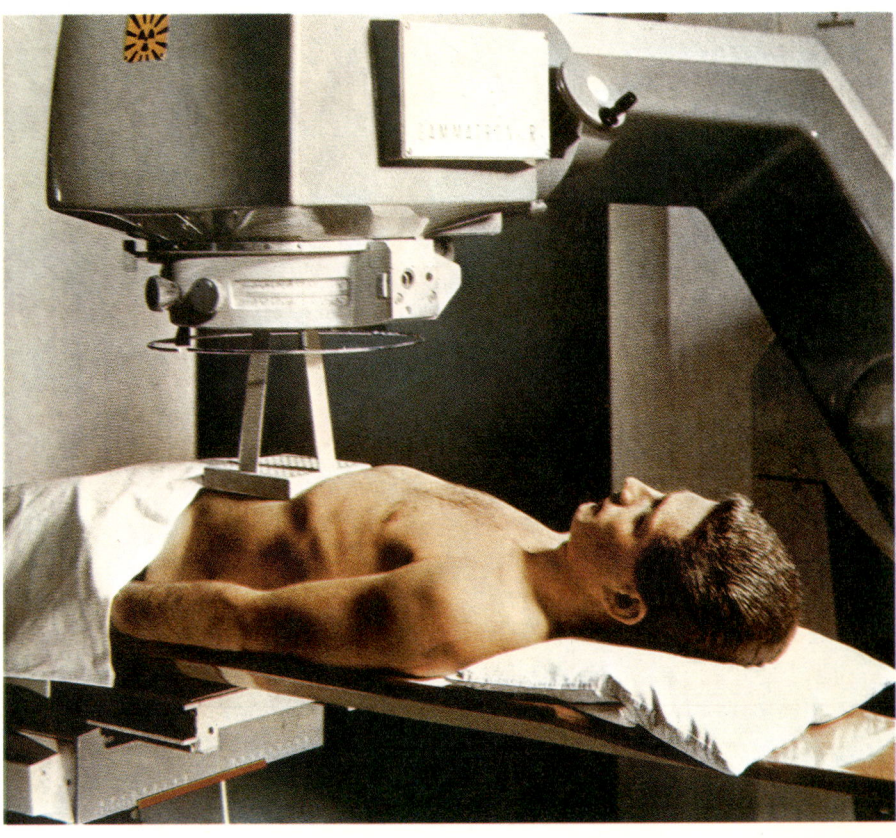

The apparatus for cobalt treatment. On top of the apparatus, on which is placed the warning symbol for the presence of radioactive substances, is the charge of the isotope, Cobalt-60. The gamma radiations emitted by the cobalt come out of a window that looks towards the patient. Automatic systems close the window after the pre-determined time of irradiation has elapsed. Irradiation with Cobalt-60 is used in the treatment of certain tumours.

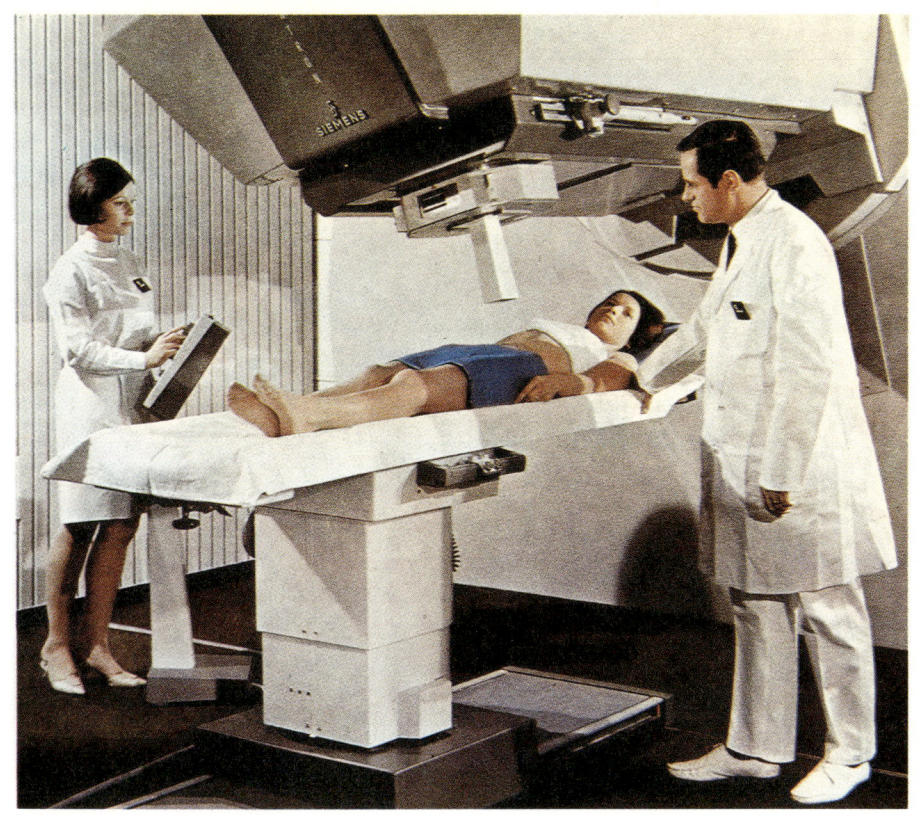

A Betatron. Electrons are accelerated in a magnetic field and are then directed through a window on to the patient. The Betatron is particularly suited to the treatment of malignant tumours that arise in the areas of the body that are relatively near the skin.

ment, once restricted to the use of special electric currents and heat supplied from a few stoves, was greatly improved by the introduction of *high-energy ionizing* radiations, leading gradually to the use of *roentgenotherapy*, *cobaltotherapy*, and the application of *gamma rays* and the *betatron*. A large series of diseases was then successfully treated with *inhalation therapy*, *diathermy*, *sinusoidal oscillating* and *exponential currents*. *Ultrasound* and *radartherapy* were applied medically after the use of ultrasonics and radar had been developed for military purposes during World War II.

In other departments, *kinesitherapy* (restoration of the sense of feeling) and *restoration of mobility* are practised. In suitable gymnasia containing baths and swimming pools, as well as special equipment and apparatus, mobility is gradually restored to young and old patients who, through injury or disease, would formerly have been condemned to immobility and total or partial inactivity.

Mention should also be made of the modern and highly effective units for the treatment of severe burns. With specialized and sophisticated equipment, these units save many lives, and with the additional aid of *plastic surgery* patients can often resume their normal daily life.

But a new factor has recently been introduced into this basic structure which promises to revolutionize the entire work of the hospital, lending futuristic possibilities to the work of the doctor—the computer.

The computer in medicine, today and tomorrow

The computer, or electronic brain, is a calculating apparatus that can classify vast amounts of data, which it retains and memorizes. So long as the request is suitably programmed,

Equipment in a physiotherapy training centre.

Exercises to strengthen the muscles of the trunk.

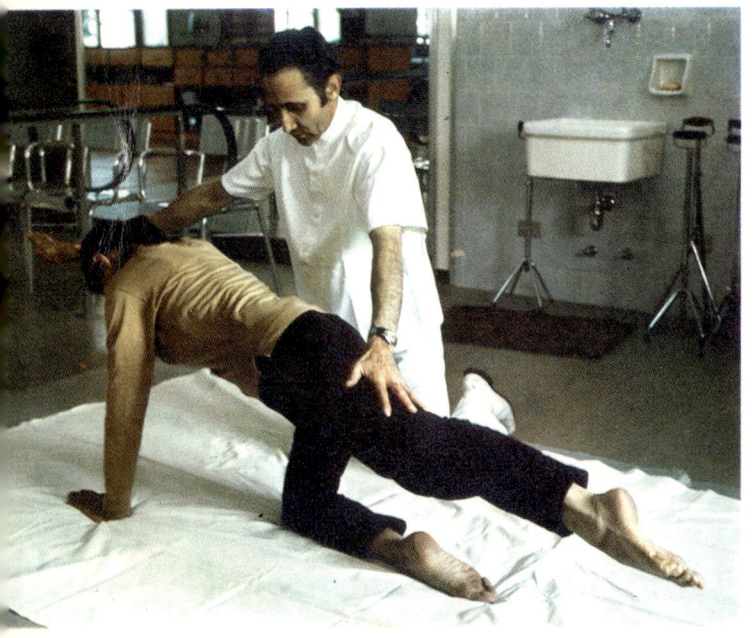

the computer can calculate answers with reference to all the information it has available, and produce its final logical result with precision.

The diseases that affect mankind number more than ten thousand, and can be identified by comparing and selecting symptoms from among a hundred thousand possible ones. The methods of treating these diseases, once identified, in turn number some hundreds of thousands, while each type of treatment will be subject to countless variations depending on the specific and general condition of each individual patient. In the light of these figures, it is easy to see how any doctor attempting to analyse and synthesise all the information available is plunging into a vast and almost unexplorable jungle of data. Obviously, if the doctor can be provided with selected and definite data, he will be able to avoid a good deal of guesswork, and his conclusions regarding diagnosis and treatment will be both more accurate and more scientific. In other words, the more he can limit the possibilities of error, the sooner and more effectively will the doctor be able to act.

The number of functioning computers in the world will soon reach a hundred thousand. Of these more than five hundred are being used in hospitals in the United States and several hundred in the hospitals of the more advanced European nations. So far, they have only been used in specific sectors dealing with single specialized fields of medicine. This is because the gathering of data and the subsequent programming can take place only one area at a time, since a long preparatory period of organization is required. However, in the future the computer will absorb data and redistribute it to the whole hospital, or possibly to an appropriate group of hospitals. Such data would consist of all the theoretical, scientific and personal information relating to the therapeutic requirements of every single individual.

Along these lines, the inhabitants of Sweden, for example, are already being issued with a small card that bears the key-data for locating a corresponding index card. This index card can be fed into a gigantic electronic computer designed for medical purposes. The information so provided means that any Swede who falls ill and is admitted to one of the main hospitals can be helped by one of the aforementioned techniques which assist the doctor to select the most appropriate treatment.

Besides these extraordinary central archives under electronic control and working on a national scale in the sphere of health, many countries have individual hospitals where computers are already transforming previous working methods.

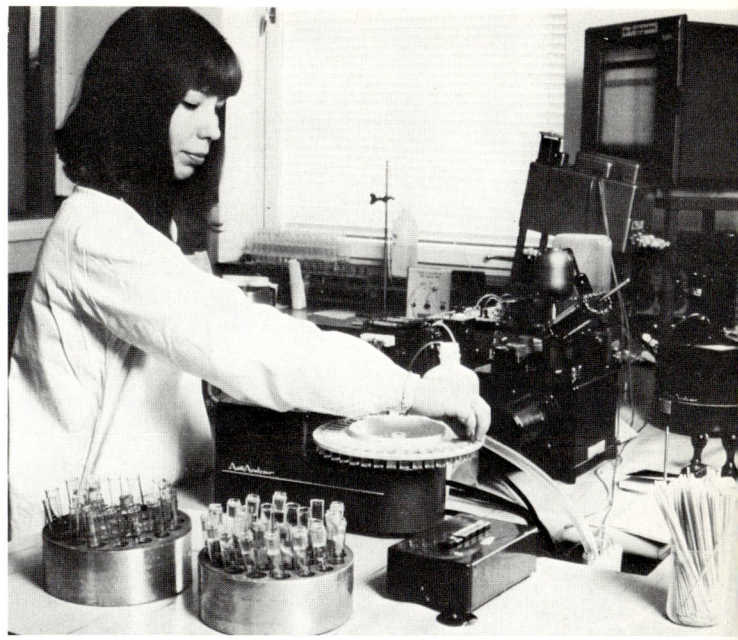

The auto-analyser (above) feeds data into the computer which converts them into numerical values and carries out the analysis.

The spirometer in the cardiological laboratory of the Gentofte Hospital (Copenhagen, Denmark) is directly connected to the computing system in order to control the processes. The data relative to the pulmonary capacity of the patient are transmitted directly to the computer for evaluation: the results appear a few seconds later on the television screen.

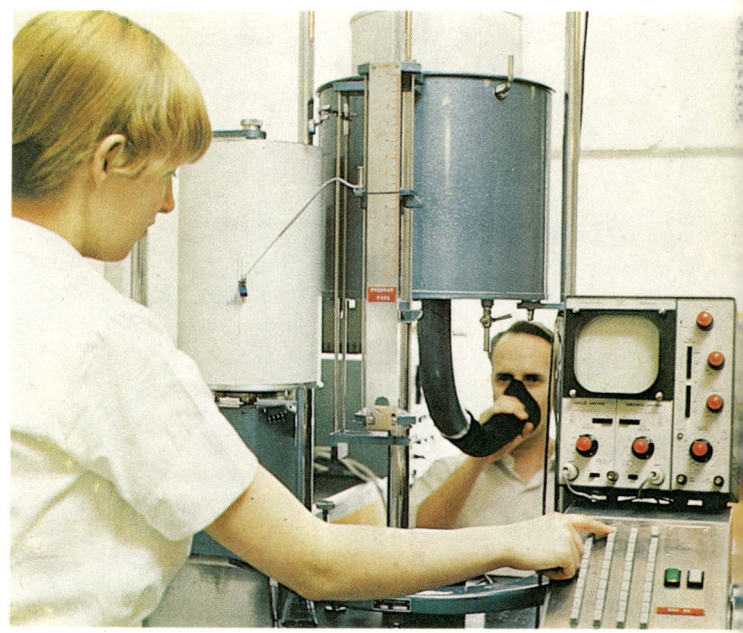

115

These computers are giving hospitals a whole set of new features. The old clinical records, stacked in piles on shelves are gradually being replaced by electronic memories, ready and available at a moment's notice to provide specific clues to immediate treatment as well as future research.

And so, apart from enormously easing the problems of hospital administration, computers are already performing the most varied tasks in the simplification and speeding up of diagnostic procedures. The computer is directly linked with the chemical pathology laboratory, so that the data relating to a particular patient can be fed into the computer directly: for example, more than fifty tests can be processed in one minute.

Apart from evaluating the results of biochemical and bacteriological tests, computers are already able to analyse and study electrocardiograms and the results of several cardiac, circulatory and respiratory tests. These electronic devices can supply the conclusive findings that enable the doctor to make a scientific diagnosis.

An even more complicated programme has been worked out, where the computer is permanently linked to the monitoring apparatus that checks day and night on the condition of patients in the intensive care units mentioned earlier. Maximum vigilance is necessary to detect variations that might occur from one moment to the next in the condition of a critically ill patient. The computer gathers the data provided by the various kinds of apparatus and processes them, checking that the recorded information remains within safe limits. If these limits are exceeded, or if some figure falls below a safe threshold, the alarm sounds immediately. The data checked in this way are not merely those that can be recorded easily, such as the respiratory rate and pulse or heart rate, but also other changeable and less obvious indices.

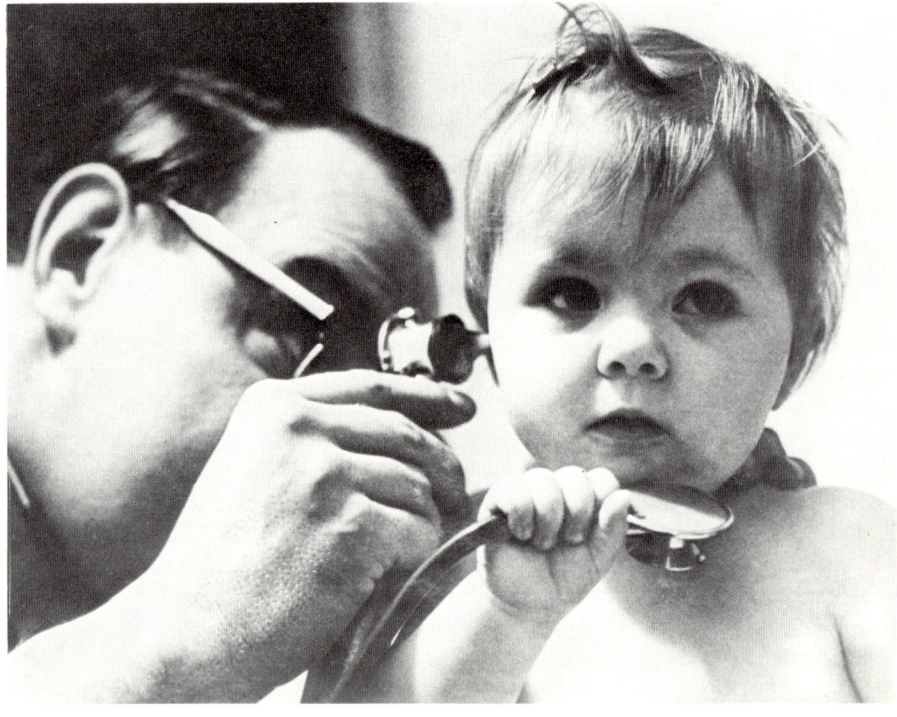

A mathematician of the Los Angeles IBM research centre has programmed an electronic calculator in such a way as to reproduce the functioning of the inner ear. The first results obtained suggest that this form of treatment is effective in easing some kinds of loss of hearing.

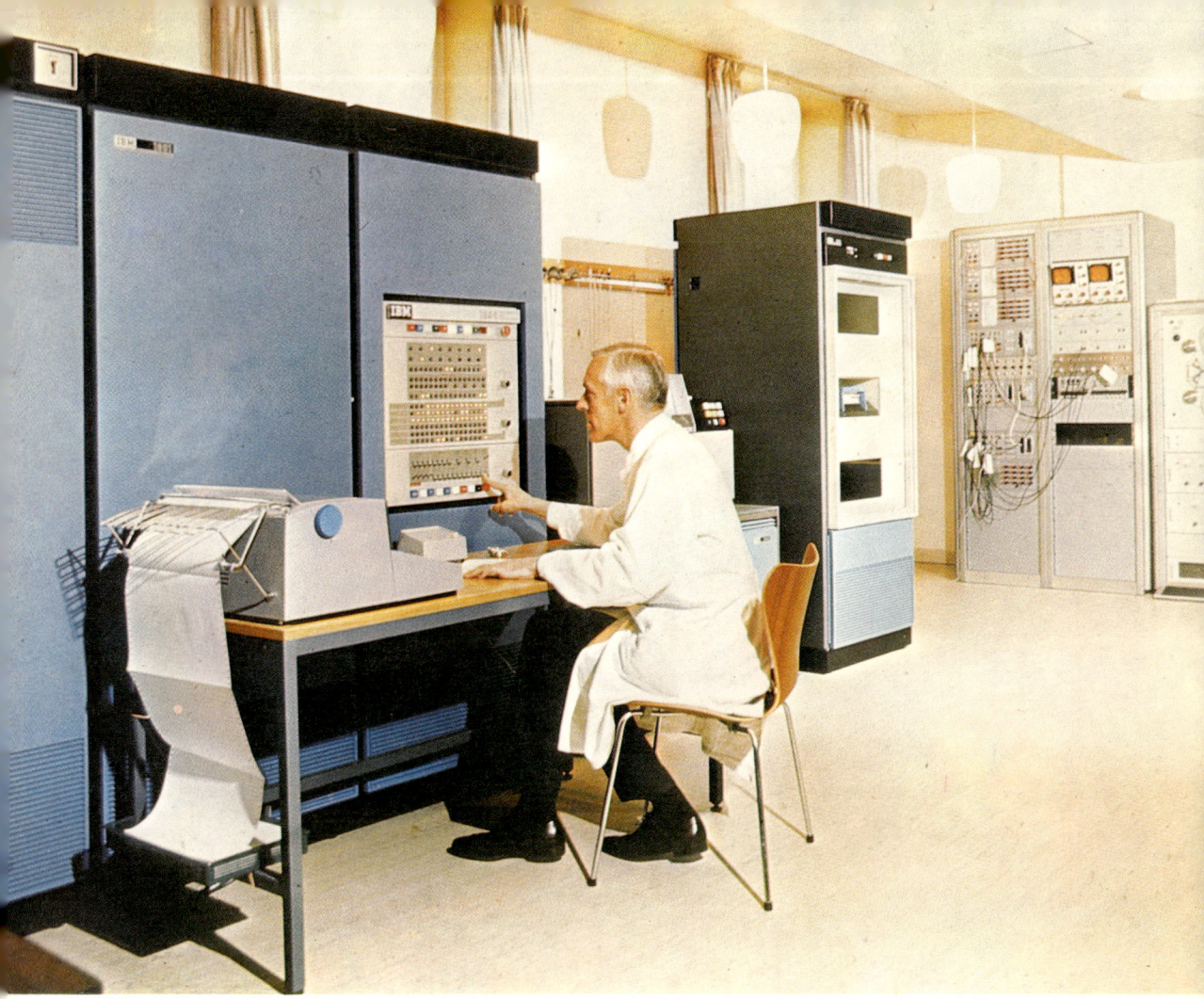

The latter include blood coagulability (which always tends to vary), and increases or decreases in many blood parameters. Changes in these indices indicate the patient's fluctuating condition and can lead to his death if the doctor or nurse is not alerted in time.

Some have expressed the belief that the computer might so mechanize and standardize the doctor's work that he might lose direct human contact with the patient. On the contrary, it can be asserted that the computer is only an instrument —even if futuristic—in the doctor's hands. It allows him to use his time more rationally, and at the same time enables him to be both more accurate and more thorough, since the computer provides him only with information which is both exact and complete—it simply does not "answer" otherwise.

The computer actually helps to raise the status of the doctor's work, inasmuch as it allows a more profound and continuous contact with objective medical science, and helps eradicate the errors of subjective judgment into which all doctors occasionally fall. At the same time, the patient can take comfort in the thought that he is helped along the painful road of his illness not only by the doctor in charge but also by the countless scientific brains that have combined to contribute their skill to the computer—and to the doctor.

The machine in the foreground is the control consol of the electronic system installed in the cardiological laboratory of the Gentofte Hospital in Copenhagen. In the background is the special unit that transmits to the computer the data relative to the patient's tests.

CHAPTER 8

SPACE MEDICINE

Although medicine is always faced with changing situations man's conquest of space has added a totally new dimension. The space venture has brought with it an imposing mass of problems demanding new answers and new solutions. These will be solutions that will not only enable man to live in an alien environment, but will also enhance man's understanding of his life and all other life forms. It could not have been originally conceived that from this enterprise, concerned with achieving a moon landing, there would spring so many important discoveries and applications relating to our daily lives, especially in the medical field. To put the idea in more concrete terms, it could not have been foreseen that within a decade, NASA would have poured out thousands of valuable inventions and discoveries of benefit to the most diverse branches of technology. The resulting miniaturizations, improvements in electronics, innovations in the field of metallurgy, plastics and mechanics have made a substantial contribution to medical research and achievements.

In fact, no matter what the technical progress, how perfect the equipment, or how brilliant the conception and realization of launching and transporting man into space, we could never have taken our first step towards the stars had we not found solutions to all the biological and medical problems that arose from man's desire to live and work in an alien environment.

The use of animals in space flights provide valuable information that could not have been gained by even the most sophisticated experimentation on planet earth. Their use permits more rigorous control than is possible with human subjects. It allows the introduction of measuring devices and techniques: the implantation of electrodes in the brain, of extended cardiovascular and urinary tract catheters and implants of miniature electronic systems deep within the bodies of the animal subjects. These are designed to transmit impulses to earth conveying information of the animal's physiological reactions.

No human being had ever before experienced the violent acceleration to which the command module would be subjected when it was "shot" out of the earth's atmosphere into interstellar space. No one had any idea how man's heart and circulatory system, and above all his nervous system, would stand up to such pressures. Conversely, no one knew how man would react physically and mentally to the equally violent deceleration at the time of re-entering the earth's atmosphere. The only certainty was that man would have to be protected and

Man has now realized his age-old dream—he has reached the moon!

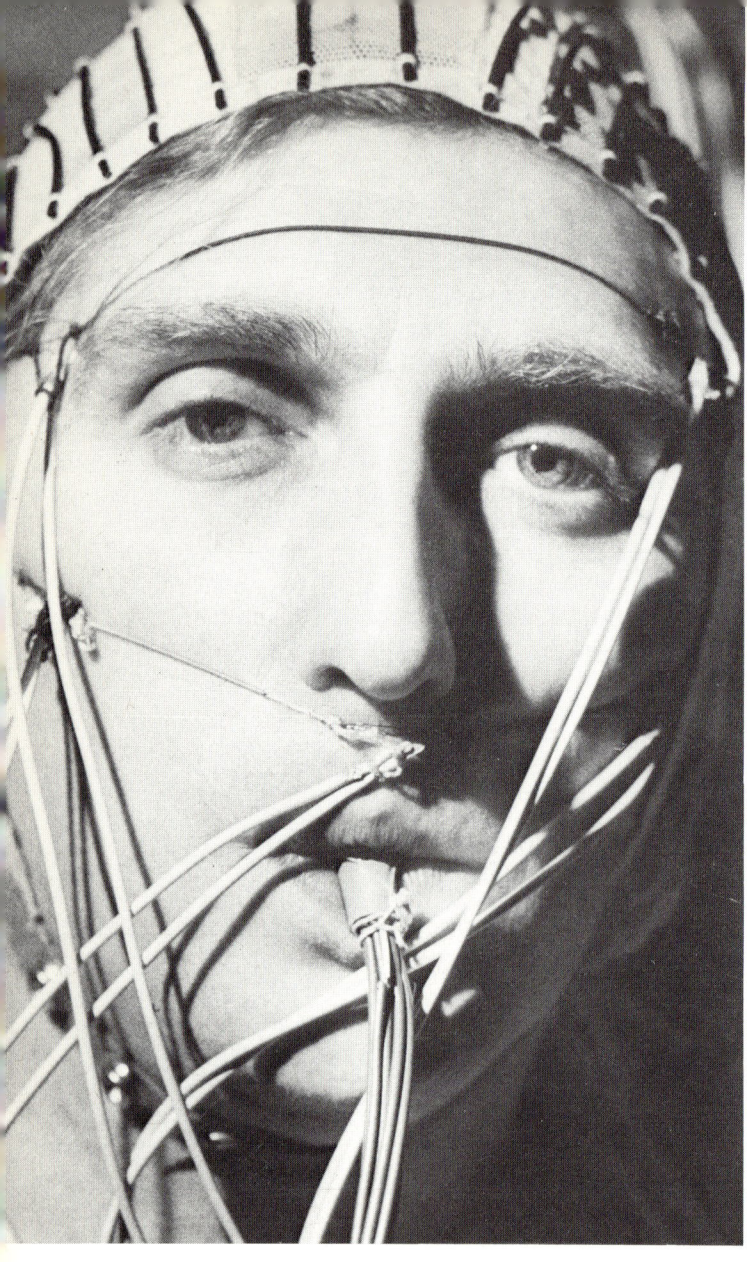

At the Farnborough Royal Air Force Institute of Aviation Medicine in England, a candidate for space exploration undergoes a series of clinical analyses to find out whether he is suitable to face the rigours of navigation in space.

completely isolated from the alien environment of space in which he would be unable to survive even for a moment. It was known that the human body, if exposed to the total vacuum of outer space, would explode and disintegrate.

The lack of atmospheric pressure along with the total absence of air posed a new and almost incalculable set of problems. The principal difficulties were: the lack of oxygen and water vapour that made breathing impossible; temperature variations amounting to hundreds of degrees, ranging from intensely hot to intensely cold; exposure to damaging ultra-violet and infra-red radiations, and above all to cosmic rays which can be deadly when unscreened by the atmosphere; a total loss of balance due to the absence of normal postural reflexes which can be maintained only under the influence of gravity. Last of all, there was the risk of mental disturbances, that might manifest themselves when men, after being launched into space, felt isolated and lost in an abyss so new as to seem unreal, and possibly overwhelming to the human mind.

These psychological hazards and the fatigue experienced by the astronauts had to be artificially simulated on earth, so that future astronauts could be carefully and gradually acclimatized. This entailed the construction of a number of controlled environment units ("simulators"), with recording instruments that would register every slightest bodily reaction to an almost endless series of tests.

After years of intensive experimentation in huge centrifuge machines it was possible to evaluate the mental and physical responses of astronauts to simulated conditions of acceleration from the launching pad. By the use of appropriate sealed chambers, the astronauts' reactions to conditions of weightlessness could also be assessed. They were connected by electric leads to an external apparatus that recorded every physiological variation and every sign of pathological change. Entire analytical laboratories, supervised by highly qualified medical experts, probed every unknown or suspected variation. Other workers devised ways of overcoming obstacles, discussing them with the technical experts in order to co-ordinate theory with practical solutions. Together they were able to invent suitable and reliable means for isolating and protecting the astronauts, enabling them to function efficiently despite the novelty of their surroundings.

It was discovered that, with an adequate period of training, the human body could withstand even the extraordinary pressures imposed by launching and space flight. This was true, however, only with the protection of a sealed capsule or at least an absolutely airtight, resistant and pressurized suit that would isolate the body from the external environment. The astronaut would also have to be connected up to a

The cosmonaut Aleksej Eliseev during the first space-flight tests.

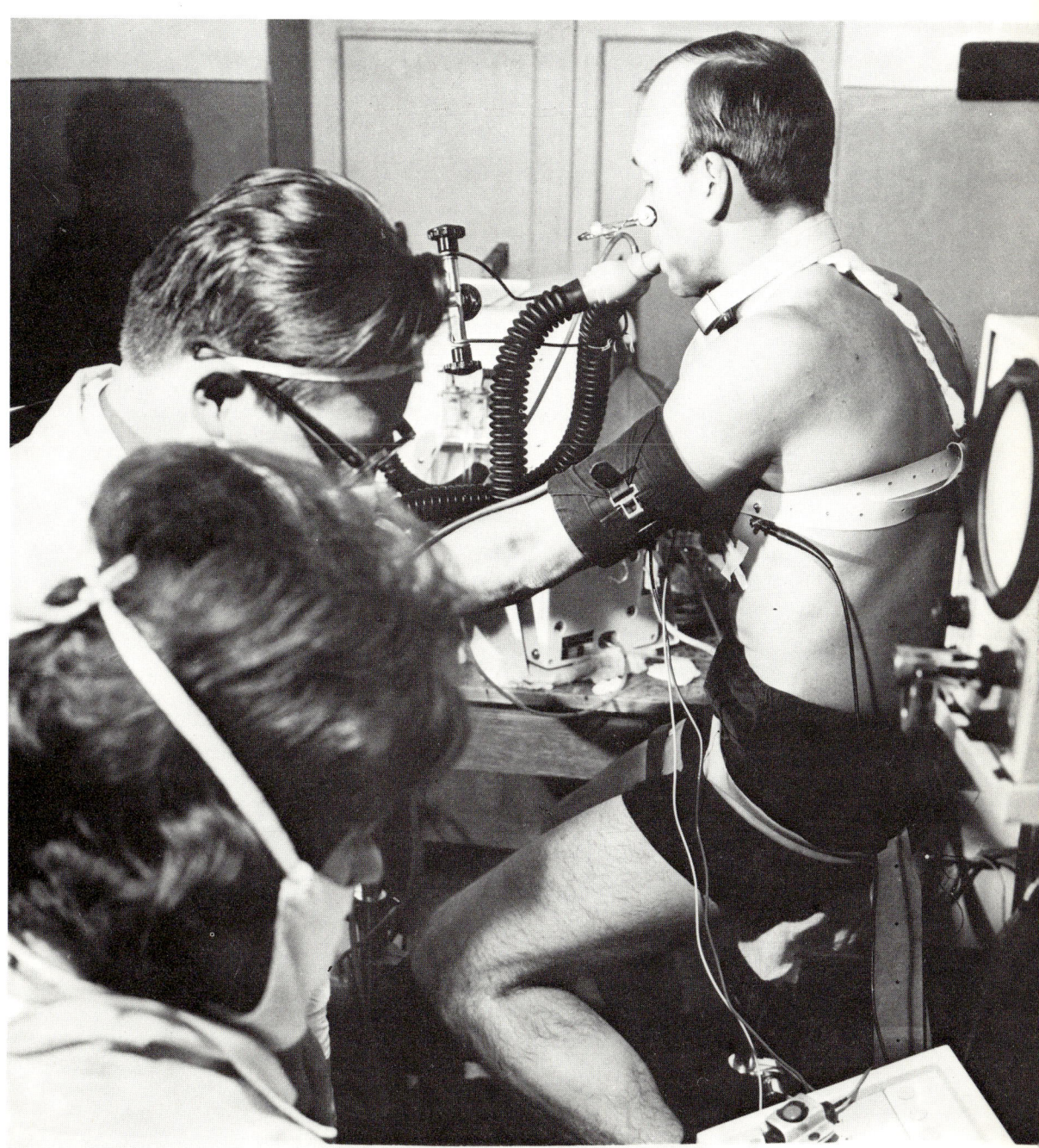

self-servicing closed circuit that provided a constant supply of oxygen for breathing. The density of oxygen required for our breathing purposes ends at an altitude of about ten miles. In outer space there is no oxygen and an astronaut must consume approximately 150 gallons of oxygen daily. Presently three sources of oxygen are available for use in a closed system: liquid oxygen, compressed oxygen in gaseous form and chemical compounds capable of releasing oxygen. Other problems that were solved included those of feeding (the type of diet and mode of food consumption), the collection of physical waste matter and how to keep the astronauts in touch with earth (a psychological as well as a physical necessity). Also, the astronauts had to be accustomed to long periods of isolation, and the problem of eliminating carbon dioxide and other toxic substances produced in the cabin by human respiration had to be solved.

Even when the solutions to all these basic problems were at hand, and the astronauts were assured of a working life-support system for the duration of their flight, they still

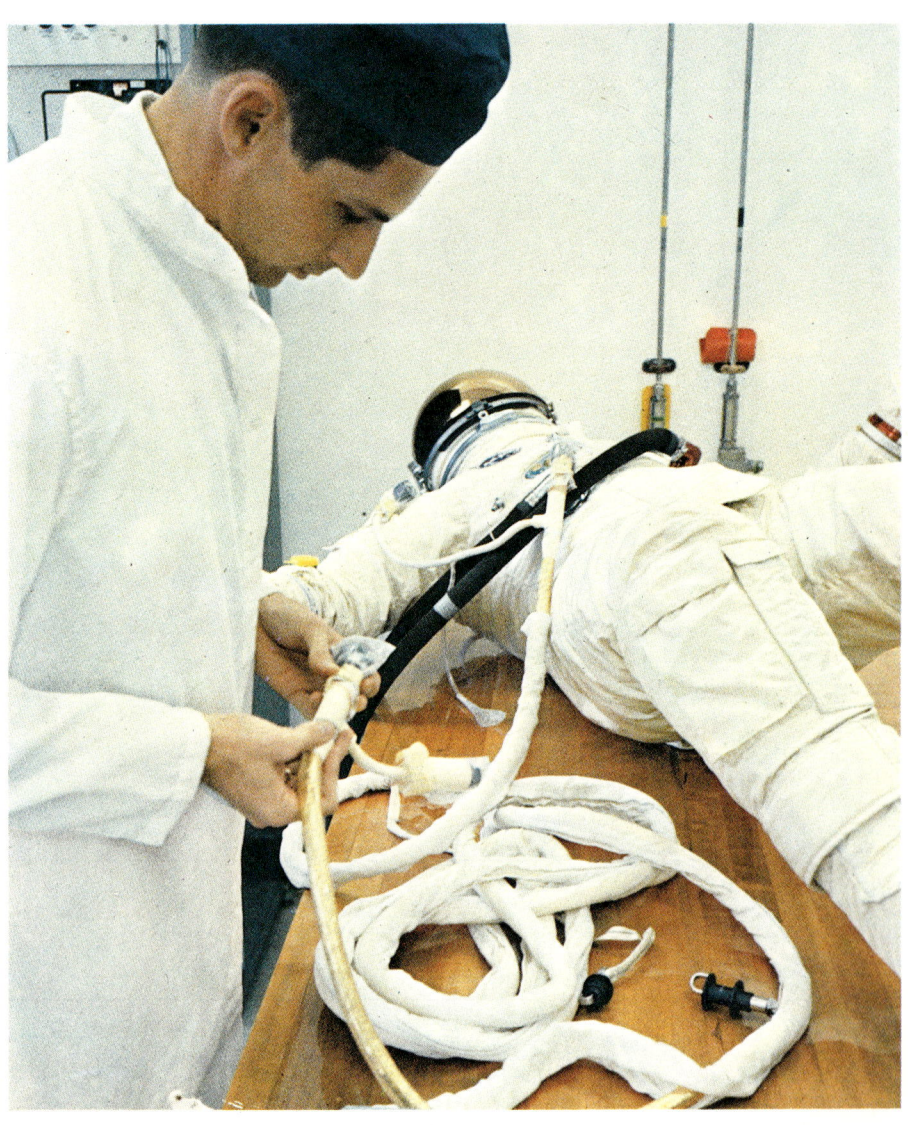

Tests on the respiration of an astronaut.

could not be flung into the unknown. There had to be some means of maintaining permanent contact with base to allow their physical condition to be checked and to maintain reliable medical assistance.

Marconi's invention, the radio, provided the answer to this problem. Radio waves would ensure a communication link-up between earth and a space ship travelling to the moon. This led to the most modern of medical developments: *biotelemetry*. This technique enables certain vital phenomena of living organisms to be recorded and measured by a device some distance away. In the case of the astronauts, a series of plates acting as electrodes were fixed to the region of the skin over the heart and other parts of the body. These plates were held in position for the duration of the space flight, and were able to pick up even the weakest bioelectric signals emitted by the body from one moment to the next. These variations in electric potential were transformed into radio waves and transmitted back to earth, as were other biological indices such as the rate and intensity of the heartbeat, and recordings of blood pressure, body temperature, sweating and emotional tension. This gave a sufficiently detailed medical picture for the astronauts to be instructed as to what safety measures to take if necessary. On reaching earth, the weak radio signals from outer space are amplified by receiving stations distributed over the whole of the earth's circumference. They are then immediately retransmitted to the American or Russian space centre. Here they are processed electronically, rapidly interpreted and studied. Answering messages reassure the astronauts that their physical well-being is being watched.

It is easy to see how this vast harvest of data and experience has provided a treasure trove for science and medicine. The knowledge gained ranges from how the human body responds when subjected to the limits of endurance, to the many technological applications specially developed for space flight that can be used in everyday medical practice.

General human progress always provides medical science with constantly growing resources, and furthers the investigation of that great mystery of biological harmony which we call the human body.

The Apollo 15 *Space Mission required a huge complex of IBM computers which was constructed and installed in the Houston NASA centre and the Goddard Centre in Maryland, U.S.A. For every day of the mission the complex at Houston carried out about 60 thousand million operations, in order to compute the vast quantity of data relative to the flight, in times of the order of nanoseconds (thousand millionths of a second).*

ACKNOWLEDGEMENTS

De Cesare: pp. 14, 16 (below), 18 (centre), 21 (above), 22 (below, both); Foto Castano: 21 (below), 40 (above), 41 (both), 43, 45, 49, 60, 61, 73, 79, 83; I.B.M.: 40 (centre), 71, 82 (both), 88 (below), 93, 105, 108, 109, 115 (both), 116, 117, 122, 123; Martini Paola: 88 (above), 89 (both), 91, 92, 95, 97, 100, 101, 103 (above), 106, 110, 111, 114 (both); Mella Arborio: 6, 10, 12, 13, 17, 20, 23, 86; Medical Times of Italy: 99 (above); Italian National Institute for the Study and Care of Tumours: 63 (both), 65 (both), 66, 67, 112, 113; Rizzoli: 16 (above), 18 (above), 22 (above), 42, 44 (both), 46, 47, 78, 98 (both), 99 (below), 104, 118, 120, 121; Rizzoli-Larousse Medical Encyclopedia: 73 (left), 103 (above); Siemens Elletra: 34.

GLOSSARY OF MEDICAL TERMS
In order of occurence

Carcinogenic Agents
Carriers which are capable of causing cancerous diseases.

Pathogenic Agents
Living organisms which, acting with other agents, are responsible for causing infectious diseases.

Anaphylaxis, Allergy
An intolerant reaction to a variety of substances, which are harmless to unaffected people. Depending on the degree of allergy, the person affected can suffer minor discomfort or acute pain.

Anaesthetics
The range of drugs used either to induce loss of feeling in a particular area of the body thus enabling surgery to take place in that area, or, to enable major surgery to be carried out, to induce total sleep in the patient.

Antibiotics
Substances, such as penicillin, streptomycin, etc., which are derived from micro-organisms, and are capable of destroying infections.

Skeletal Systems
The bone structure around which the body is built.

Catheterization
The introduction (by natural means or by incision) of a small, flexible, hollow tube, called a catheter, which is pushed along a natural channel, eventually reaching deep seated organs of the human body. This is done for diagnostic or curative reasons.

Diagnostic Screening
The tracing of specific symptoms, and their acceptance as scientific proof of the presence of disease, or the pre-disease state.

Haemolysis
Damage to blood cells caused by the use of surgical instruments.

Morphological Entities
The characteristics which distinguish the form and composition of an entity.

Physiology
The study of the human body.

Phlebotomy
The now outdated practice of blood-letting whereby the veins of a patient were cut, in the mistaken belief that this would be beneficial to the patient.

Immunology
The means of inducing a non-harmful reaction when a human organism finds itself in contact with an unknown agent. The study of immunology is especially relevant today, in view of the increased occurrence of transplant surgery.

Macromolecule
A large molecule formed by a number of simpler molecules.

Venereal Disease
The range of infectious diseases which are passed on from the carrier to the recipient during sexual contact.

Bubonic Plague
An infectious, epidemic disease, the main characteristics of which are fever, swelling of the lymphatic glands, a rapid course and a very high mortality rate.

Bacteriostatic Power
The power to reduce the aggression and reproductive habits of bacteria without destroying the bacteria themselves.

Non-specific Immunology
The injection of proteins foreign to the human body, in order to strengthen the defence mechanisms and to build up resistance to various illnesses.

Receptor
The recipient of a transplanted organ.

Serum Therapy
The treatment of disease by the administration of serum containing antibodies of the bacteria or toxin causing the disease.

Synthetic Drugs
Drugs produced artificially by the pharmaceutical industry after detailed research and specialist procedures have been carried out. The manufacture of synthetic drugs enables the substitution of the scarce natural product, at a comparatively low cost and in limitless quantity.

Autonomic Nervous System
That part of the nervous system that influences the functioning of the internal organs of the human body, which function independently of will-power.

Staphylococci
Bacteria which appear in small clusters under the microscope.

Streptococci
Bacteria which appear under the microscope in a chain-like formation.

Technology
The range of scientifically proven data which has helped man to achieve the present level of advancement in science, medicine, etc.

Viscous Tissue
The tendency for the platelets in the blood to stick together and clog any breakdown in a blood vessel, and thus prevent leakage.

INDEX
Italic page numbers refer to illustrations

A
Acetylcholine, 75
Acetysalicylic acid, 80
ACTH, 78
Adrenal glands (see glands)
Alcmaeon, 12
Allergic reactions, 46
Allergic rhinitis, 84
Allergies, 83–5
Amino acids, 30, 70, 79
Anaerobic bacteria (see bacteria)
Anaesthesia, 54–6, 87, *88*
Anaesthetics, 8, 56; general, 56; infiltration, 56; local, 56; nerve block, 56; topical, 56
Analgesics, 87
Anaphylactic reactions, 46, 84
Anatomy, *11*, 12, 14, *87*; study of, 13, 16; microscopic, 25
Anthrax, 43–4
Antibiogram, 48
Antibiosis, 43
Antibiotics, 42–50, 68, 102
Antibodies, *38*, 52
Antigen, *38*
Antihistamine, 84
Antiviral antibodies, 52
Aristotle, 12
Arteries, 72, *73*
Arteriosclerosis, 72–4
Arthritis, rheumatoid, 82, 104
Arthroplasty, 104
Artificial devices (see prosthetics)
Artificial kidney machine, 110, *111*
Asepsis, 8
Aspirin, 80
Asthma, 84
Astronauts, 120–3
Atebrin, 40
Atheromas, 72
Atherosclerosis, 72
Automatic respirator, 90, *91*
Autonomic nervous system (see nervous system)
Averroes, 12
Avicenna, 12, *14*

B
Bacilli, 38, *40*
Bacteria, 38–52, *57*, 97; anaerobic, 41; pathogenic, 38, 52; rod-shaped, 38, *40*; rounded, 38, *40*; spiral-shaped, 38, *40*
Bacteriostatic action, 41
Barnard, Christian, 96
Berger, 104
Bichat, 16
Biochemistry, 28
Biology, history of, 7–24
Bionics, 104
Biotelemetry, 123
Blood, 8, *37*, 70–1; banks, 90, 112; circulation, 14, 72, *73*; corpuscles, 37; groups, 90; transfusion, 90, *92*; vessels, 11, 68, 71, *77*, 90
Botallo, 13
Bovet, 84
Brain, 75–6, *79*, 104–5
Bronchial asthma, 84

C
Cajal, Ramon y, 75
Cancer (see diseases and tumours)
Capillaries, 71
Carcinogenic, 63–4, 66–7
Cardiac stimulator, 93–4, *95*
Cardiography, 68; ballisto-, 68; electro- 68
Cardiology, 68–9
Cardiovascular, research, 69; specialist, 68; surgery, 68, 90–5
Carotid artery, 104
Carrel, Alexis, 90
Catheterization, *77*, 92–3
Cell, 14, 16, 25–8, *26*, 30, 35, 59–62, 72, *78*, *83*; (division, 32; metabolism, 30; nucleus, 27, 34, 35)
Celsus, 12
Central nervous system (see nervous system)
Cerebellum, *79*
Cerebral ventricles, 104
Cesalpino, Andrea, 14
Chain, Ernst Boris, 44, *44*
Charcot, 22
Chemical pathology laboratory, 110
Chemotherapy (see therapy)
Chicken pox, 52
Chloromycetin, 48
Choh Hao Li, 78–9
Cholera, 16–18
Cholestrol, 72
Chromosomes, 32, 34, *34*, 35
Circulatory system (see systems)
Cobalt treatment, *112*, 113
Co-carcinogenic, 63
Cocci, 38, *40*
Computers, *109*, 113–17, *115*, *116*, *117*
Conjunctivitis, 52, 85
Contagium Vivum, 16
Cooley, A. Denton, 96, 99
Cooper, 105
Coronary units, 110
Corpuscles, red, *37*; white, *38*
Cortisone, 78, 80
Cranium, 11
Crick, Francis, 32
Croton oil, 63–4
Crythromycin, *48*
Curie, Marie and Pierre, 21, *22*
Cushing, 105
Cyclic adenosine monophosphate, 79
Cytoplasm, 27, 32, 62

D
d'Acquapendente, Fabrizio, 13
Dante Alighieri, 13
da Vinci, Leonardo, *11*, 13, *16*
De Bakey, Michael, 90, 96, *98*
Defibrillators, 110, *110*
Demikov, 96
Dendrites, 75
Deoxyribonucleic acid (DNA), 30–5, *32*, 50, 61–2
Diabetes, 70–1, 78
Diagnosis, 12
Digestive system (see systems)
Dioscorides, 12
Diptheria, 37
Diseases, 59–85; cancerous, 54; heart, 68–9; infectious, 37; mental, 76; metabolic, 70; occupational, 107; rheumatic, 79–83; social, 107; viral, 52
Domagk, 40, *42*
Double helix, 32
Dubost, 90, *98*

E
Eccles, Sir John, 75
Echo-encephalograph, 105
Ehrlich, Paul, 38
Electrocardiographs, 68, *75*, 91, *92*, 110
Electrocoagulation, 105
Electrodes, 104, 119
Eliseev, Aleksej, *121*
Encephalitis, 52
Endocrine gland (see glands)
Endoplasmic reticulum, 27
Enzymes, 30, 64, 78
Epidemic parotitis (see mumps)
Epidermis, 7, *9*
Ether, 54
Eustachio, 13

F
Fallopio, 13
Fertilization, 34
Fleming, Alexander, 42–4, *44*
Florey, 44
Follicles, hair, *9*
Forsmann, Werner, 92
Freud, Sigmund, 21–3, *22*, 76

G
Galen, 12, 14
Galilei, Galileo, 14
Gangrene, gas, 41
Genes, 34, 61–2, 98
Genetics, 30, *30*, 32, *32*, 34–5, 62, 98
German measles, 52
Gerontology, 108
Gibbon, 94
Glands, adrenal, 78, 80; endocrine, 78, *85*; pituitary, 78, *83*; secretory, 11; thyroid, 78
Glandular bulbs, *9*
Graft, 98
Granulocytes, *37*, 73
Groote Schuur hospital, 96
Growth, 78–9

H
Haemodialysis, *107*, 110, *111*
Haemolytic streptococcus, 82
Haemophilia, 91
Harvey, William, 14
Hay fever, 84
Health services, 107–17
Heart, 8, 11, *77*, 93; block, 94; disease, 68; surgery, 90–5
Heart-lung machine, 94, *97*
Heparin, 90
Heredity (see genetics)
Hippocrates, 12, *12*
Histamine, 83
Histocompatibility genes, 99
Histology, 16, 25, *79*
History, of biology, 7–24; of medicine, 7–24
Hodgkin, 75
Hormones, 64, 76, 78–9
Huxley, 75
Hygiene, 18
Hyperglycaemia, 70
Hypophysis 78, *83*
Hypothermia, 94

I
Infantile paralysis (see poliomyelitis)
Infarction, 69
Influenza, 52, *53*
Infusoria, 14
Immune reactions, 64, 69, 98, 102
immunization, 18, *23*, 37, 42, 54
Immunology, 18, 64
Immunosuppressive drugs, 99–102
Inorganic molecules, 28
Insulin, 70–1, 78

125

Intensive care unit, 110
Interferon, 52
Intrathoracic surgery (see surgery)
Ions, 75–6
Isoniazid, 47

K
Kidneys, 110, *111*
Koch, 8, 16, 18–19, *21*
Koch's bacillus, 19, *21*
Kolff, 110

L
Labial herpes (see cold sore)
Leriche, 90
Leucocytes, *37*
Leukaemia, 54, 91
Lillihei, 94
Loewi, 75
Lymphocytes, *37*, 98, 102
Lymphograph, *67*
Lymphoma, 62
Lymphosarcoma, *66*, *67*

M
Macro-molecules, 28, 30
Magic, 8, 11, 16, 107
Malaria, 40
Malpighi, Marcello, 14, *16*, 25
Measles, 52
Mendel's Laws, *30*
Meningitis, 52; tubercular, 48
Mental disease, 76
Metabolic processes, 72
Metabolism, 94, 108; cell, 30
Microbes, 7, 16–18
Microbiology, 16
Microscope, 14, 25–6, *25*
Mitochondria, 27
Molecules, 27–8, *27*, 30, 32, 35
Morgagni, Giovanni Battista, 16, *18*
Morton, William, 8, 54
Moulds, 42–4, 47–8
Mumps, 52
Muscles, 11
Mutations, 32
Myocardial infarction, 69, 72
Myxovirus, *53*

N
NASA, 119, *123*
Neoplasms, 60
Nervous system, 11, 75–6; autonomic, 76; central, 11, 76, *80*, 102; peripheral, 11, *81*
Neurons, 75
Neurosurgery (see surgery)
Nitinol, 104
Noguchi, 38
Non-specific protein therapy (see therapy)
Nucleic acids, 30, 35, 61–2
Nucleus, 27, 34

O
Occupational disease (see diseases)
Olivecrona, Herbert, *104*, 105
Open-heart surgery (see surgery)
Organic molecules, 28
Osteocarcoma, *65*

P
Pacemaker, 93–4, *95*
Pacini, 16
Pancreas, 70
Para-aminosalicylic acid (PAS), 47
Paratyphoid, 37, 48

Paré, Ambroise, 13
Pasteur, Louis, 8, 16–18, *20*, 37, 43
Pasteurization, 18
Pathogen, 18, 19
Pathogenic agents, 17–18, 40, 82
Pathological anatomy, 110
Pathology, 16, 116
Penicillin, 44–47, *44*, 83; reaction, 46; resistance, 47
Penicillium notatum, 42–4, *43*
Peripheral nervous system (see nervous system)
Phagocytosis, *38*
Phlebotomy, 14
Physiology, history of, 14
Physiotherapy (see therapy)
Pituitary gland (see glands)
Plague, 12, 47
Plasmochin, 38
Plastic surgery (see surgery)
Pliny, 12
Pneumonia, 41, 50
Poliomyelitis, 46, *47*, *51*, 52–4
Pollinoses, 84
Polyoma, 63
Prontosil, 40, 41
Prosthetics, *100*, 102–4, *103*, 112
Proteins, 30, 32, *32*
Psychiatry, 21–3, 75–6
Psychoanalysis, 22–3
Psychopharmaceuticals, 76
Psychosomatic illness, 75–6
Psychotherapy (see therapy)
Psychotropic drugs, 76

R
Radiation, 21, 113
Radiology, 21, 112–13
Rejection, 69, 97–102
Rembrandt, *87*
Renal insufficiency, 110
Research, 38–44, 47, 54, 62–9, 75, 95, *109*
Respiratory system (see systems)
Rheumatic diseases (see diseases)
Ribonucleic acid (RNA), 32, *32*, 50, 61–2
Ribosomes, 27, 32, *32*
Roentgen, Wilhelm, 20–1, *22*
Rolandi teachers, *7*
Roman Empire, 12
Rous, 62

S
Sabin, Albert *47*, 54
"Saccules", 14
St Ambrose, 12
St Augustine, 12
St Benedict, 12
Salernitana school, 12
Salk, Jonas, *46*, 54
Salvarsan, 38
Sarcoma, 62
Sauerbruch, 90
Scarlet fever, 52
Scintigraphy, 63
Scintiscanning, 105, *105*
Semmelweiss, 8
Serotherapy (see therapy)
Serum, 37, 84
Servetus, Michele, 14
Shumway, 96
Skeleton, 11
Skin, 7–8, *9*
Smallpox, 18, 52, *55*
Smoking, 64–6
Sodium salicylate, 80
Space medicine, 119; 123

Spallanzani, Lazzaro, 16, *18*
Spirilla, 38, *40*
Spores, 38
Stappylococci, 40–1, 82
Stefanini, Professor, *93*
Stereotaxic apparatus, 105
Steroids, 102
Streptococci, 40–1, 82
Streptomyces griseus, 47
Streptomycin, 47–8; resistance, 48
Sulphonamide, 38, 40–2; resistance, 42, 48
Surgery, 87–105, *93*; cardiovascular, 68, 90–5; intrathoracic, 90; neuro-, 104–5; open-heart, 69, 94–5; plastic, 113
Surgical instruments, 88–90, *88*, *89*, *99*
Sutherland, Earl, *78*, 79
Symptoms, 28
Synapses, 75–6
Synthesis, 78–9
Systems, circulatory, 14, 72–4, *73*, *97*, 108; digestive, 11, 52, 108; nervous, 11, 75–6, *80*, 102; respiratory, 11, 52, 71, *74*, 108; urinogenital, 11, 71, 108

T
Tetanus, 37
Thalidomide, 44–6
Therapy, chemo-, 38; non-specific protein, 42; physio-, 68, 112–13, *114*; psycho-, 76; vaccine, 37, 40, *47*, 54
Thyroid gland (see glands)
Thyroxine, 78
Tiberio, Vincenzo, 42
Tissues, 14, 25, 60–2, 72, 98–9, 105
Tobacco, 64–6
Toxins, 37, 97
Transplants, 69, 90, 95–102
Trepanning, 11
Tuberculin, 19
Tuberculosis, 18–19, 41, 47–8; pulmonary, 47; septicaemia, 47
Tumours, defences against, 66–8, *71*, 79, *112*, *113*; development of, 62–6; endocranial, 105; malignant, 50, 54, 59–68, *59*, *63*, *65*, *66*, *69*
Thyphoid, 37, 48

U
United Nations, 67
Urethrane, 63
Urinogenital system (see systems)

V
Vaccination (see immunization)
Vaccine therapy (see therapy)
van Leeuwenhoek, Anton, 14, *18*
Varolio, 13
Veins, *73*
Vesalius, Andreas, 13
Viral hepatitis, 52; tumours, 62–3
Viruses, 50–54, *51*, *53*, *55*, 62–3
von Haller, 16

W
Waksman, 47
Washkansky, Louis, 96
Watson, James Dewey, 32
Witt, *82*
World Health Organization (WHO), 70

X
X-rays, 20–1, 64, *71*, 93–4, 112

Y
yellow fever, 50, 52

FURTHER READING

Brain, Lord. *Doctors, Past and Present.* London: Pitman, 1964

Caiden, Martin, and Caiden, Grace. *Aviation and Space Medicine.* New York: E. P. Dutton, 1962.

Calder, J. *Drugs, Medicine and Man.* London: Allen and Unwin, 1962.

Christie, A. B. *Infectious Diseases.* London: Faber and Faber, 1968.

Donizetti, Pino. *Shadow and Substance.* London: Pergamon Press, 1967.

Glaser, Hugo. *The Miracle of Heart Surgery.* London: Lutterworth, 1961.

Grundy, Fred. *Preventive Medicine and Public Health.* London: H. K. Lewis, 1960.

Herber, Lewis. *Crisis in Our Cities: Death, Disease and the Urban Plague.* Englewood Cliffs, New Jersey: Prentice-Hall, 1965.

Maurois, André. *The Life of Sir Alexander Fleming, Discoverer of Penicillin.* New York: E. P. Dutton, 1959.

Nolen, William A. *Spare Parts for the Human Body.* New York: Random House, 1971.

Norten, Alan. *The New Dimensions in Medicine.* London: Hodder and Stoughton, 1969.

Riedman, Sarah P. *Masters of the Scalpel: The story of Surgery.* Chicago: Rand Macnally, 1962.

Riedman, Sarah P. *How Man Discovered His Body.* Rev. Ed. New York: Abelard-Schuman, 1966.

Rouche, Berton. *Eleven Blue Men and Other Narratives of Medical Detection.* Boston: Little Brown, 1953.

Rouche, Berton. *The Incurable Wound.* Boston: Little Brown, 1957.

Silverberg, Robert. *The Dawn of Medicine.* New York: G. P. Putman's, 1966.

Smith, Alwyn. *The Science of Social Medicine.* London: Staples, 1968.

Warwick, Roger (ed). *Regional Anatomy.* London: J. & A. Churchill, 1968.

Wright, Helen, and Rapport, Samuel (eds). *The Amazing World of Medicine.* London: Gollancz, 1960. New York: Harper and Row, 1961.